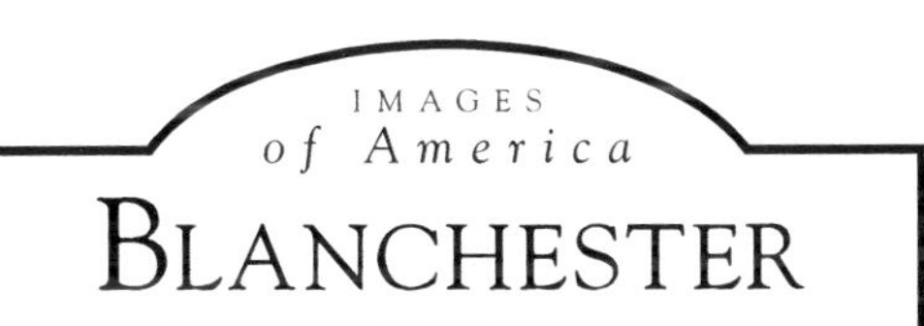
IMAGES
of America
BLANCHESTER

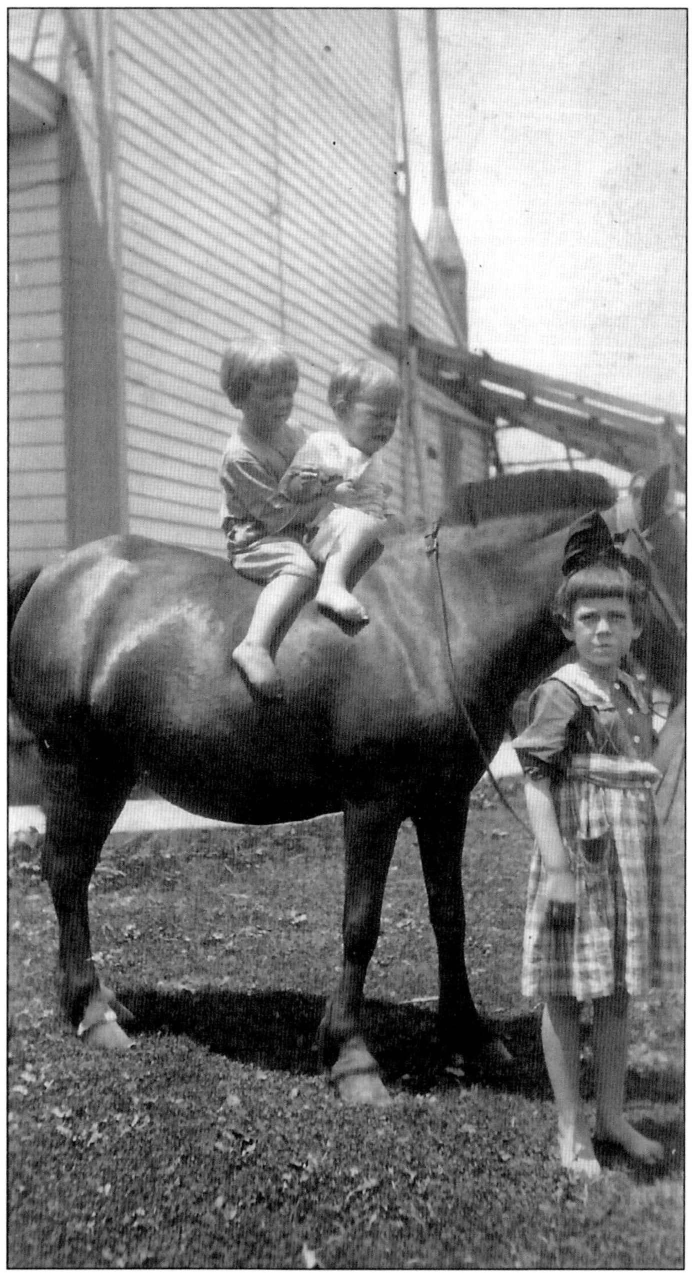

The Irvin family lived on East Center Street in an old farmhouse that had been much expanded on over the years. Pictured here are three of the daughters—Florence, Hazel and Reva—on their pony in the side yard. This photograph is notable, as this is the house that the author's grandparents resided in while she was growing up and served as her home away from home in town. (Courtesy of the Blanchester Area Historical Society.)

On the Cover: Taken in 1933, this photograph shows the children of Blanchester and the surrounding areas standing beside the railroad and waving white flags of welcome. The train was bringing Gov. George White to the community to celebrate the Blanchester centennial and the ribbon-cutting for the new road. (Courtesy of the Blanchester Area Historical Society.)

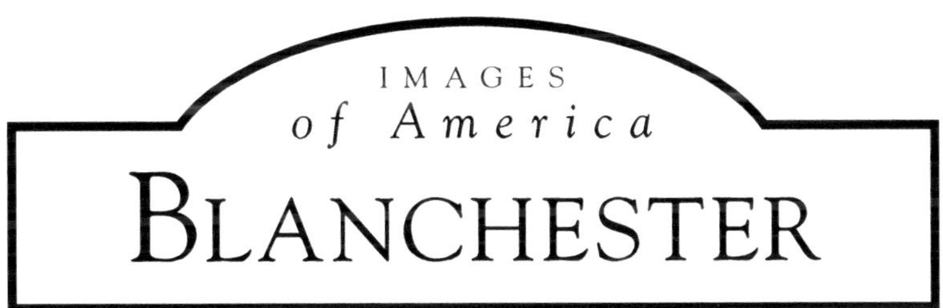

Robyn Stone-Kraft and Richard Read

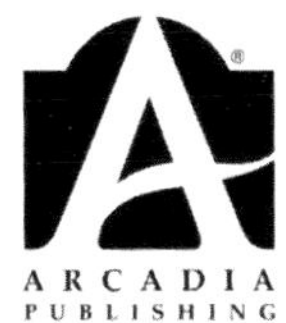

ISBN 978-1-4671-1414-1

Published by Arcadia Publishing
Charleston, South Carolina

Printed in the United States of America

Library of Congress Control Number: 2015955298

For all general information, please contact Arcadia Publishing:
Telephone 843-853-2070
Fax 843-853-0044
E-mail sales@arcadiapublishing.com
For customer service and orders:
Toll-Free 1-888-313-2665

Visit us on the Internet at www.arcadiapublishing.com

To Grandma Jeanne and Battery Grandpa, who let me visit, play, and dream in their lovely small town

Contents

Acknowledgments 6

Introduction 7

1. Notable Locals 9

2. Fire and Ruin 21

3. The Centennial Celebration 27

4. Trains and Traction 37

5. School Days 43

6. Touched by War 57

7. A Sense of Community 65

8. Business and Commerce 93

9. Street Fairs and Celebrations 113

Bibliography 126

About the Blanchester Area Historical Society 127

ACKNOWLEDGMENTS

This book would not have been possible without the help and support of the Blanchester Area Historical Society. Members were gracious and generous with their time, insight, knowledge, and old postcards. I am forever indebted to them and others like them who seek to retain the fascinating histories of their homes. It is important work, more than just being interesting. Special appreciation goes to John Simpson and Jane Richardson, who gave me their time and encouragement. It goes without saying that they told me everything correctly, and any errors in the text are entirely my own. All images in the text, unless otherwise noted, are provided courtesy of the Blanchester Area Historical Society.

Many thanks go to Debbie Blocker from the Blanchester Church of Christ, the "I Remember Blanchester" *Facebook* group, and Peggy Schildmeyer from the Tufts Schildmeyer Funeral Home for answering my questions and providing information, insight, and support.

Thanks must also go to my grandparents, who provided me a wonderful place to stay and introduced me to the joys of living in a small town. Grandma Jeanne encouraged in me a love of history that cannot be denied and was the one who introduced me to the historical society when she did some work for them involving some antiques in their collection. It was 20 years until I found my way back, but it is all in her memory. And as for Grandpa, this could not have been done without him, as he kindly supported my efforts to put everything together for this book, running errands and fetching images for me when I was unable to do so myself. Thanks, Grandpa.

I feel I need to thank my cats as well, since they were my primary company during the writing of this book. So, thank you Dova for napping nearby and providing moral support. Much less thanks to Rowan, for routinely unplugging my laptop while it was charging, and Arthur and Morgana, who made it incredibly hard to work with all of their walking on my keyboard and climbing on me. Fortunately, you are all very cute.

Most of all, I need to thank my husband, Edward, for his love, support, and willingness to drive me the hour up to Blanchester and help me explore cold cemeteries on rainy days. Without you, I would have given up my writing dreams by now. I love you more than I can possibly say. Most importantly, Grandma approved of you, so I know you are good.

INTRODUCTION

Driving into Blanchester from Cincinnati is an interesting experience, almost like passing into a completely different world. After getting off the highway, a driver will pass through Milford. Both sides of the road are cluttered with chain stores and restaurants, making the driver imagine that anything they need will be right at hand. On the other side of Milford, though, is a long stretch of road that is increasingly lined with open fields, farms, and stables. Here and there one might get caught behind farm equipment moving from one end of a large field to the other. There are places to stop off and ride a horse or buy a pumpkin or flowers for a garden.

Then, just as the driver starts wondering if the destination will ever be reached, there is a curve in the road, and then the road passes under a rusty railroad overpass that was not visible even seconds before. And just like that, on a gently winding country road, the driver will suddenly find Blanchester, greeted at the outskirts by a friendly sign welcoming visitors.

Keep going forward, and the driver will find the historic downtown area, though Blanchester is too modest to bill itself as having a historic downtown. The old buildings on Main and Broadway Streets are just the buildings that have always been there, and while some of the locals know their history, origins, and who had originally sold their wares from those locations, for many it seems more like the everyday. It is not designed to attract tourists, though it is certainly worth a visit while passing through the area or looking for somewhere new and interesting to visit on a day trip.

The shops on South Broadway Street in downtown Blanchester do not just sell antiques and the work of local artists, they also provide a place for socializing within easy walking distance of the library, the bank, and a smattering of restaurants. Those who pass through the small village in Clinton County, adrift somewhere between Milford and Wilmington, will overhear talk about neighbors, local events, and family gatherings. Old stories from years past will be told, usually referencing people from the same graduating class, and calling the shops by names they have not gone by in years, sometimes with talk about the previous owners and their families. It seems as if everyone who had the pleasure of growing up there knows everyone else, their families, and their entire family trees. This can render things dangerous to newcomers who do not know how all the families are connected, making gossip risky. In many ways, Blanchester, Ohio, seems like a small town like any other, and while it may share some characteristics, it is wholly unique. There are no other towns named Blanchester in the entire country, a fact that the locals take pride in.

In the farthest back corner, half overgrown with trees, the curious wanderer of cemeteries will find old gravestones badly worn by the years, many bearing the name Baldwin. Jonathan Baldwin was the first settler in Marion Township in 1814, but it was his wife Harriet's family, the Blancetts, that really left their mark on the immediate area. John and Joseph Blancett arrived from Pennsylvania and laid out the original settlement in March 1832. Originally, there were 24 lots, and all of the original buildings were made of log. Unfortunately, many of these buildings were burned in the fire of 1895. Originally, according to an article in the *Star Republican* from

1933, the Blancett brothers wanted to name the town Manchester, but finding that another town of the same name existed in Ohio, they were forced to find another option. In the end, the Blancetts left their name on the growing village, the "Blan" of the name originating from their own last name, and the "chester," meaning "village," thus Blanchester means the village of Blancett. While the name is not the most common in the Blanchester IOOF Cemetery, and the tombstones are not the most obviously situated, the name Blancett can not be forgotten by residents, even if they do not realize they are referring to it.

Blanchester is the sort of town that has regular yearly events, from yard sales in spring and autumn to a Fourth of July parade and street fair that seems to grow every year. It is the sort of town where everyone relates to each other by what year they graduated from the local high school, and many can rattle off where each of those graduates ended up and whom they married. There are a multitude of community groups and clubs that organize events, and it is a small enough place to close entire streets down to set up the street fairs. After all, it is easy enough to walk from one end of the town to the other. Those used to a faster pace of living might be amazed at how quiet it is, walking down the sidewalks in front of historic houses. There are dogs barking and the laughter of children, but the roads are not brimming with cars that may have loud stereos. It is the kind of place that makes one feel safe walking around, just enjoying the day.

Still, despite its quaint small-town feel, Blanchester is a growing village. As of the 2010 census, it had 4,243 inhabitants. The school system is good and pulls in students from the surrounding area, a practice with historical precedence. Businesses are setting up locations to service residents. Kroger opened a superstore in 2007, its fifth location in 100-plus years of serving Blanchester, as well as Dollar General and Family Dollar, though they are still considered new to the area. Change comes slowly to Blanchester, and things are regularly referred to by their old names, such as the old bank or old opera house.

It is a surprisingly exciting place to live, providing more than Fourth of July fireworks and apple picking at area orchards to entertain locals and visitors alike. While the trains and traction line originally provided a boon to the local economy, these days they have fallen largely into disuse; however, that does not stop progress from passing through. For several years, the small village of Blanchester has served as a time station for Race Across America, the 3,000-mile bicycle race that starts in California and ends in Maryland. So, even today, people pass through the area and get a glimpse of the country charm and the friendly people who line the streets to cheer bicyclists on.

When telling someone about Blanchester, the question "Where is it?" may often come up, but at least the residents know they have the distinction of not having to hear, "Oh, which one?" Truly, it is a unique place and will continue to be so for a long time in the future, which hopefully promises only better for this little rural village.

One

Notable Locals

For a small village, Blanchester has produced a good number of noteworthy individuals. In addition to the Blancetts, who originally laid the town out, Blanchester was the birthplace of Clarence J. Brown Sr. and Clarence J. Brown Jr., who both served Ohio on a national level.

Other notables include George B. Shanor, who served as a US Army colonel; Hazel Losh, a PhD and a professor of astronomy at the University of Michigan; Robert E. Lucas, who served as the 15th president of Wilmington College; Sam B. Nicely, a state representative from 1943 to 1955; H. Cooper Snyder, who was a state senator; and Dr. Joy Garrison Cauffman, an OSU graduate, professor at University of Southern California, and advisor to five US presidents for health education and physical fitness.

Truly, Blanchester has a lot of which to be proud.

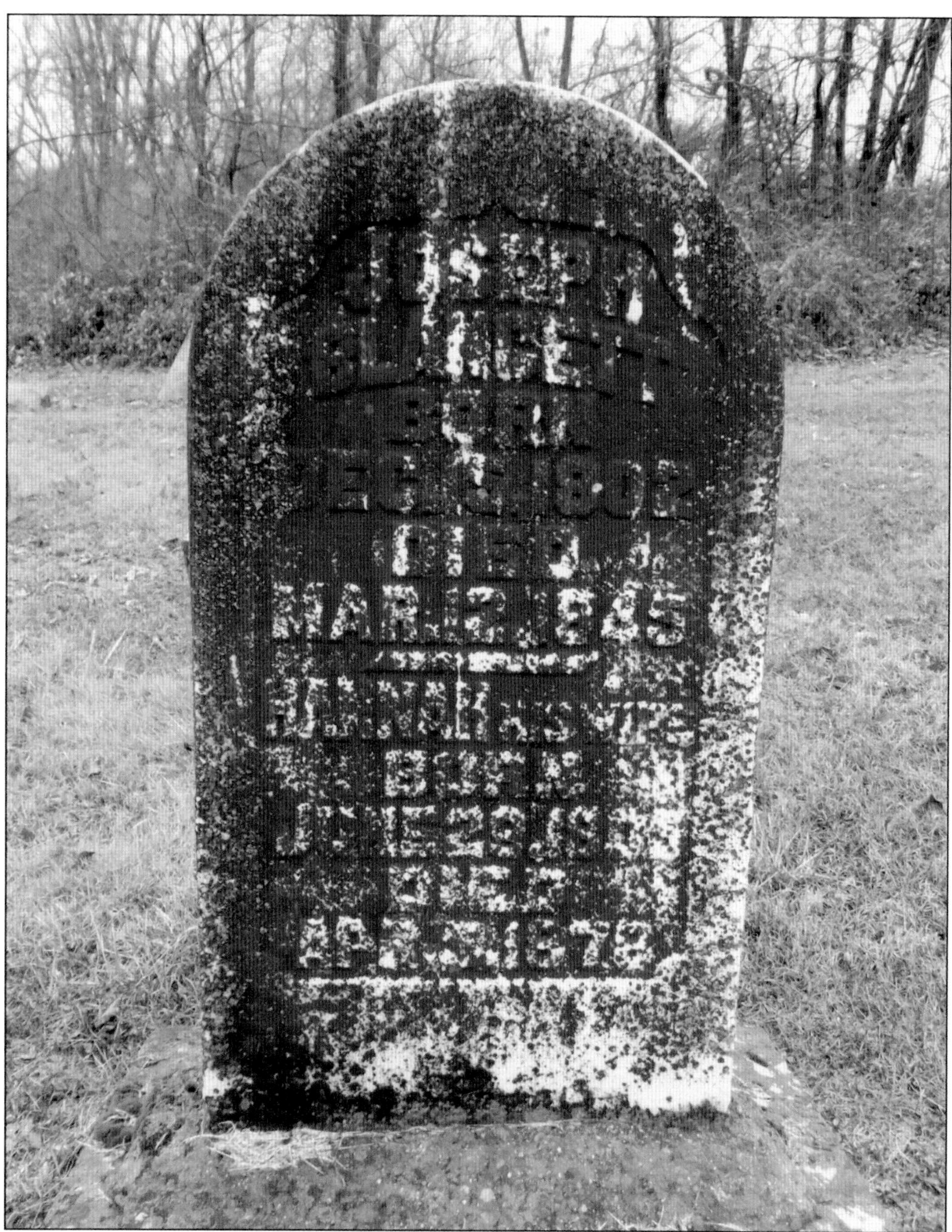

Joseph and John Blancett arrived in Ohio from western Pennsylvania and drew up the original plans for the village of Blanchester in March 1832, giving the original settlement both shape and name. Joseph was born in 1804 and married Hannah Beedle. They had four boys and five girls who were known to have survived. Joseph was also the first merchant in the village, carrying a line of general groceries and notions. The store was located on Plot 1 in the oldest part of town and was built of hewn logs. Joseph died in 1845, leaving a large family. Hannah was later listed with several children in the Woodville census, indicating that maybe they moved away from Blanchester after his death. Nonetheless, Joseph and Hannah, as well as their son Elias and daughter Alamira Blancett, are all buried in the Blanchester IOOF Cemetery. (Photograph by the author.)

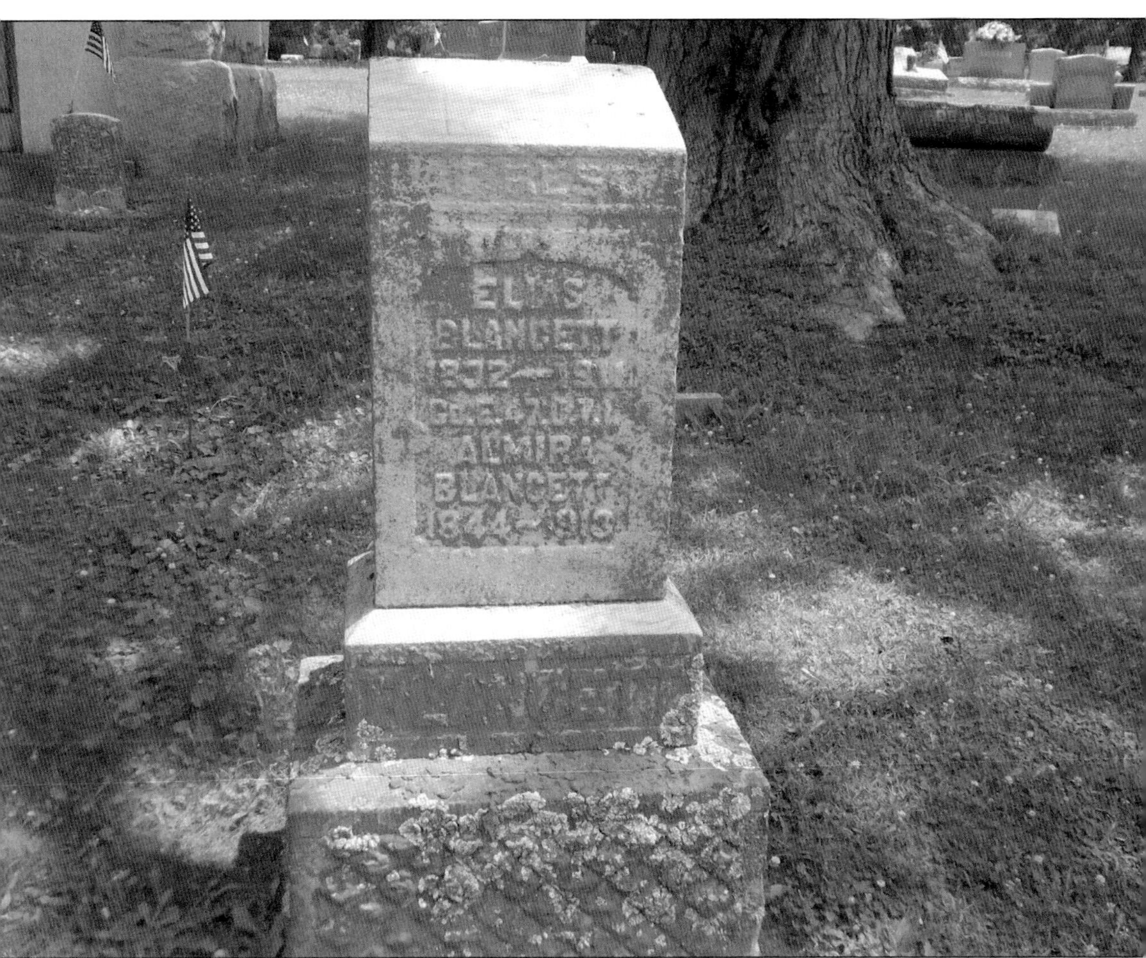

Elias Blancett is the most well-remembered son of Joseph and Hannah, though that has as much to do with his burial location as anything else. While he was buried at the opposite corner from his parents, the cemetery is otherwise surprisingly devoid of the family that gave the town its name. He was born on January 22, 1832, and died in 1911. It was from his obituary that the death date of Joseph Blancett was learned, as before that point it was uncertain. It also appears that the family moved to Woodville after the death of Joseph, which may account for the lack of Blancetts buried in Blanchester. (Photograph by the author.)

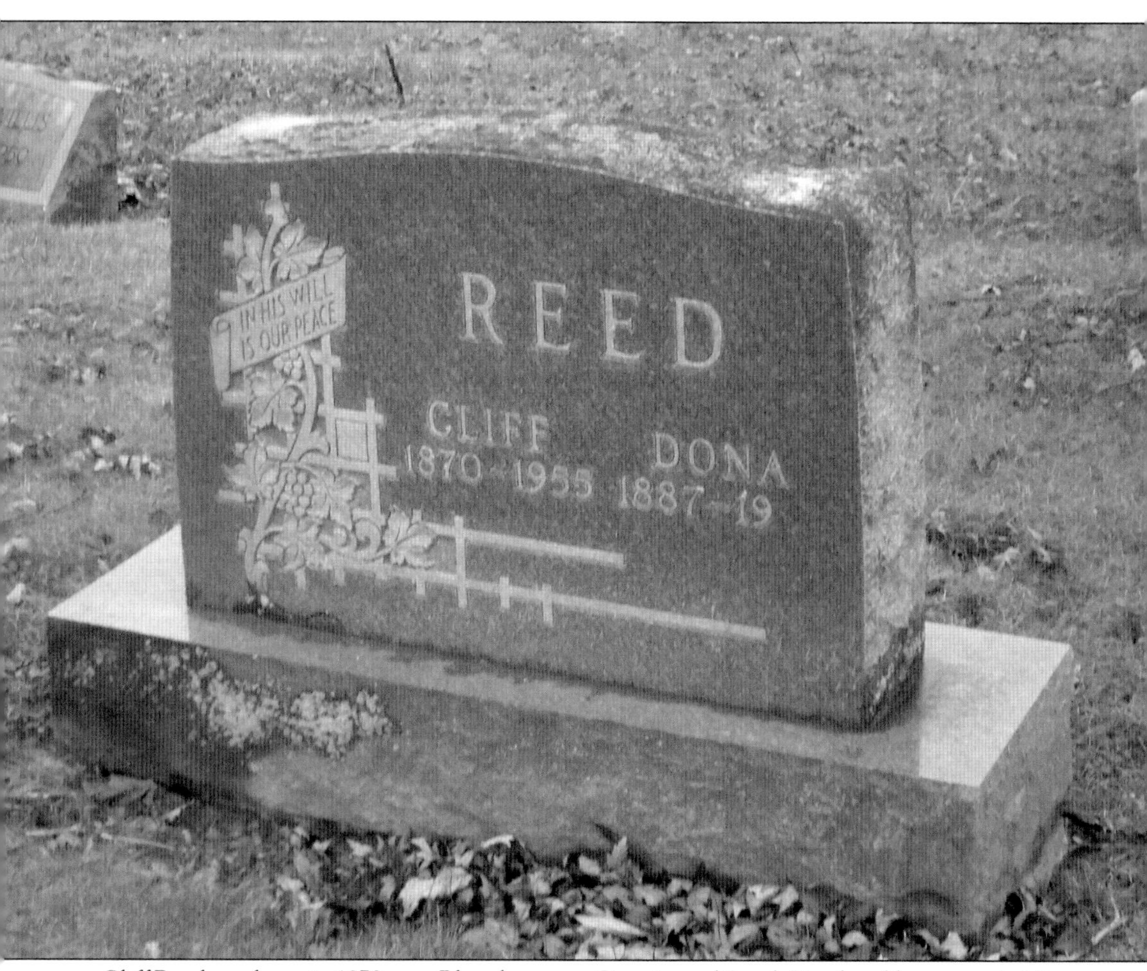

Cliff Reed was born in 1870 near Blanchester to Corwin and Sarah Reed and later married Dona Parr Reed (1887–1970). Reed served as the 17th recorded mayor of the village of Blanchester. His dates of service run from January 1, 1930, to December 31, 1937, which means he presided over the Blanchester centennial celebration. He helped organize and plan the event and welcomed Ohio secretary of state Clarence J. Brown as honorary chairman to the village for the ribbon-cutting ceremony to officially open the new brick-paved road. He spent the last 20 years of his life serving as justice of the peace for Marion Township. He passed away in 1955 and is buried in the Blanchester IOOF Cemetery. He was survived by two daughters from his previous two marriages, Mrs. Frances Robertson and Mrs. Leon Schwartz. (Photograph by the author.)

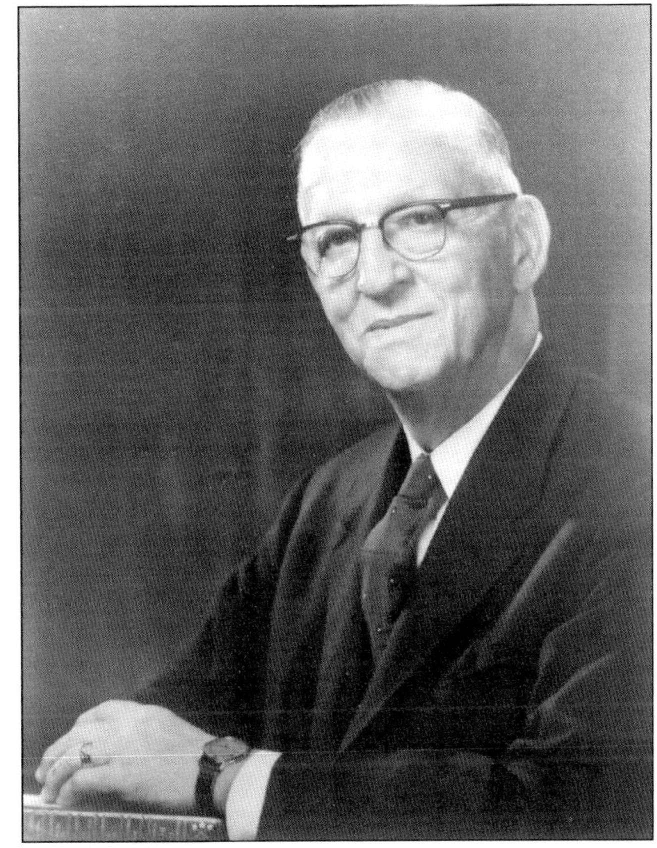

Clarence J. Brown Sr. was born in Blanchester to Owen and Ellen Brown on July 14, 1895, in the house pictured below. He graduated from Blanchester High School in 1912, and on his 21st birthday he married Ethel McKinney. In 1919, he became the 36th lieutenant governor of Ohio, at the age of 25, making him the youngest to ever hold that position. He held the title until 1923. From 1939 until his death in 1965, he represented Ohio in the US House of Representatives. Brown was a devoted isolationist during the presidency of Roosevelt, and he did not agree with Truman's Fair Deal.

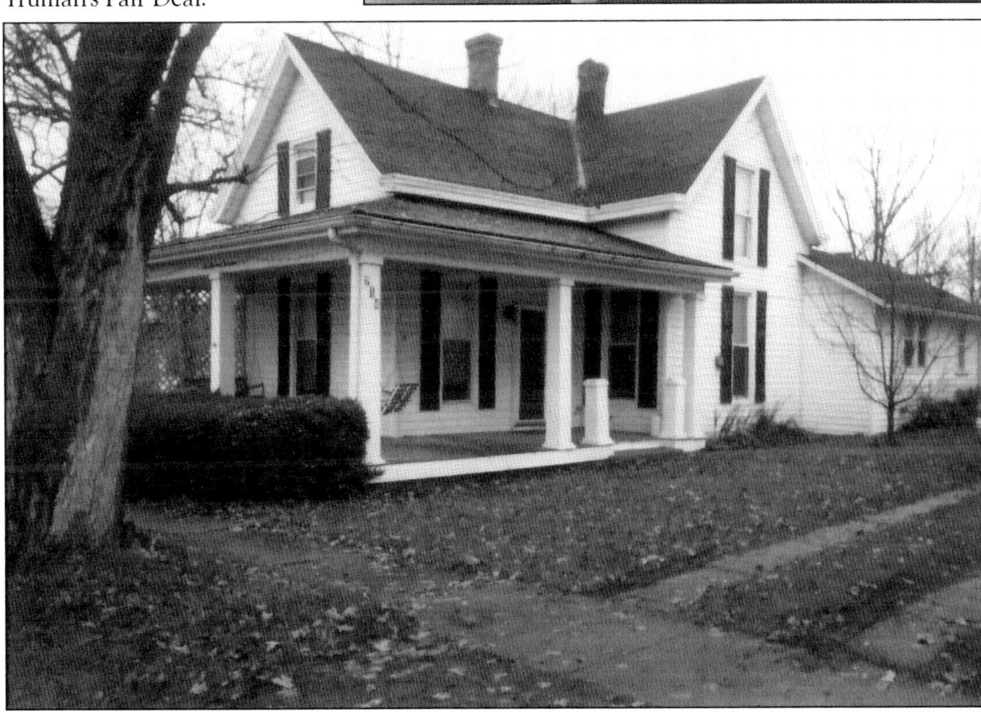

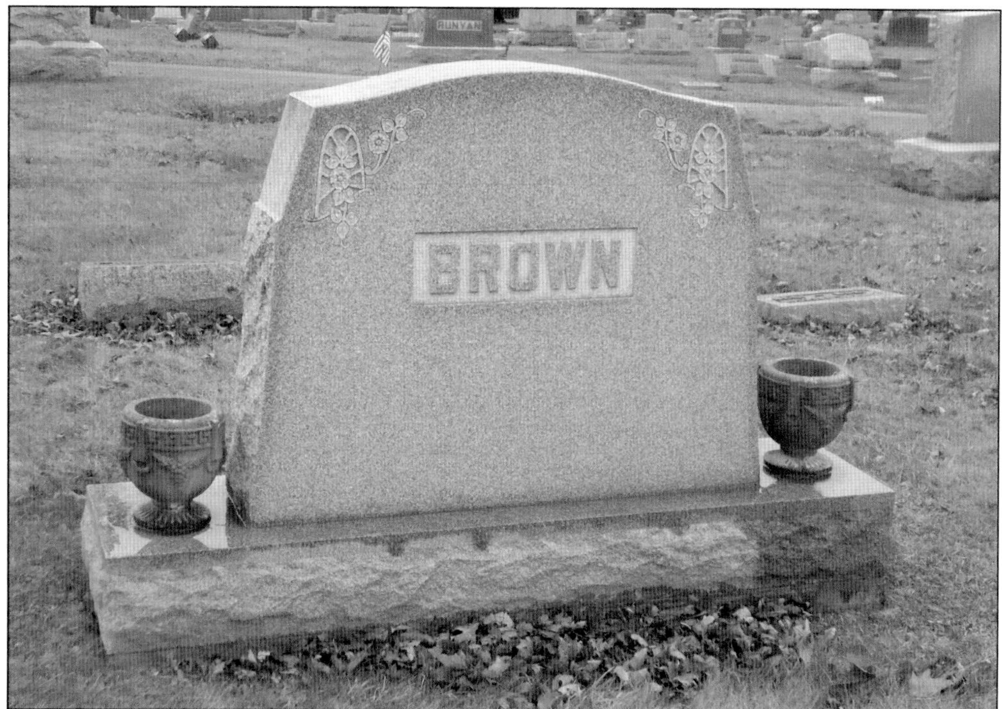

Though he tended to vote conservatively as a Republican, Brown helped pass the Voting Rights Act of 1965, allowing an equal right to vote for all citizens, even though he was dealing with failing health at the time. Brown also established the Brown Publishing Company in 1920 in addition to his political work. At one point, the company produced 18 daily newspapers, 27 weekly newspapers, and 26 free weeklies. The publishing company remained a family business for 90 years, though the Blanchester division became Curless Printing in 1953 after a fire destroyed the location. Under that name, it remains in business. Brown is buried in the Blanchester IOOF Cemetery in a surprisingly modest grave for all of his accomplishments. (Photographs by the author.)

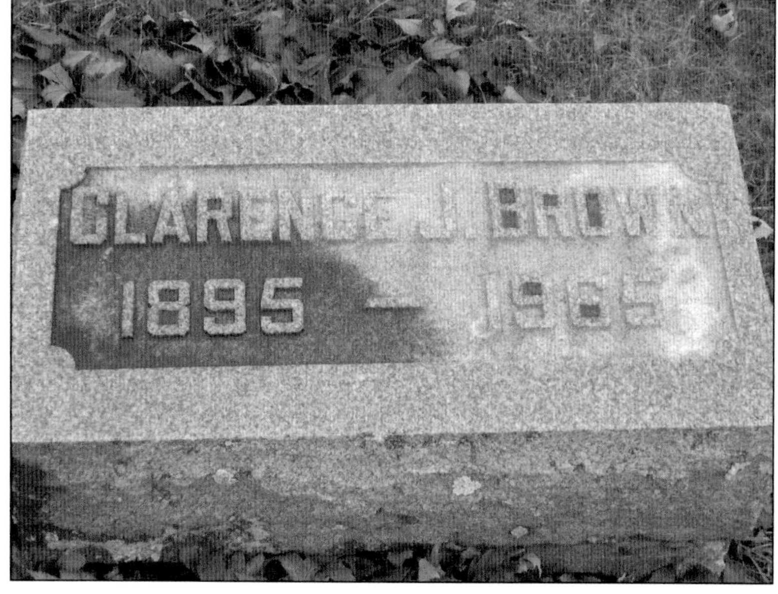

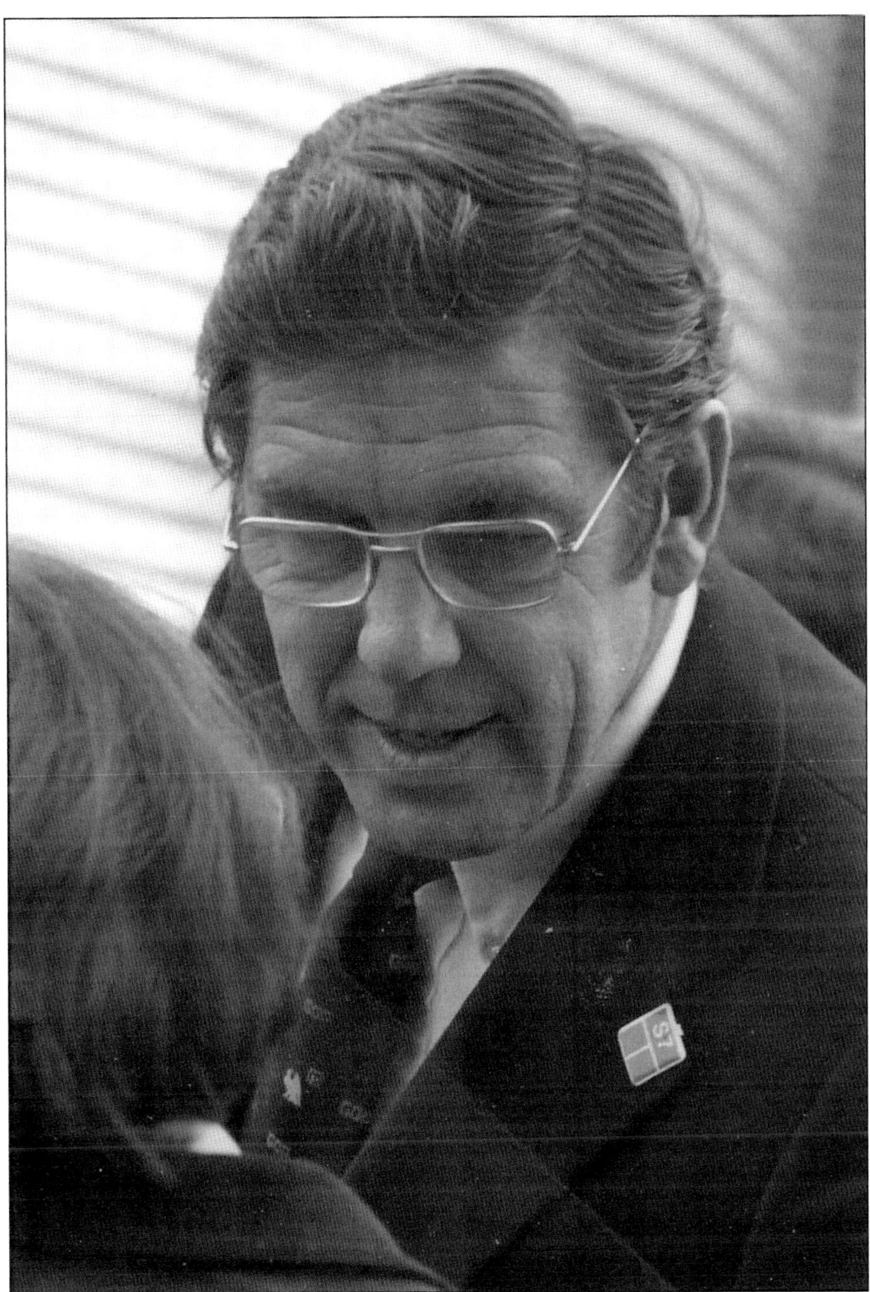

Clarence J. "Bud" Brown Jr. was born in 1927 in Columbus to Clarence J. Brown Sr. and his wife, Ethel. He spent some time attending school in Blanchester, so he got to know the town where his father was born. He married Joyce Eldridge, and they have three children. He served in the US Navy from 1944 to 1946 and then again from 1950 to 1953 during the Korean War. In addition to working for the Brown Publishing Company from a young age, he became a Republican US representative in 1965, replacing his father, who had died in office. He served in that capacity until 1983. He made an attempt to win the position of governor of Ohio but lost the election. After that, he was appointed by Pres. Ronald Reagan to serve as US deputy secretary of commerce and then secretary of commerce from 1983 to 1988.

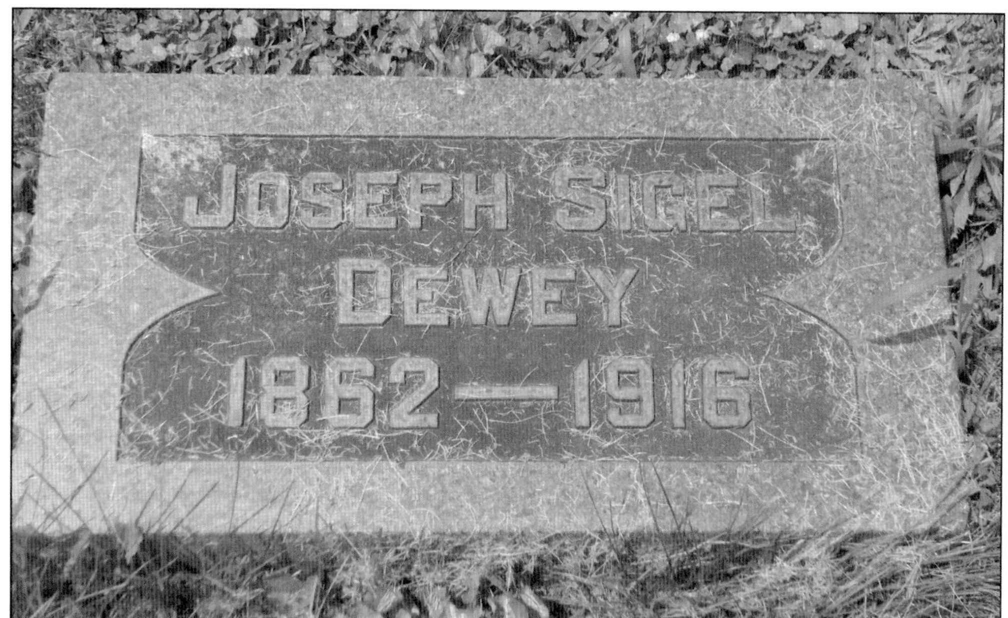

The Dewey brothers brought a great deal of commerce to Blanchester with their family business. It was on August 26, 1889, that Joseph Sigel Dewey and Lewis Wilson Dewey started their successful partnership. They were the sons of John P. and Catherine L. Dewey, and Joseph was the elder of the two boys. He had two sons, Joseph Collier and Raymond Ball, who both joined the Dewey Bros. Company after they graduated from high school. Joseph, or J.S., was a well-respected member of the Blanchester community, serving as a member of the board of directors of the First National Bank of Blanchester as well as being active in the local Masonic order. In addition, he served as treasurer of Marion Township and was a member of the town council. (Photographs by the author.)

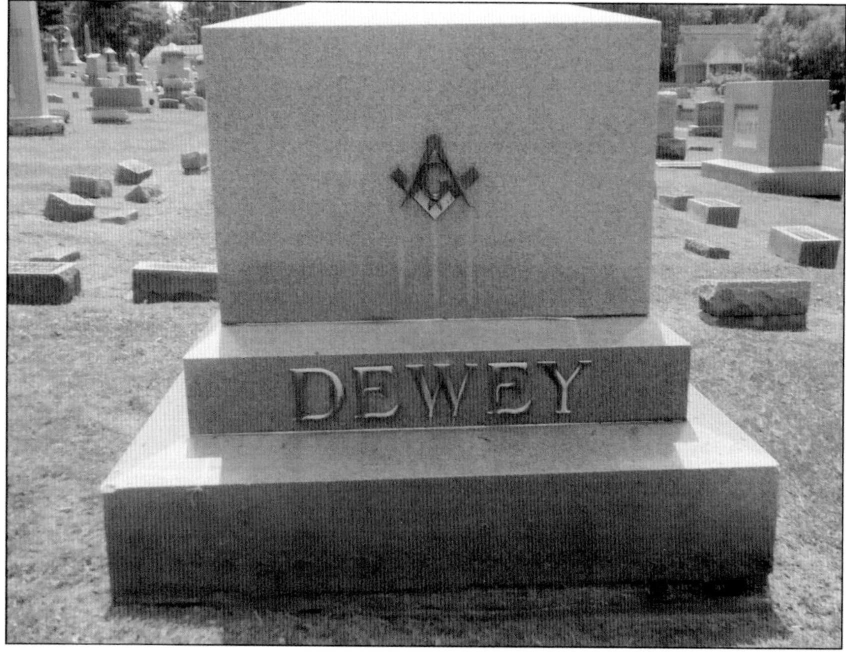

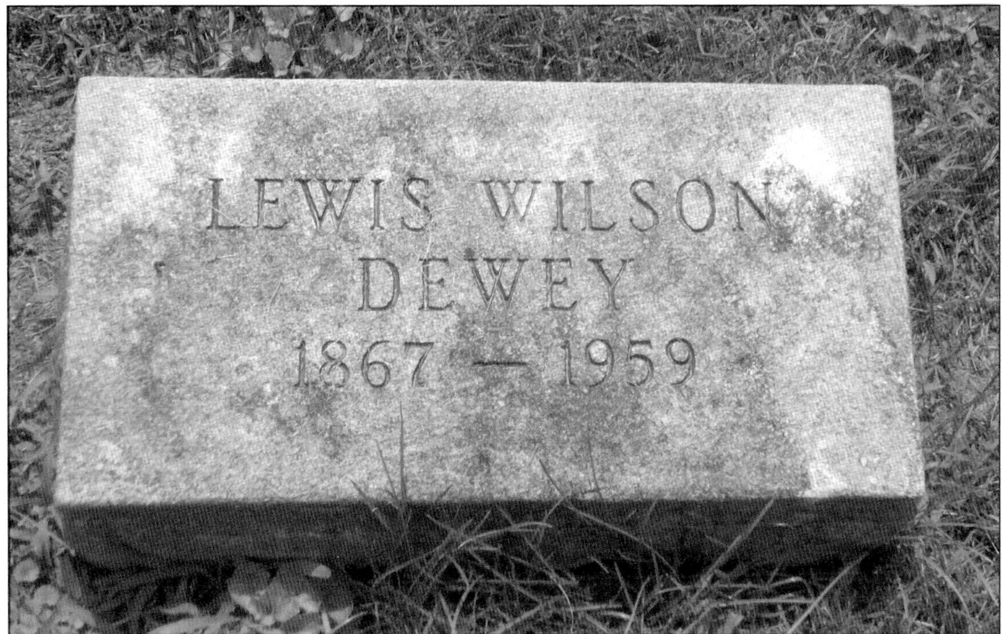

Lewis Wilson Dewey, or L.W., was born in 1867. He had three sons: William, John, and George. After they graduated from college, they also joined the company. Lewis was a member of the Masonic order like his brother and continued to run the company after J.S.'s death in 1916. Also like his brother, he was active in the community life of the town that served as their headquarters. Lewis was succeeded as president of Dewey Bros. Company by Joseph C. Dewey, keeping the company in the family, where it remained until 1975, when the business was finally closed. (Photographs by the author.)

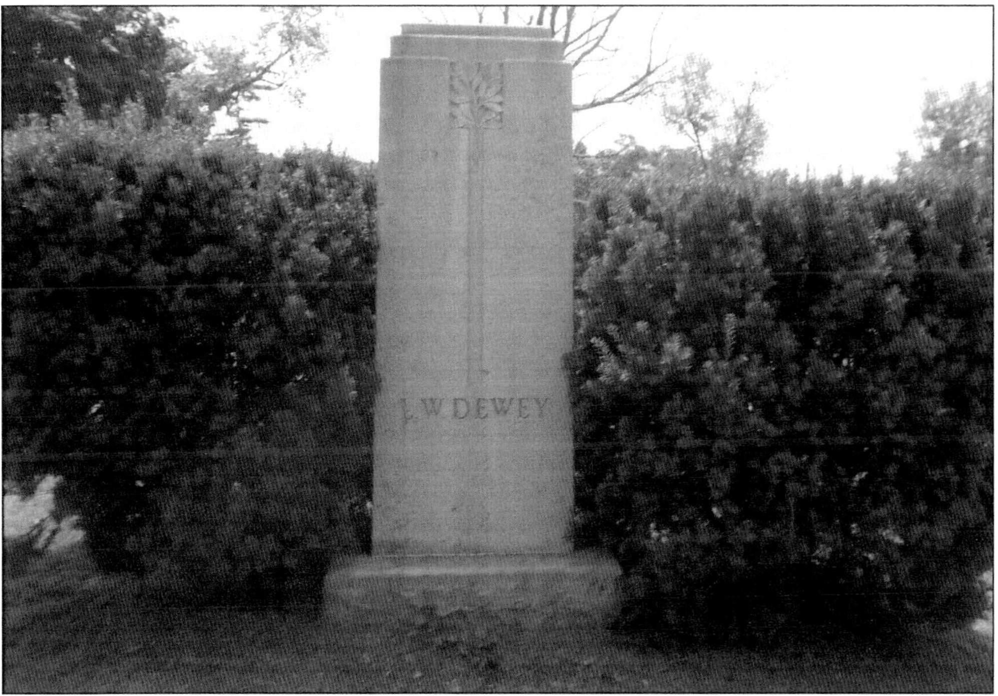

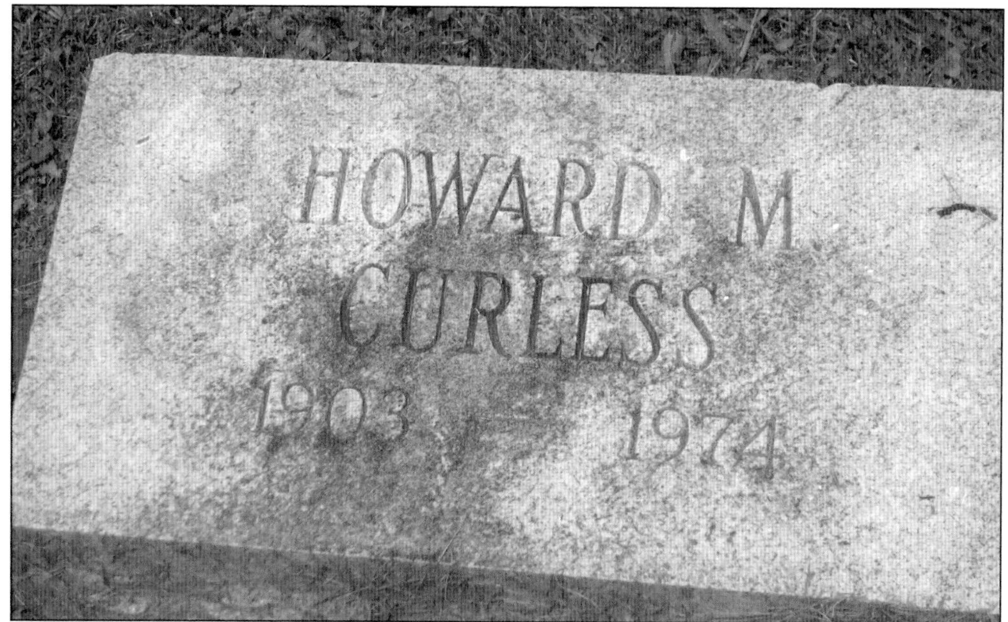

Howard M. Curless, born in 1903, bought the Curless Printing Company from Brown Publishing Co., which was owned and operated by Clarence J. Brown Sr. Upon purchase, he moved the operations to a building he and his wife, Mary, had previously purchased in Blanchester. Unfortunately, a fire destroyed the original building in April 1953. Undaunted, Howard made arrangements to keep the business and employees he cared for while the building was being reconstructed, and the business continued on at the same location by the end of the year. After Howard's death 20 years after the fire in 1974, Mary continued on as president. (Photographs by the author.)

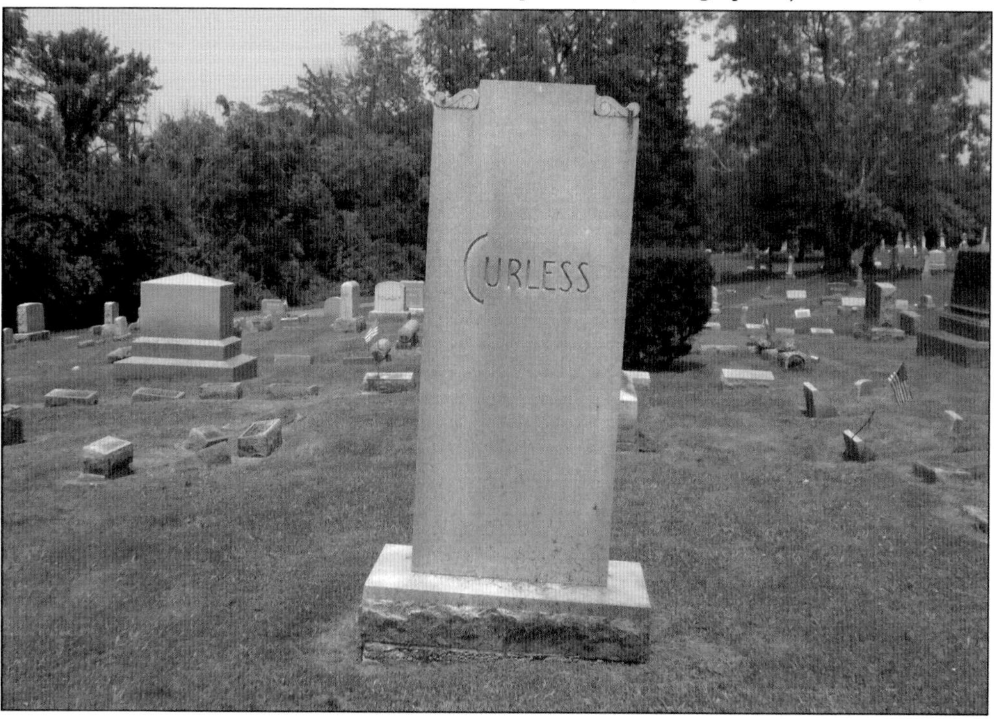

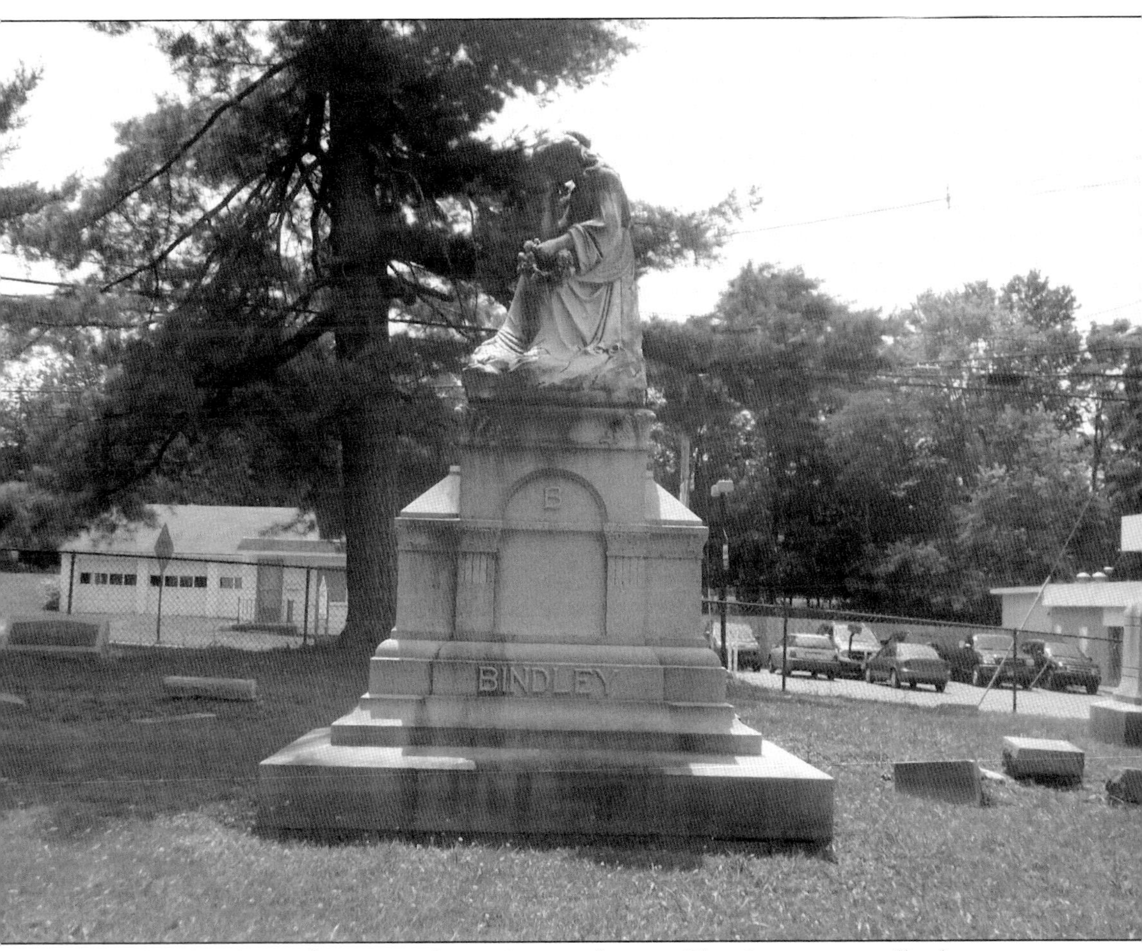

The Bindley family is still mentioned on a frequent basis in Blanchester, especially if one goes downtown, where the heart of the business district is dominated by the magnificent building constructed in 1896 by John Bindley to revive the commerce of the town after the fire of 1895. The building stands out even today, though the businesses occupying it are no longer the same. Originally it primarily hosted the Merchant and Farmer's Bank. Over the years, it has been bought and sold and broken up into smaller businesses, but the magnificence of the wrought iron and brickwork are still visible to anyone walking by on the street. Truly, John Bindley accomplished his goal of preserving commerce in the town, and even modern-day residents can remember him with appreciation and pay respect at this beautiful monument in the Blanchester IOOF Cemetery. (Photograph by the author.)

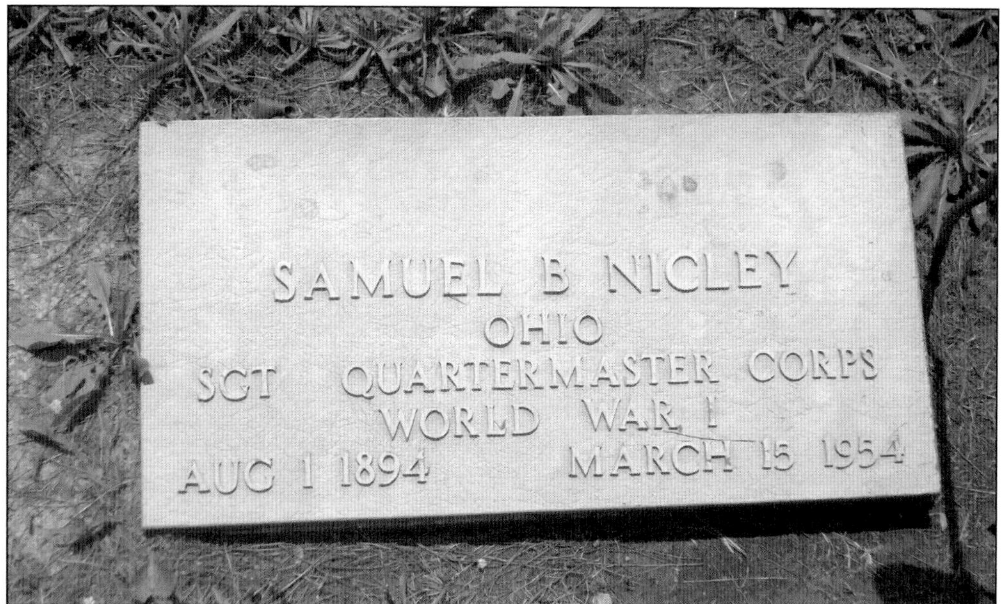

Samuel B. Nicely operated a restaurant with his brothers Burt and Henry. In 1920, he purchased a laundry and dry-cleaning business on South Broadway. He actually changed the spelling of his last name to serve as the trademark motto "Nicely Does It Nicely." He served six consecutive terms in the House of Representatives of the Ohio General Assembly. Nicely was born in 1894 and served in World War I as a sergeant quartermaster. He passed away in 1954, and his widow, Hazel, continued to operate the dry-cleaning business for 20 years after his death. He is now memorialized in the Blanchester IOOF Cemetery by a monument that serves as a bench, continuing to provide nicely for anyone who feels like visiting the peaceful spot. (Photographs by the author.)

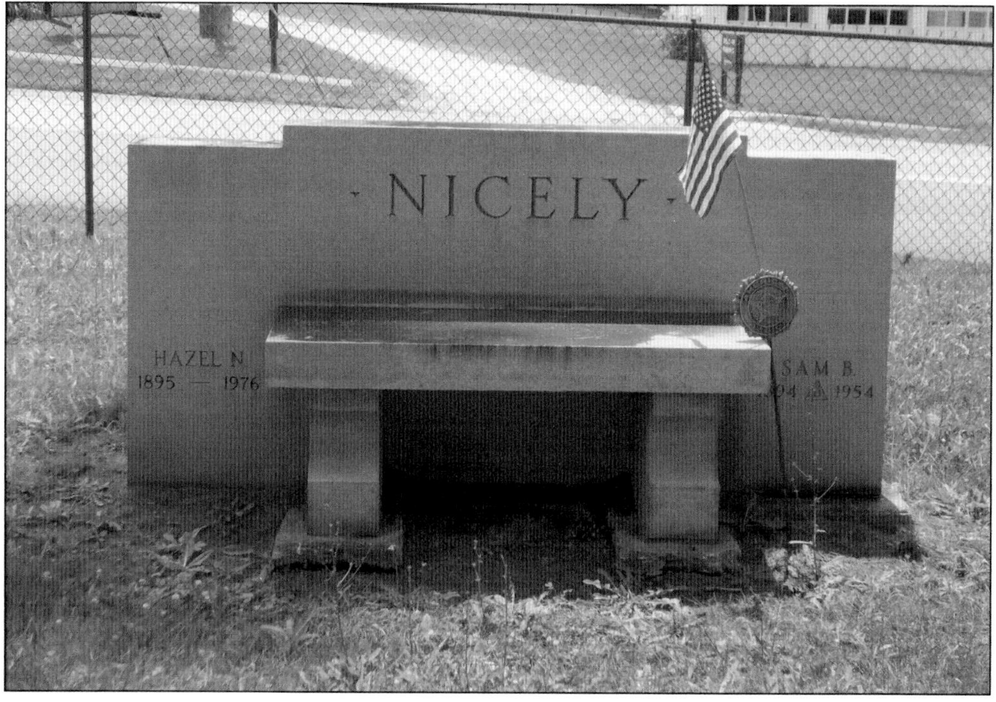

Two

Fire and Ruin

Any growing town will face some sort of calamity, and Blanchester is no exception. Early postcard images show the aftermath of fire, tornado, and snow, each disaster arriving fairly shortly after the recovery from the previous calamity. Damage to buildings is inevitable, and many of the original structures situated in the heart of Blanchester have been burned down or lost parts of roofs or facades. Fortunately, the people of Blanchester are resilient and have rebuilt, not allowing these tragedies to stop the growth of their village or harm their sense of community.

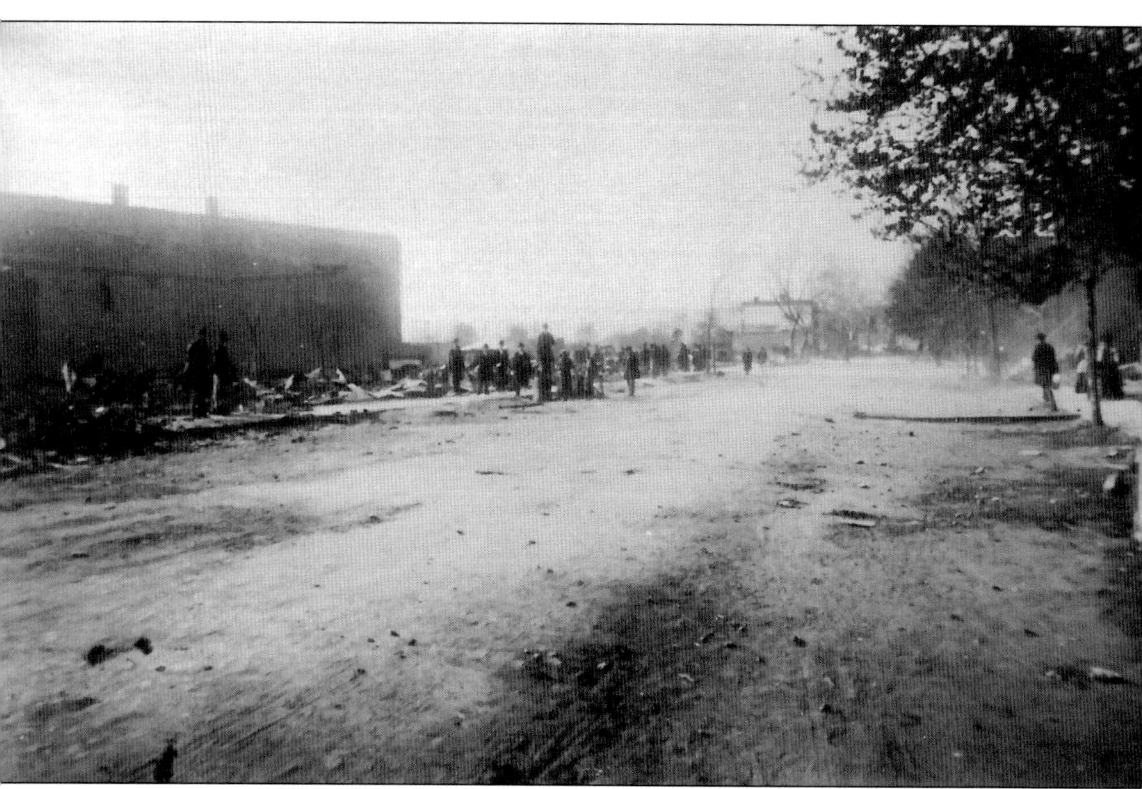

This is a view of the damage done to the business district of downtown Blanchester after the fire of 1895, looking west from the original Universalist church. The fire occurred on October 18, starting at around 1:30 p.m. in the old livery stables of W.W. Burke on South Broadway Street. At the time, the fire department had only hand engines and had to pump water from the area wells and cisterns, which quickly dried up, leaving the only source of water the Second Creek some blocks away. It was a windy day, causing the fire to spread more quickly than it could be contained. The fire raged out of control for several hours, devouring the original wood buildings that made up much of the original settlement. Ash is thick on the ground in this photograph, as the inhabitants try to determine what can be recovered and how to go about repairs.

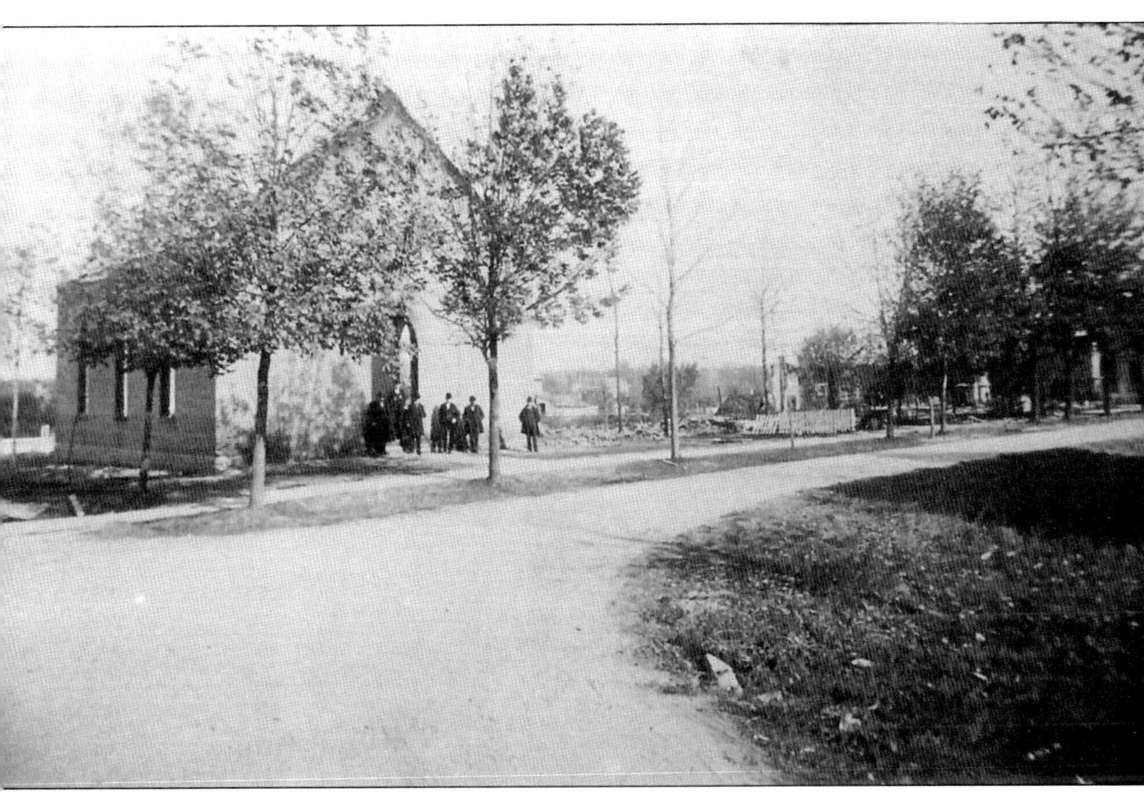

This is a photograph of the Methodist church after the fire. The church and neighboring buildings sustained heavy damage in the conflagration. The collapsed walls and rubble in the background give an idea of what it must have been like to see a once-familiar sight totally destroyed. When the fire started, the neighboring communities of Hillsboro, Lynchburg, and Loveland all responded quickly and arrived by rail to help battle the flames, and after six hours the fire was finally contained; however, 72 buildings were burned, including most of the business district, many homes, and stables. Fortunately, and somewhat amazingly, there were no injuries and no loss of life. Still, the total loss amounted to $125,000, only some of which was covered by insurance. In the wake of the tragedy, there was shock at the huge losses sustained by the community.

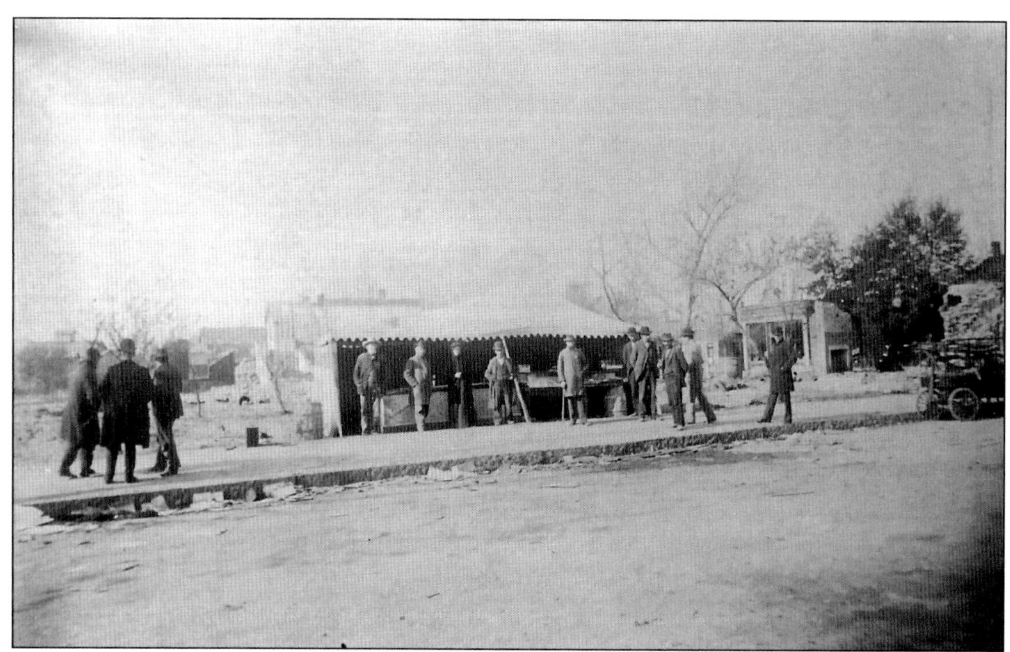

Fortunately, the businessmen of Blanchester had an enterprising spirit and did not let a fire destroying most of the business district detract from their work. Following the fire, P.E. Snyder Hardware set up a tent in the ruined business blocks from which to continue doing business for their Christmas sale, as depicted above. In 1896, a great deal of rebuilding was done, spearheaded by John Bindley, who oversaw the construction of new brick buildings in the business district. From him this commercial block took the popular name it is still referred to by today, the Bindley Block, pictured below. While the businesses have changed, much of the original building looks the same.

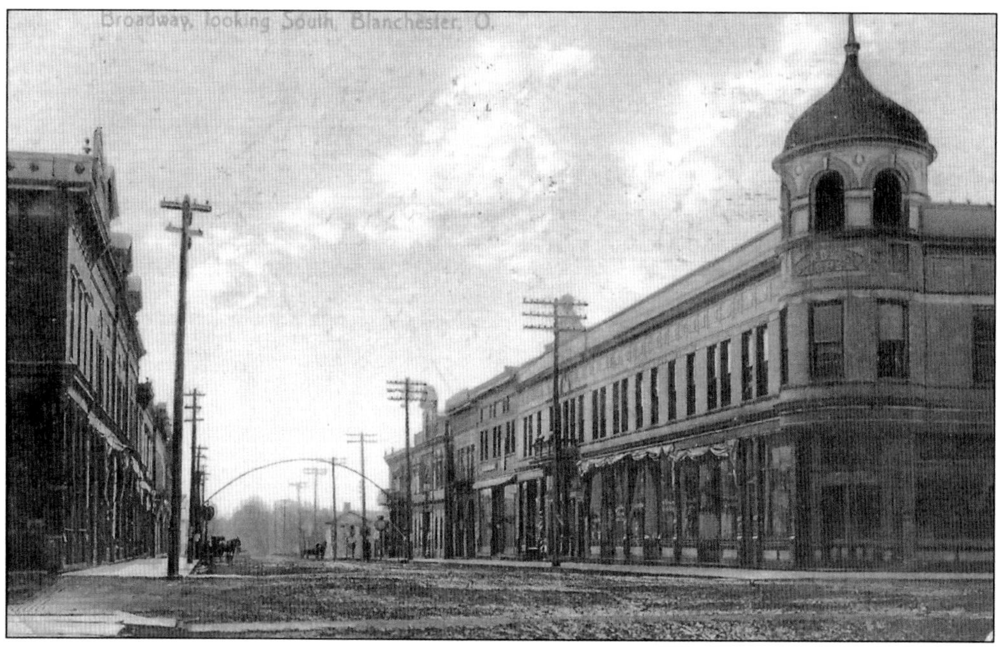

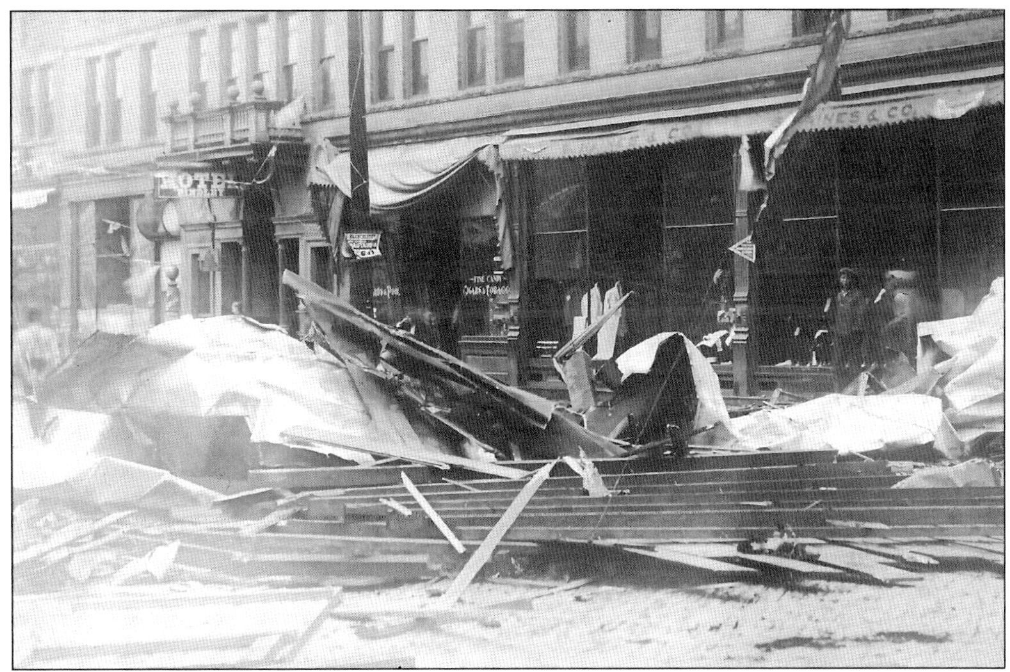

Unfortunately, the fire was not the only calamity the business district of Blanchester was forced to endure. Around 1910, a tornado struck the area, doing quite a lot of damage to the storefronts in the recently built Bindley Block. These photographs show the broken glass and damaged roofs as well as the debris in the street, while the locals assess the damage they will have to repair this time. However, by this point being well versed in rebuilding, the tornado, while frightening, was much more quickly recovered from, and soon the storefronts were repaired. These photographs specifically capture the damage to the buildings on South Broadway Street.

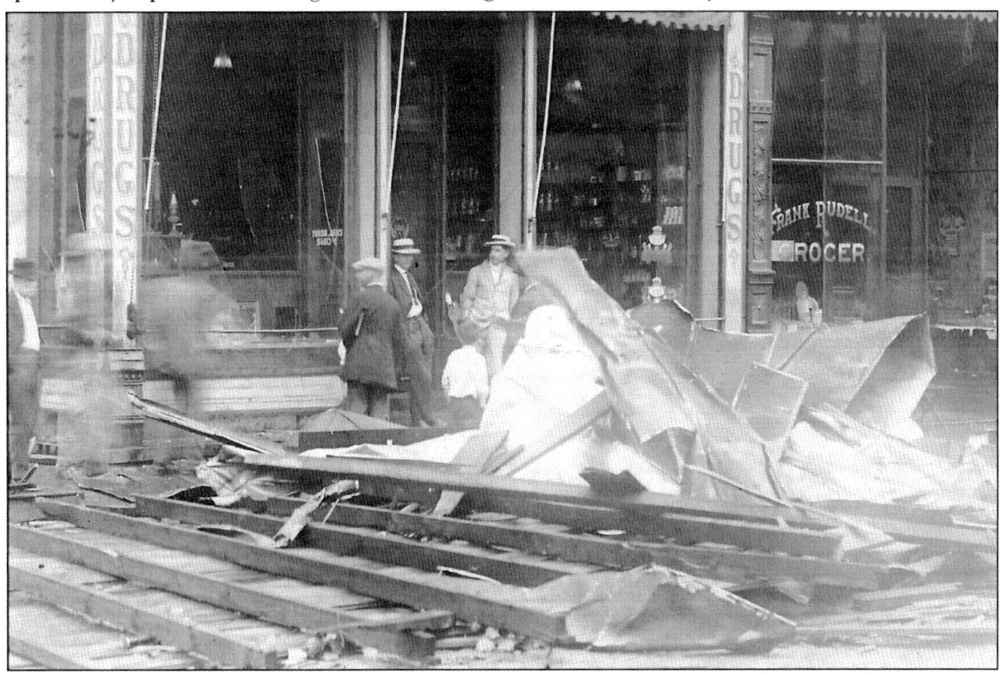

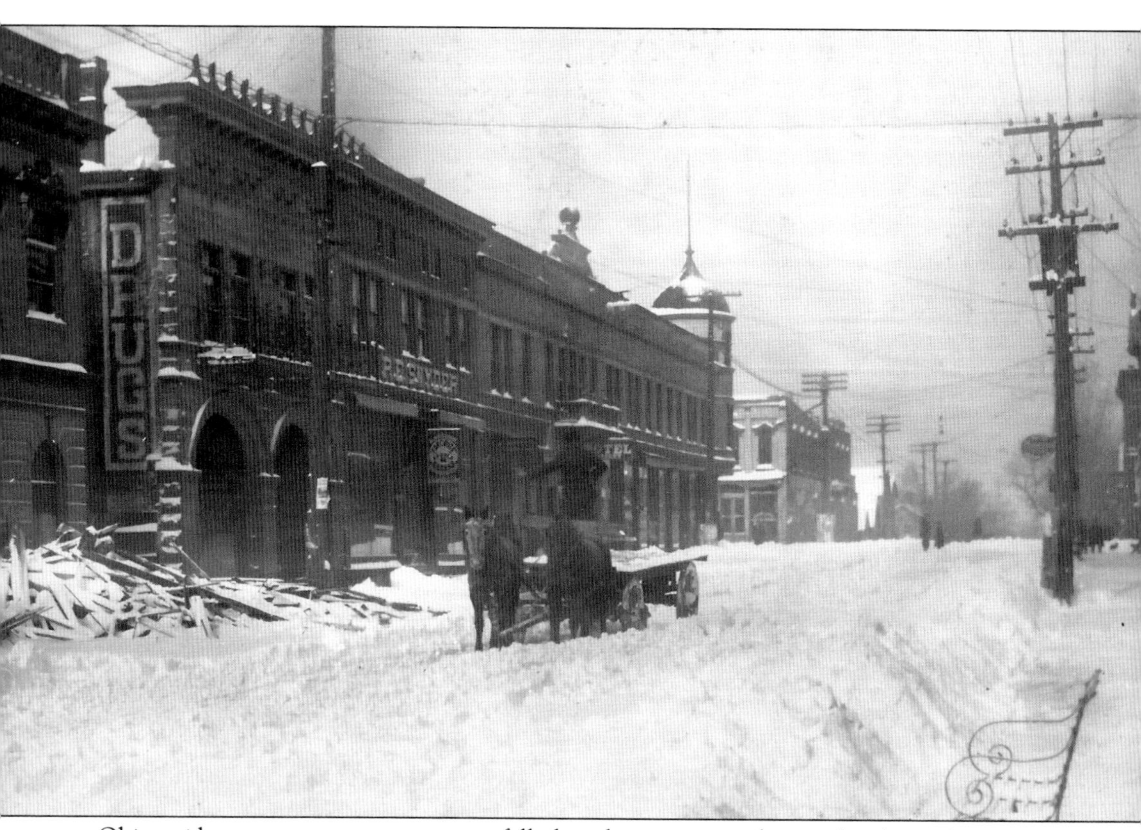

Ohio residents are not strangers to snowfall, though most storms do not often leave the mountains of snow that are regularly experienced by more northern states. Blanchester, located at the southern end of the state, is even protected from most of the lake-effect snow that can make life interesting for those closer to Lake Erie and Cleveland. Still, damaging snow can occur, and just such a heavy snowfall arrived in Blanchester during the winter of 1917–1918, blanketing the streets and the buildings that had just recovered from the tornado of 1910. In some places, the snow fell heavily on structures that were not designed to withstand the weight. At the far left of the image is the rubble from the skylight of the arcade building in the business district, which collapsed, leaving much debris in the street.

Three

The Centennial Celebration

On June 22, 1933, the *Star Republican*, a local newspaper, published the following article:

> Many Blanchester persons have expressed themselves favorably as the result of suggestions that a centennial celebration be held here when Blanchester's new Main Street is completed later in the year. Blanchester was first laid out in 1832 and officers were elected after additions were made to the village in 1833, making this the centennial of the town. Local business and civic leaders are expected to take the proposal up in the near future and plan for a celebration of several days' duration.

Those "Blanchester persons" did not have to wait long for their celebration, which was held September 27–30, 1933. The celebration included concerts from local bands, parades, floats telling the history of the town, and visits from local government officials. The local Tuesday Club even presented a display of the changing fashions of the last 100 years. The crowd numbered roughly 80,000 people over the four days, and the celebration is still looked back on fondly.

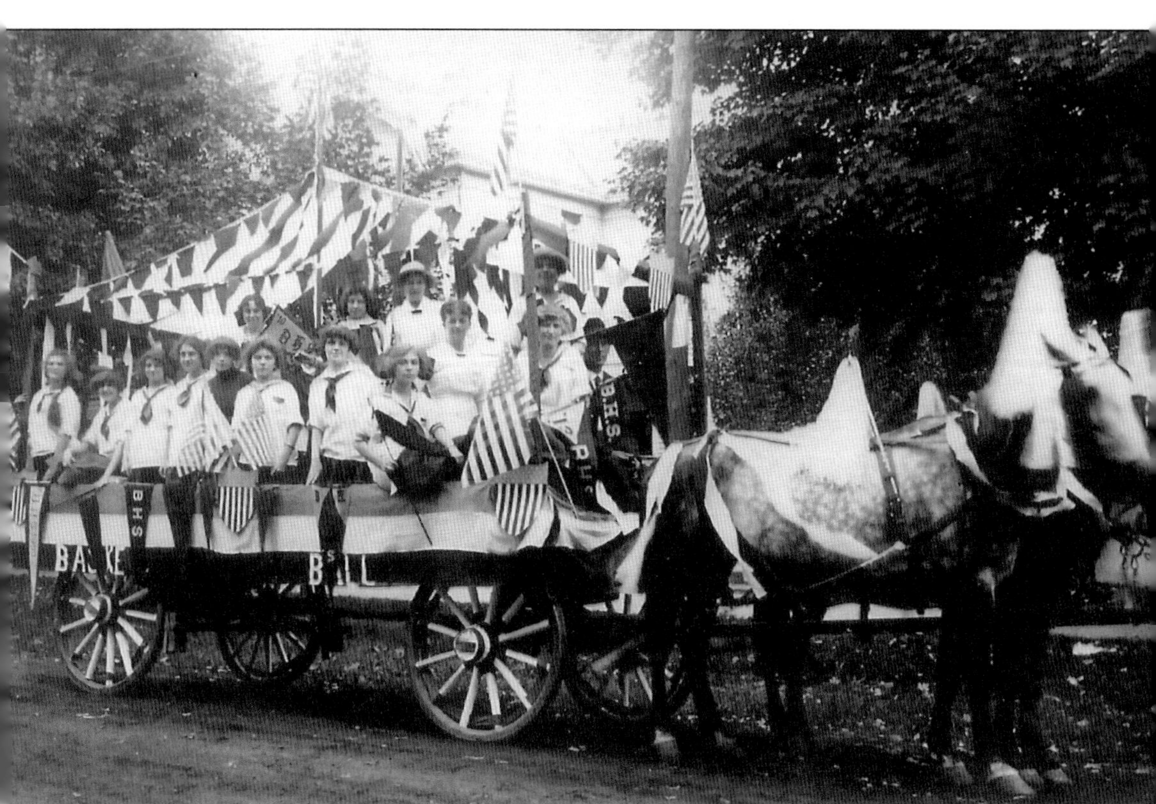

Pictured here is a float put together by the Blanchester High School to participate in the Blanchester centennial celebrations. The high school was a major focus of the community at the time and has remained so to this day. The matching school uniforms worn by those on the float really emanate a sense of solidarity.

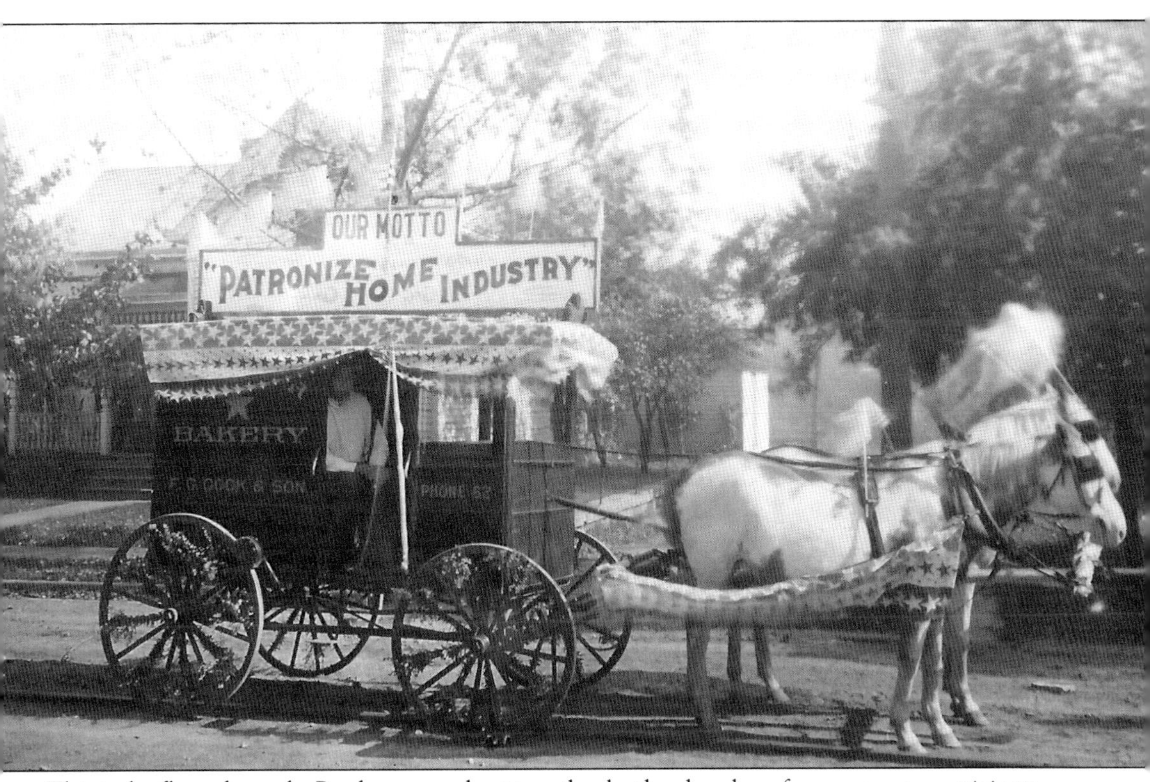

This is the float, drawn by Percherons and put together by the chamber of commerce to participate in the centennial celebration, encourages the throngs of spectators to patronize home industry. The side features an advertisement for a local bakery as well as F.G. Cook and Son.

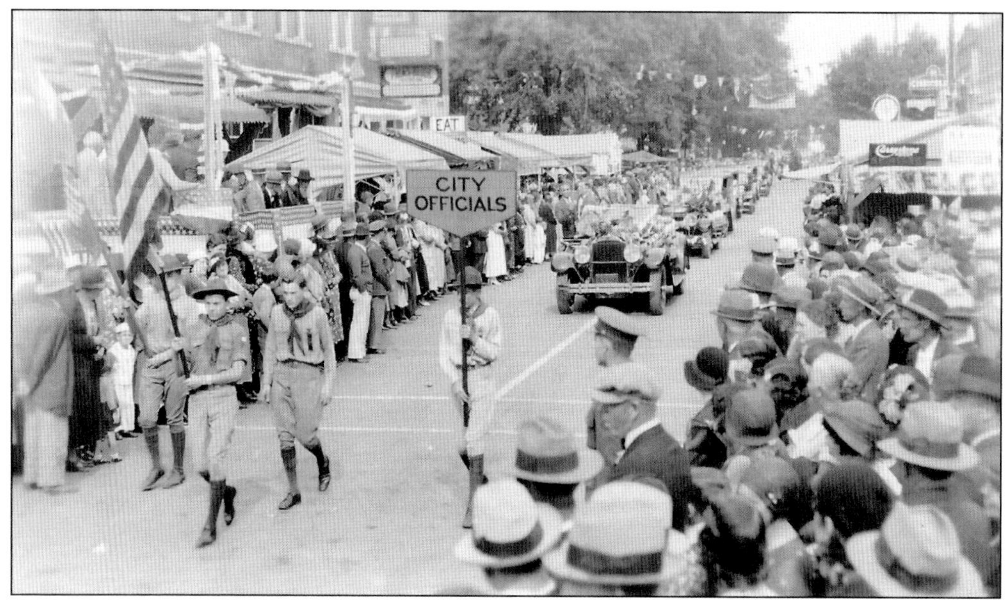

There were many parades that took place over the four days of the celebration. The streets were thronged with onlookers as local groups and musicians all came to march and show their support for the village that had grown so much over a century. Marching here are groups of Boy Scouts, local officials, and many others. School bands from all over the surrounding area arrived to march. The *Star Republican* reported that people came to see the parades from Brown, Clermont, and Highland Counties, and during the evening parades one could only "get through the vast crowd with the greatest of difficulty." Friday alone drew in an estimated 30,000 people, and that was only the third day of the festivities. In the end, it was not just a parade to celebrate Blanchester, it celebrated the entire region.

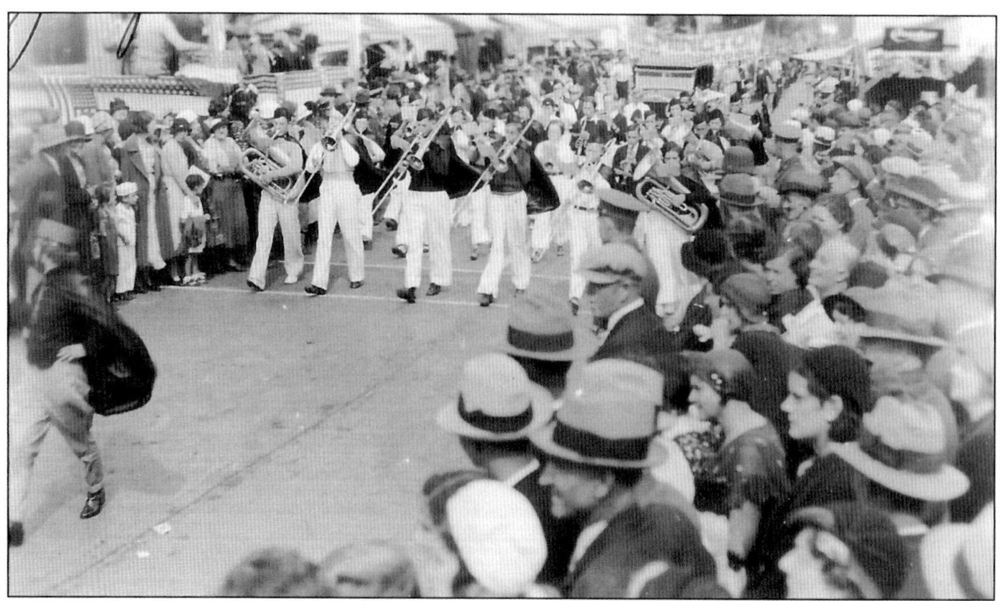

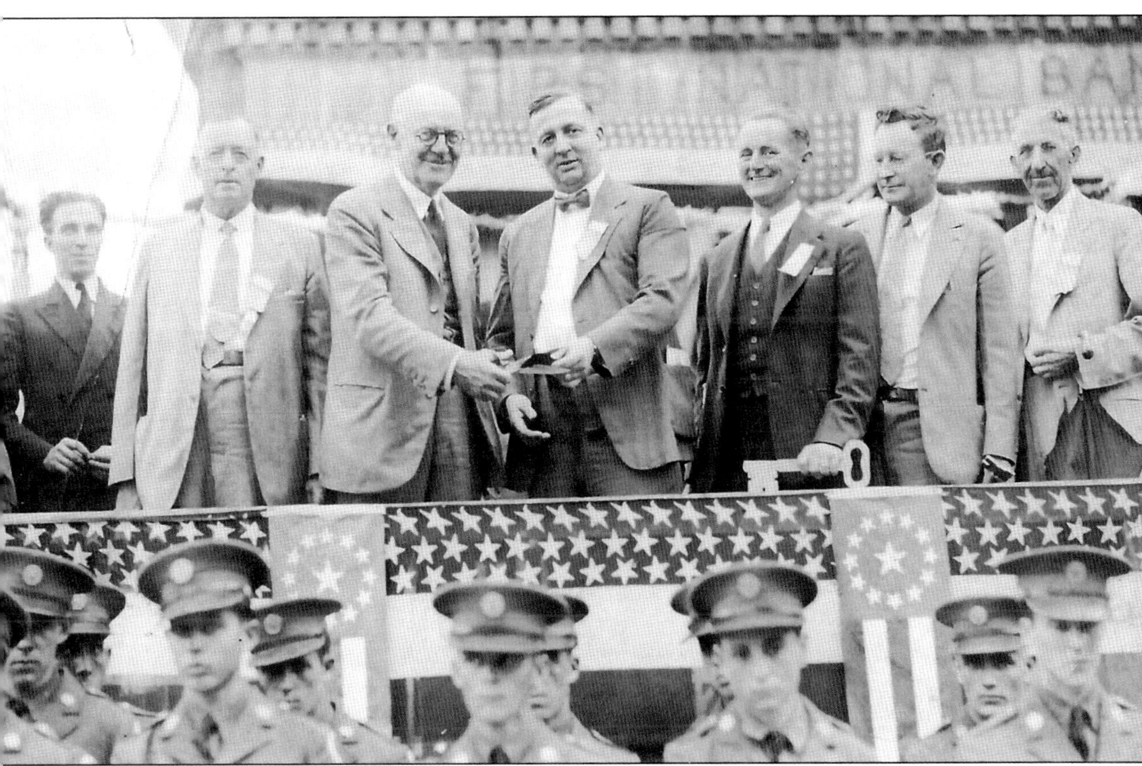

The main event of the centennial celebration, taking place on Wednesday, the first day of the festivities, was the ribbon-cutting and dedication for the nine-tenths of a mile of road that had just been repaved with brick over the new sewer system. It was this construction that had caused the delay in the celebration, which should have taken place in 1932, the actual centennial date of the laying out of the town. Pictured here is the honorary chairman for the festivities, Clarence J. Brown Sr., along with Mayor Cliff Reed, Gov. George White, the Honorable O.W. Merrell, who was director of highways, and Joe Bennett, a 1925 graduate of the high school who devised a new technique for printing images in the newspaper. The ribbon-cutting took place at 2:30 p.m., and then Mayor Reed presented the honored guests with keys to the city.

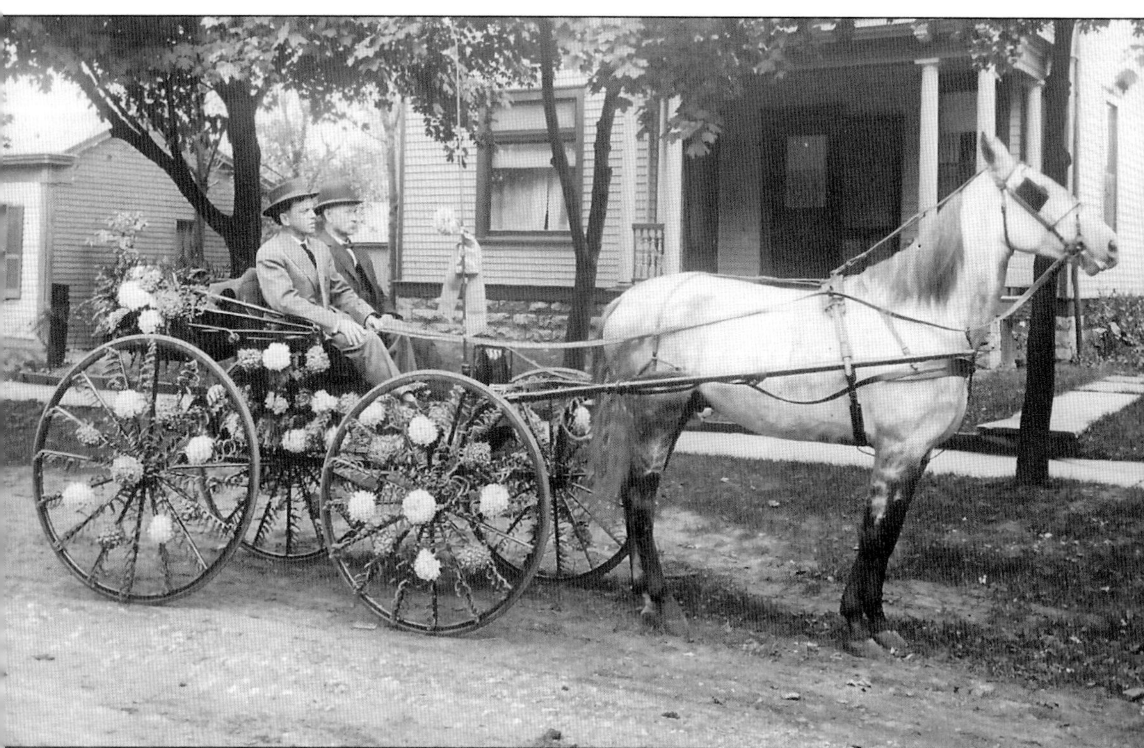

The Hannah Funeral Home, which had opened in Blanchester in the early 1900s on East Main Street, participated in the centennial parade by decorating its carriage with flowers. For the occasion, employees gaily attached flowers to the wheels and attached the canvas top. Festively decorated, it looks nothing like the carriage of a funeral home. Today, the business is carried on by Tufts Schildmeyer Funeral Homes.

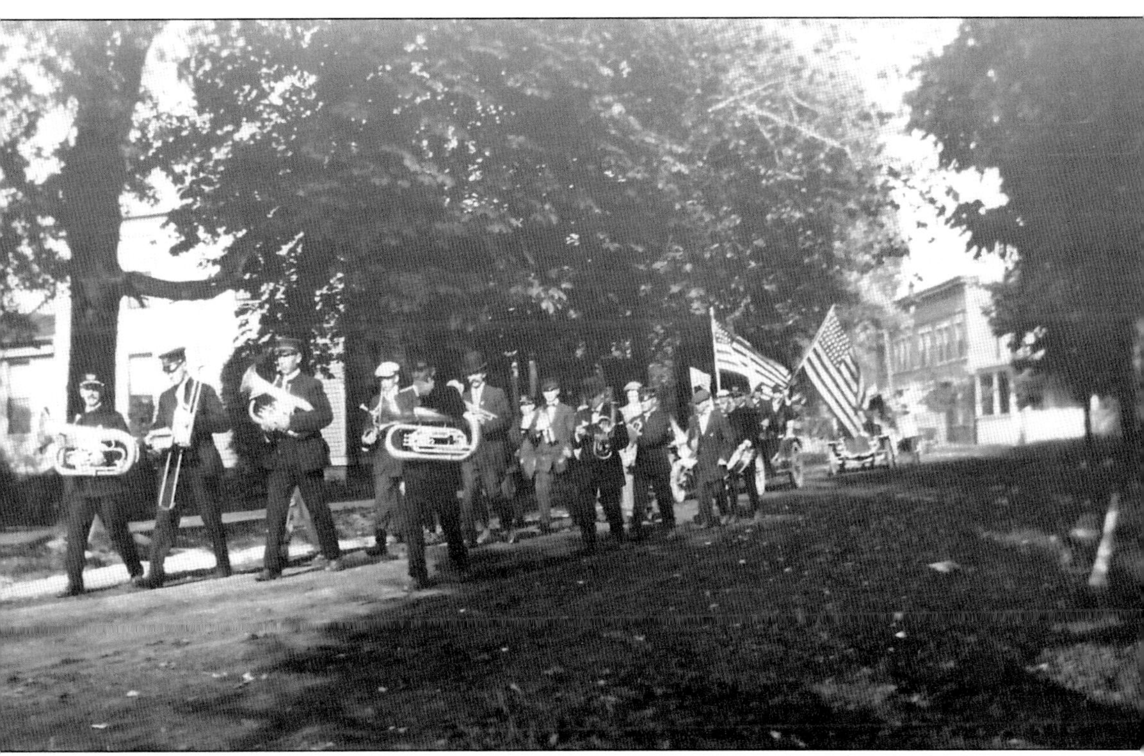

Seen here marching down a residential street is the local National Guard unit band. The director and leader of the band, George Shanor, was a Blanchester resident from a musical family. He served in World War I, World War II, and Korea and retired as a lieutenant colonel. This band also led the 1915 dedication of the newly constructed JROUAM (or Junior Order) building at the corner of North Broadway and East Center Streets. The building is still in use today by the Fraternal Order and the Exchange of the Church of the Nazarene.

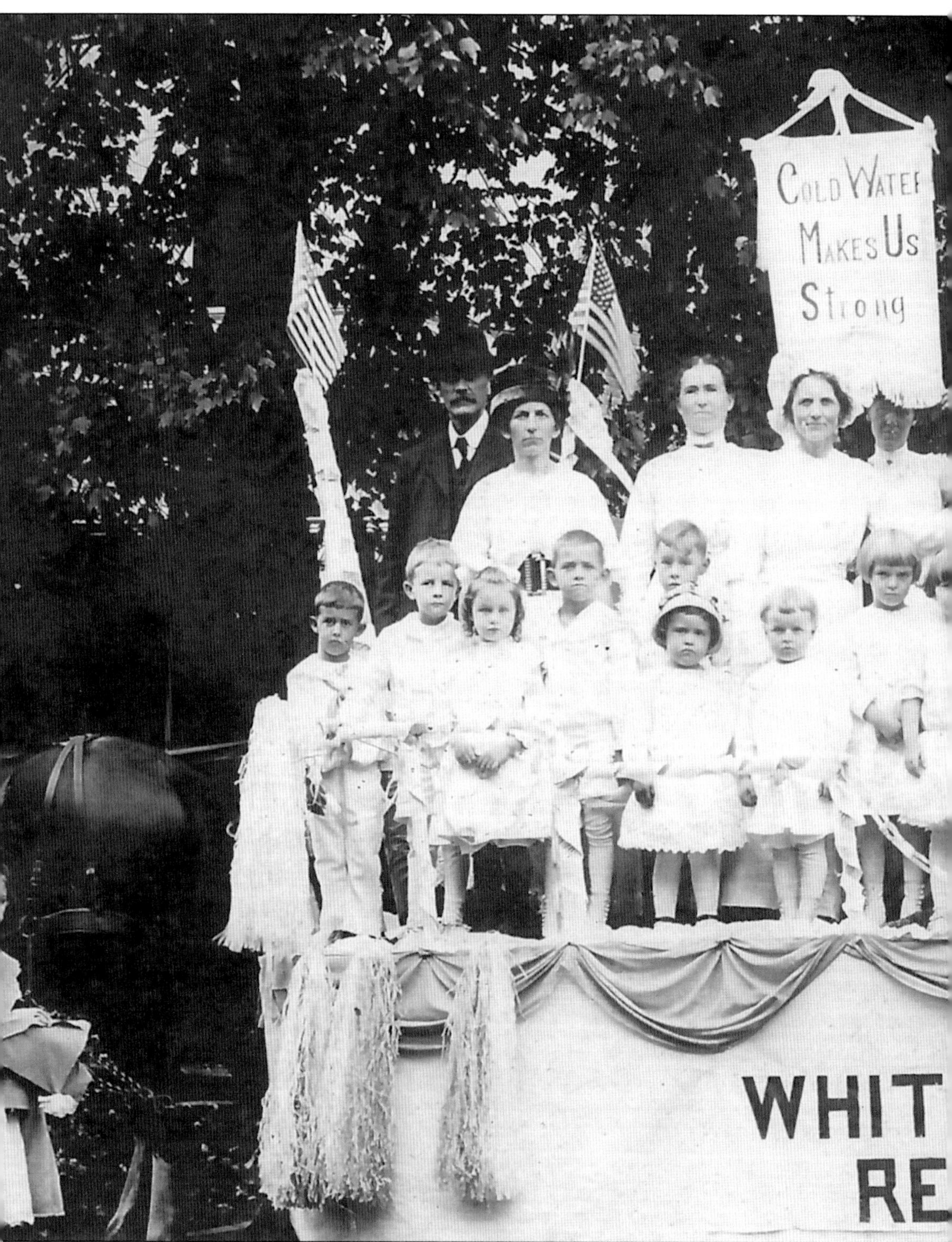

This float represents the White Ribbon recruits of Blanchester. At the time, Prohibition had recently come to an end, and to counter the return of alcohol to communities, the White Ribbon

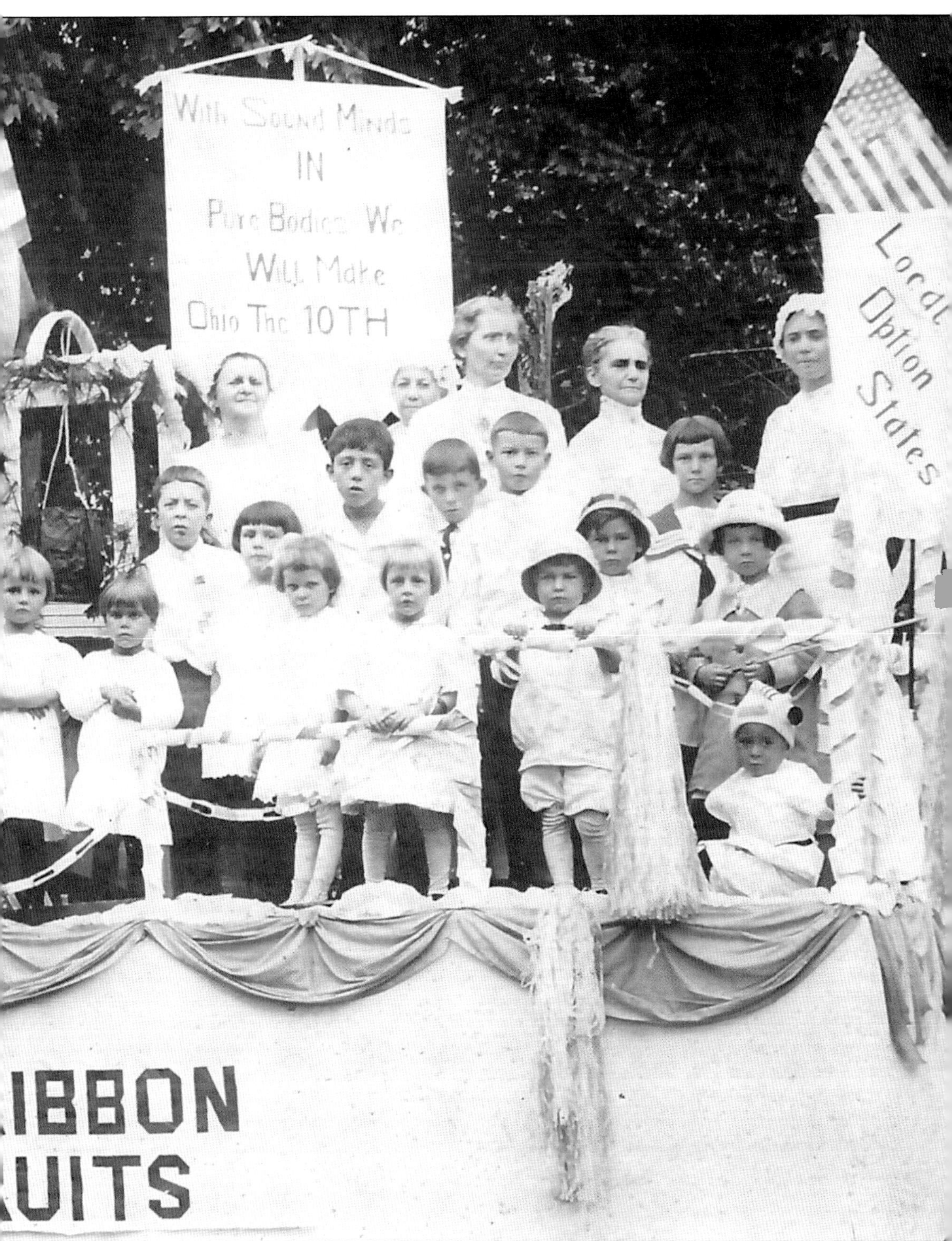

group went to local schools to recruit students for their cause. These students then rode in the parade wearing white ribbons to show their support.

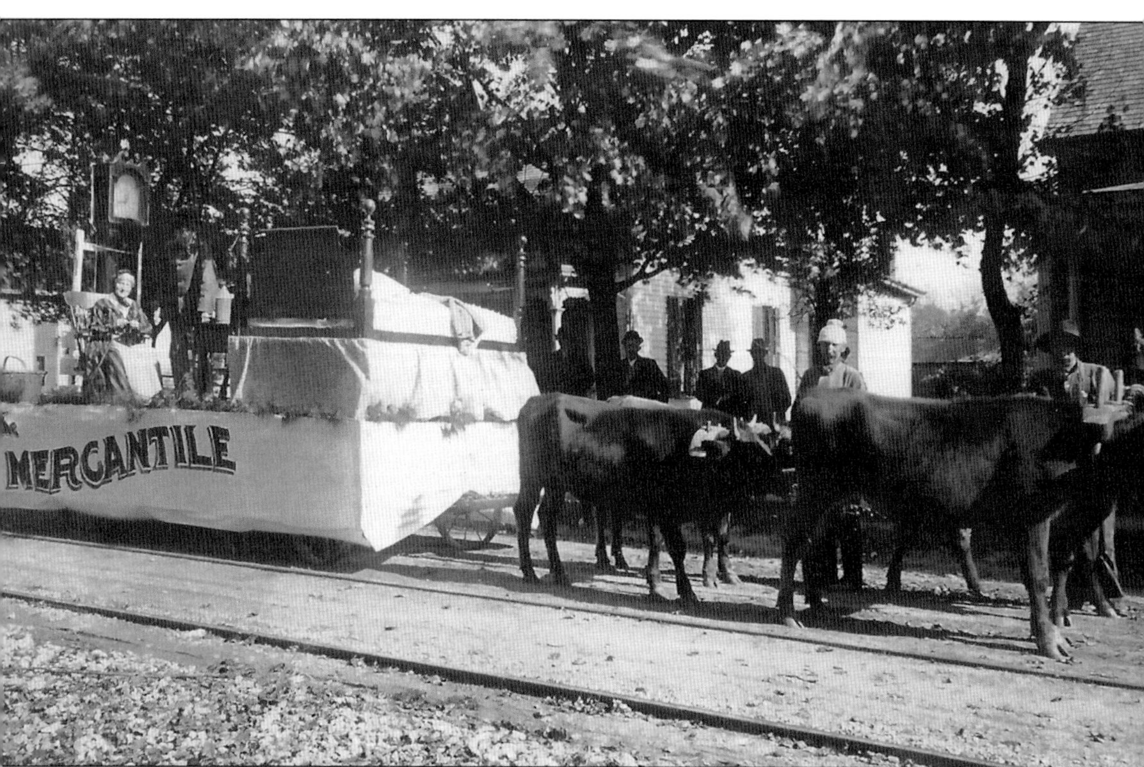

This float was sponsored by the local mercantile store for the centennial parade. Here it is pictured on South Broadway Street, near the heart of the celebration. It is notable that the float is drawn by oxen rather than the horses seen pulling the rest of the floats. The oxen were meant to represent the hardworking nature of those associated with the float.

Four

Trains and Traction

The village of Blanchester gained a great advantage over some of the other small villages in the area when the railroad decided to pass through town rather than the originally planned Woodville. Residents were also blessed with a traction line, which brought business, students, passengers, famous locals to celebrate Blanchester events, and in times of need help to the growing village, which suddenly found itself a hub of industry in the midst of acres of farmland.

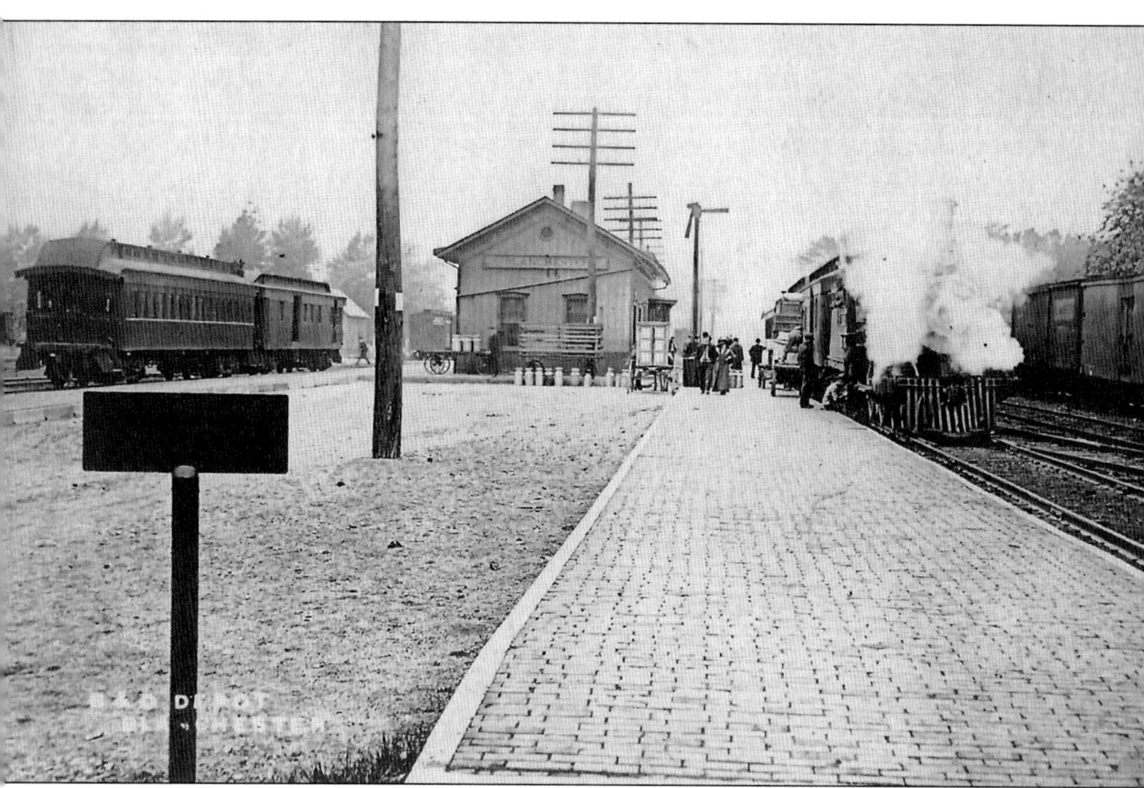

Pictured here is the local depot during the years when Blanchester was an exciting hub. On the left side is the passenger train on the Hillsboro line. On the right side is the South-West Railway on the east- and west-bound rails. They were part of the Marietta and Cincinnati Railroad, which was important in southern Ohio. The full route ran from Marietta through Vincent, Athens, Hamden, Chillicothe, Greenfield, Blanchester, and Loveland. One of the main branches of the route was the Blanchester to Hillsboro section. Unfortunately, there is not as much need for trains to pass through the area now, with most original freight being carried by cars or trucks. Though the tracks remain, and sometimes a train will pass through on the rails, the business and excitement that the railroad brought to Blanchester is a thing of memory.

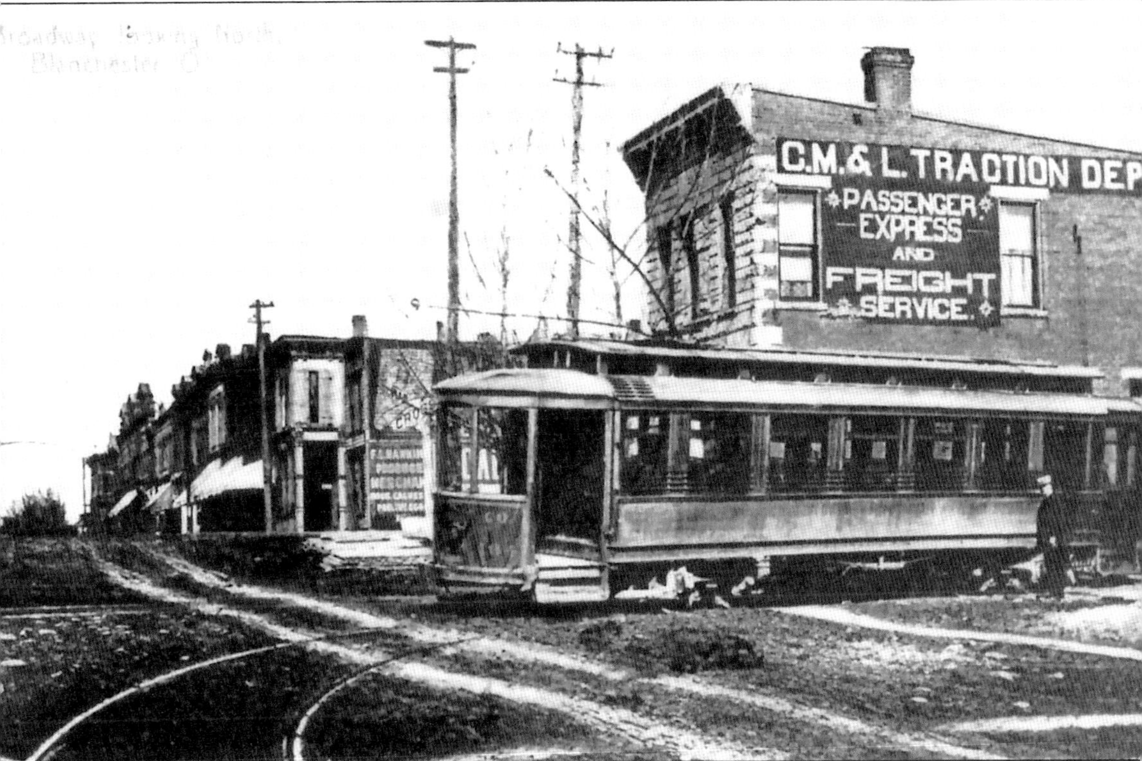

The traction line ran in Blanchester from 1906 to 1926. Originally, it was meant to be the CM&L Line, as seen painted on the side of the traction depot building in the image, running from Cincinnati through Milford and ending in Loveland. Instead, it ended up running to Blanchester and served as a way for area students to attend school in the village when the more far-flung school systems merged with the Blanchester schools. One student was even known to ride her horse and buggy to the traction depot to board the line and then ride the rest of the way into Blanchester, which gives a good impression of how rural much of the area still was at the time. The depot, shown here in 1907, was the old Acton Artistic Monument company building, which was appropriated to serve the traction line.

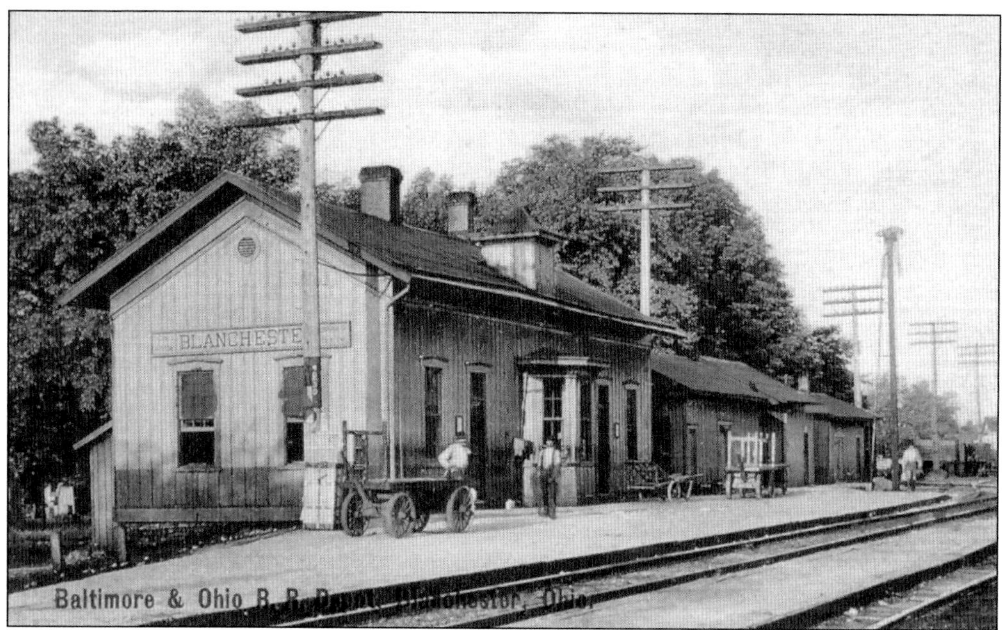

This is an image of the original Blanchester Railway Depot when it was located closer to Broadway Street, dating the image prior to 1910. After 1910, the location was moved farther away from Broadway Street and thus the heart of the village and the business district. The railroad tracks, however, still cross Broadway Street.

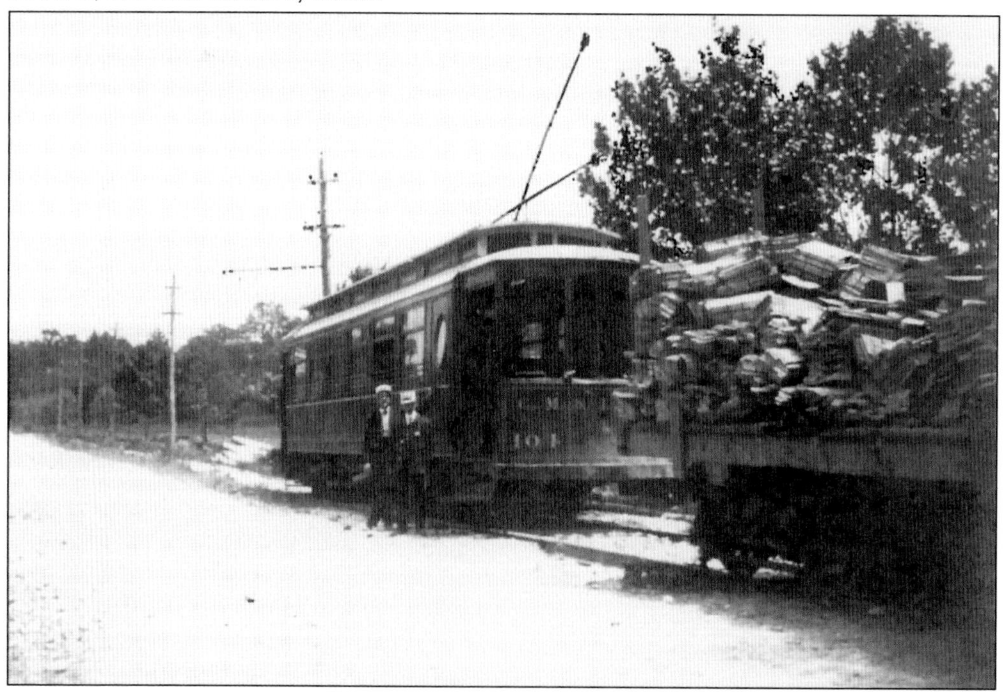

Pictured here is one of the old traction cars that passed through Blanchester regularly for the 20 years that the traction line ran through the area. The first arrival of such a car to Blanchester took place on June 11, 1906. Unfortunately, the traction lines no longer run, though the community remembers them fondly.

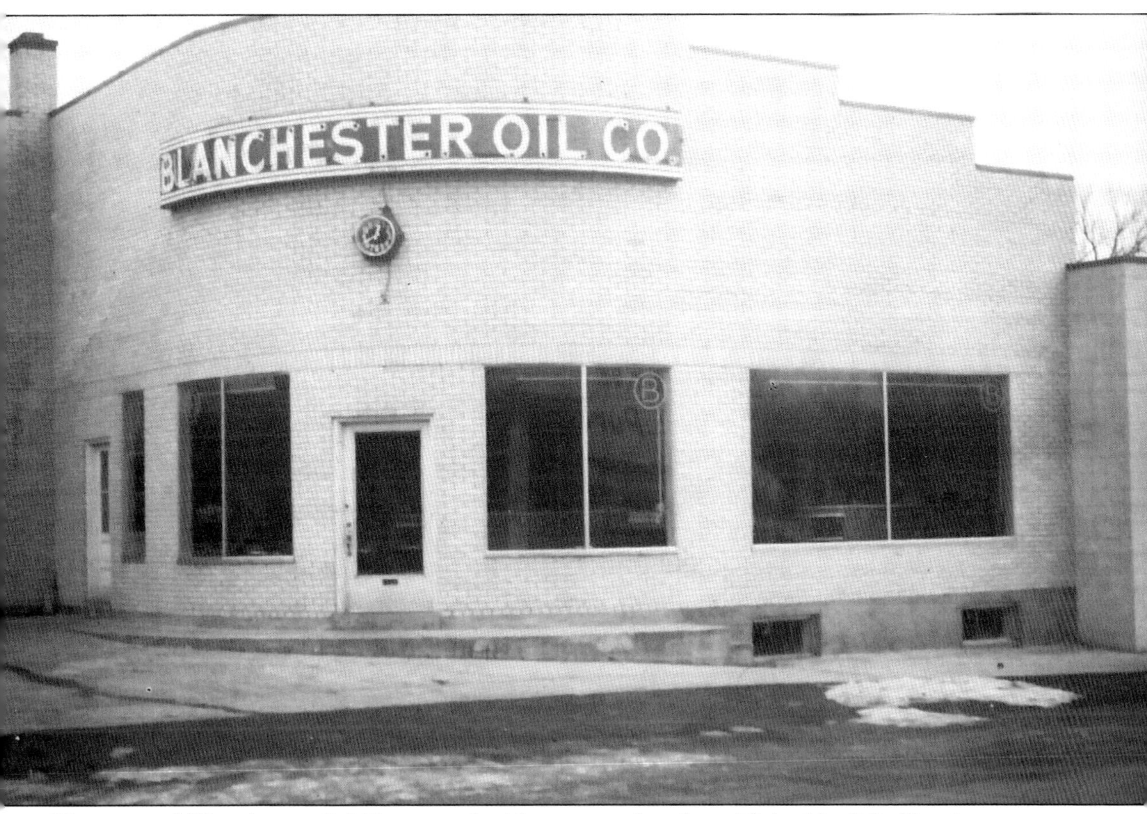

The original Blanchester Oil Company building, owned and established by R.L. Kruckemeyer, who also owned the Foundry and Engineering Company with his business partner, a Mr. Shrader, was burned in a fire in 1944 and had to be reconstructed. This image features the new building, which is made of white brick and still standing, with the sign proudly displayed. Though much of the building is now used to house a few novelty shops, it is still a highly recognizable landmark. More importantly, it is located right by the remaining railroad and traction lines, mostly neglected these days but still running across Broadway Street, just at the outskirts of the business district of downtown Blanchester. It was on the side of this building that a local artist, Ronald D. Keith, painted a mural to commemorate the history of the traction line in town.

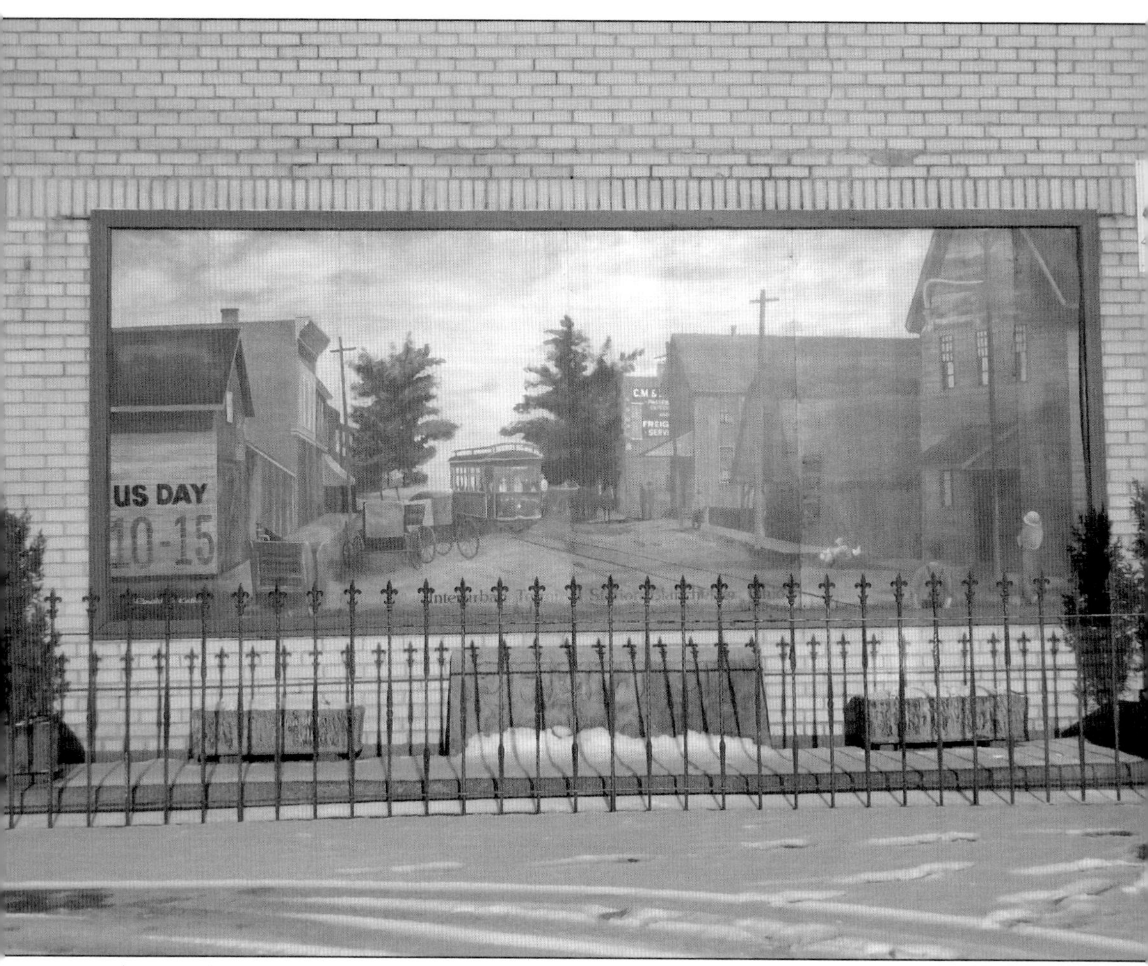

This mural was painted by local Blanchester artist Ronald D. Keith on the side of the Blanchester Oil Company building to remember the former traction line that had brought such prosperity to the small village and had run through just feet away. While he paints a wide variety of subjects, including nature scenes, pastoral views, and landscapes, the residents of Blanchester know Keith best for re-creating scenes from village history on his canvases and murals on the walls of town buildings. Many of the paintings are in the hands of the Blanchester Area Historical Society, though they were created to be put up for bid at the Blanchester auction. They are highly prized—and with good reason. The traction line painting was done in 2006 to celebrate the 100th anniversary of the arrival of the first traction car to Blanchester in 1906. (Photograph by the author.)

Five

School Days

Blanchester has a lot to be proud of in regards to the school district. Community schools are consistently highly rated and serve much of the surrounding area. Of course, for locals this is not much of a surprise, as the schools have increasingly served the educational needs of area young. The schools are also the primary organizers of community events and a way for locals to continue to relate to each other, ensuring the focus on community, which is such a central part of life in Blanchester.

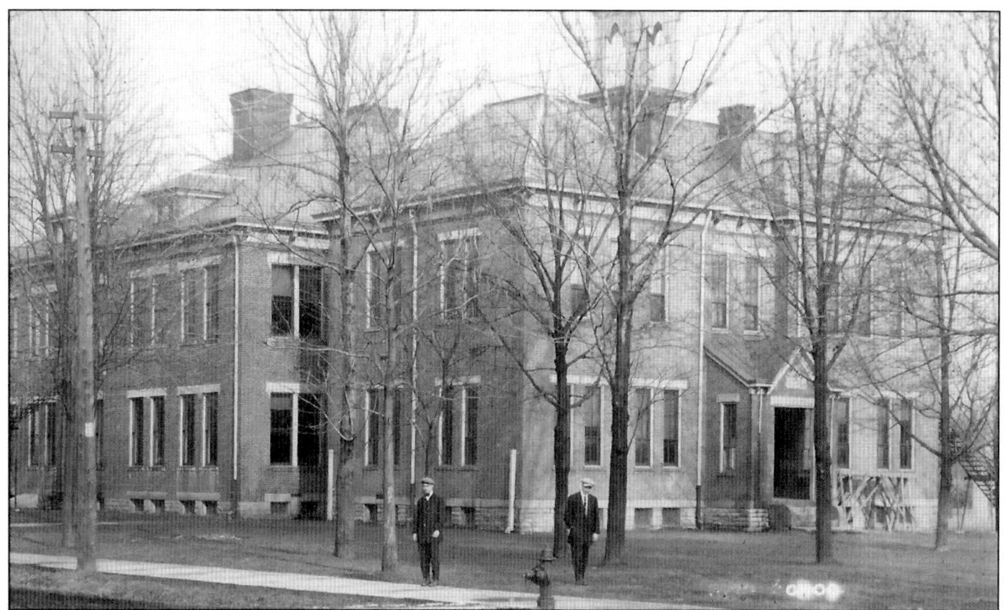

Pictured here in the early 1900s is the Main Street school building, which was located near the heart of Blanchester. While it was not the first school in town—the older ones having been burned down or torn down in previous years—it is generally considered the old schoolhouse nonetheless, likely because many residents have fond memories of attending school there.

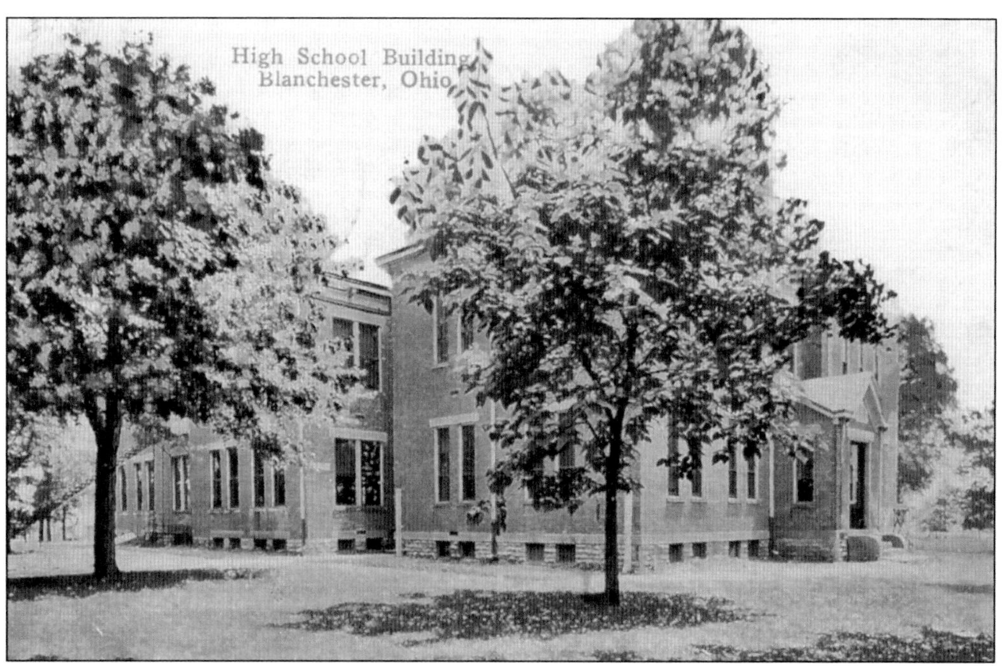

The Main Street school served as the early high and elementary school for Blanchester and the surrounding area. This original building was torn down in 1967. It was located in front of the future high school building, which is now the municipal building. As the student body grew, the building was given new additions to accommodate children.

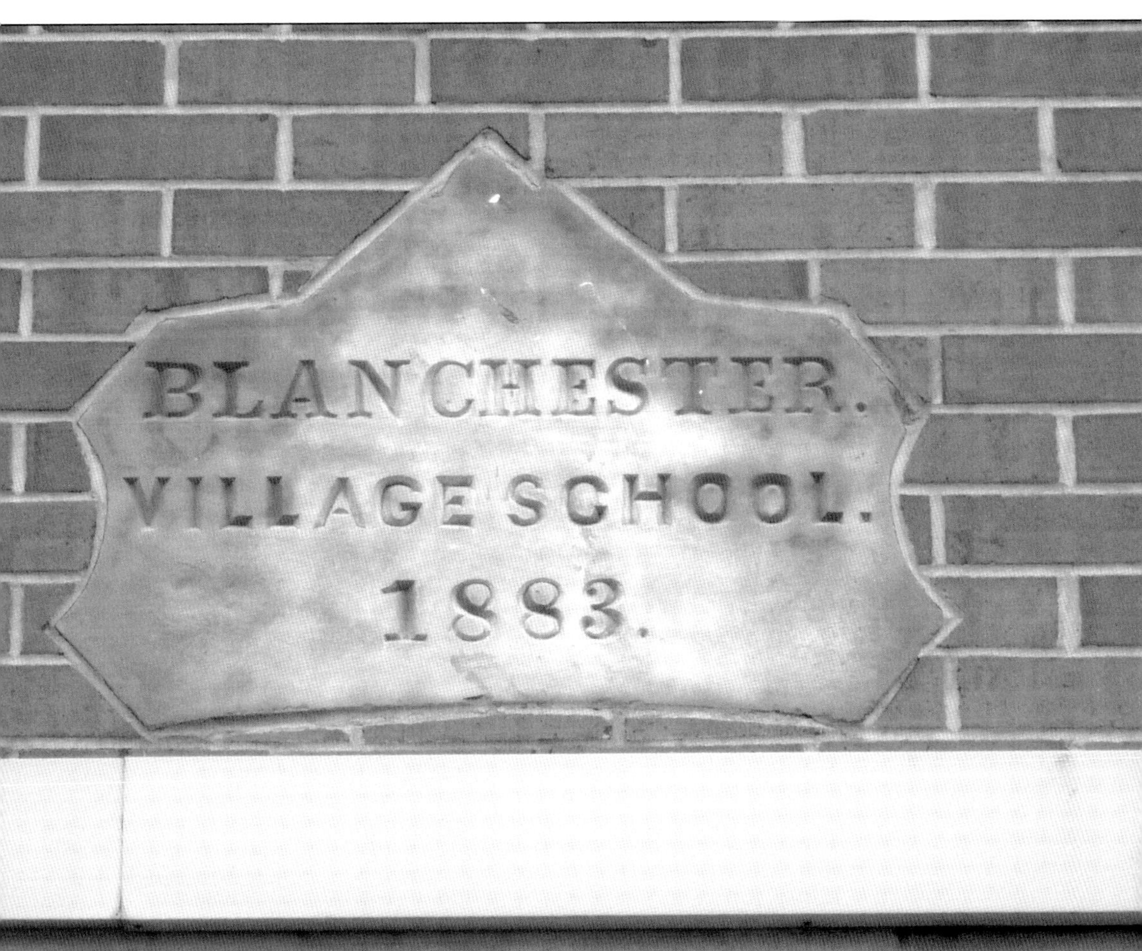

This is an image of the top arch of the ticket booth at the current Blanchester High School sports and athletic complex. It was taken from the original building, where it was placed to commemorate the graduation of the first high school student from the school system, George W. Gustin. Gustin graduated in 1883, and he was the first because prior to his graduation most of the students who went through the schools stopped after their elementary education was completed. This signified a changing of the times and priorities of the surrounding communities. The following years had small graduating classes as well, but more graduated nearly every year. The preservation of this stone is largely thanks to the Blanchester Area Historical Society, which insisted that the history be preserved and given a place of honor in the local community. (Photograph by the author.)

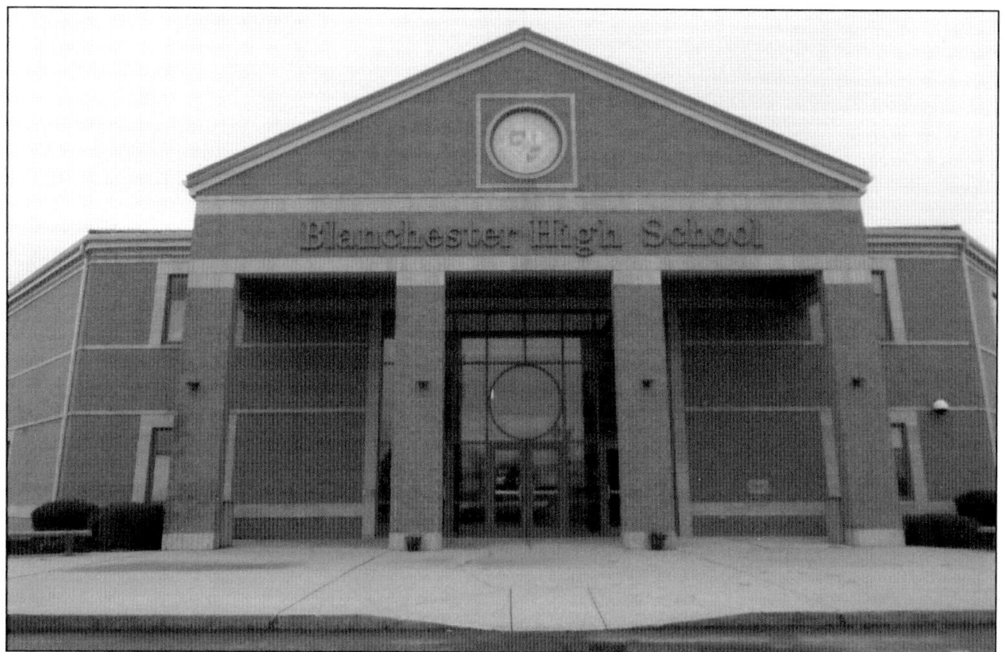

The new Blanchester High School opened 2002 and is on Cherry Street next to the former high school that opened in 1967. That building was remodeled as the middle school. The "school complex" began development in 1967 and currently includes the board of education office, athletic fields, bus compound, and all school buildings except Putman Elementary School. (Photograph by the author.)

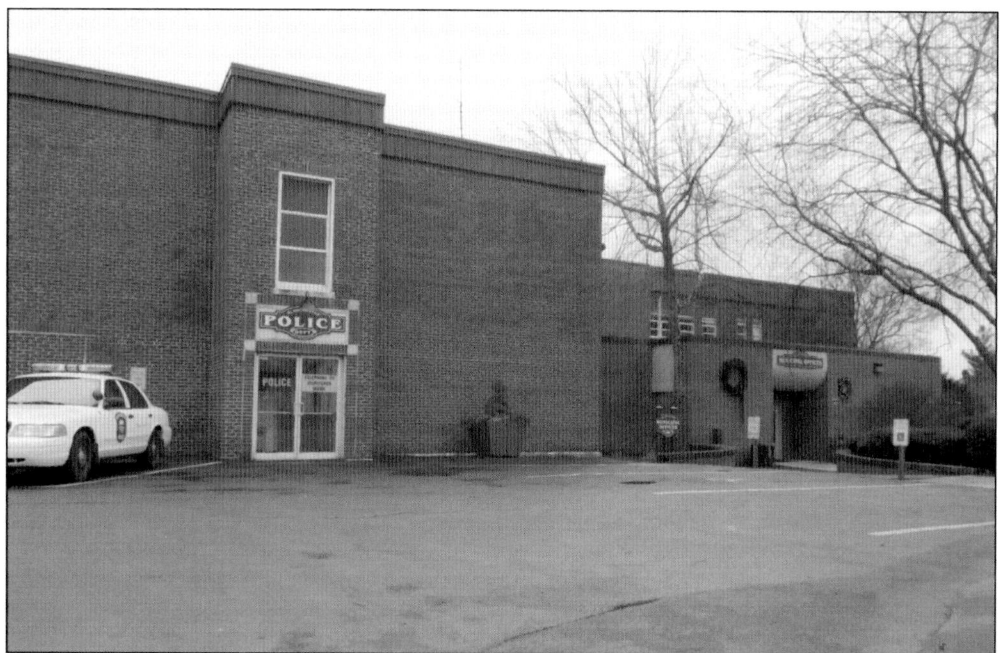

Now serving as the municipal building and police department, this structure was the previous high school, still known as the Main Street School. The additions to the building as the student body expanded are obvious in the construction. (Photograph by the author.)

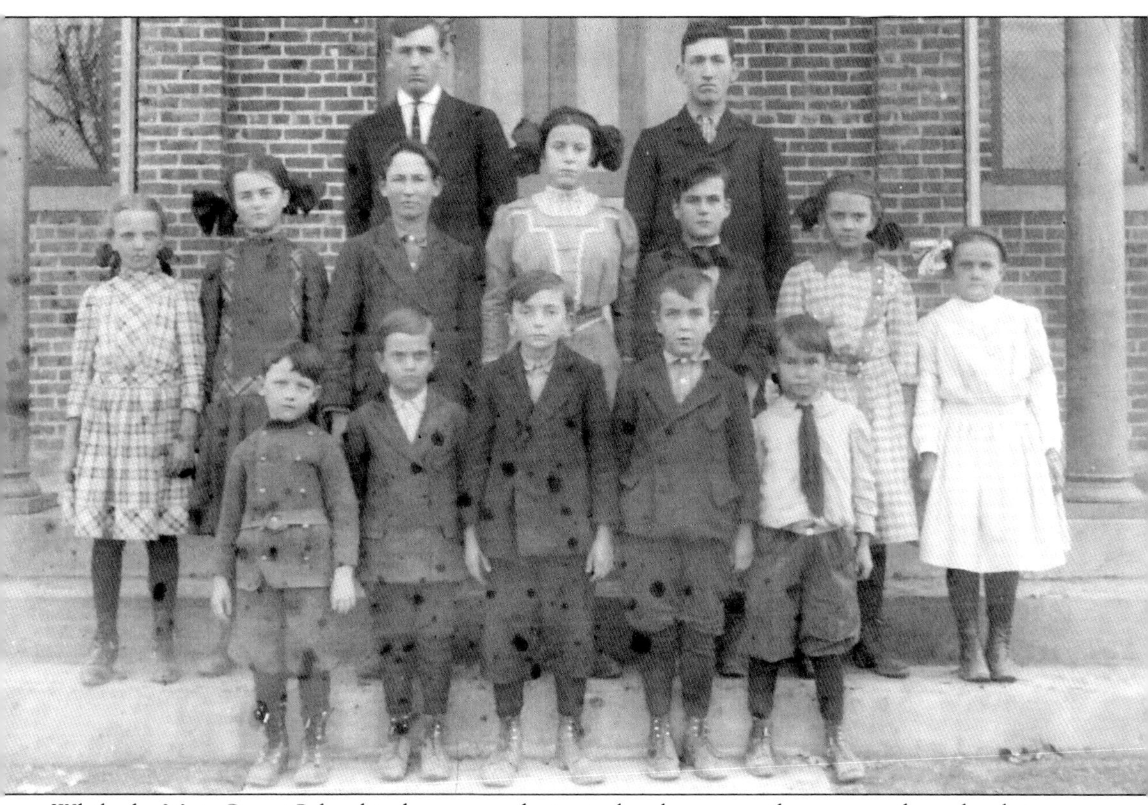

While the Main Street School is the most enduring in local memory, there were other schools in the Blanchester area over the years, many of which then fed into the ever-growing high school. Pictured here is the student body of the Second Creek School, including teacher George Simpson (back left) and student Everett Penquite (back right), who became a farmer and rural postal carrier. The photograph was likely taken between 1909 and 1912, the years Simpson was a teacher at the school. The school itself was in operation until 1931, and the students were merged with the larger Blanchester School District, along with students of other smaller area schools, especially as the buildings were expanded. This school building still exists and now serves as a private residence. It is thought that the original school in Blanchester was perhaps along Second Creek near this location, though the exact spot of that building, a roughly hewn log structure, is uncertain.

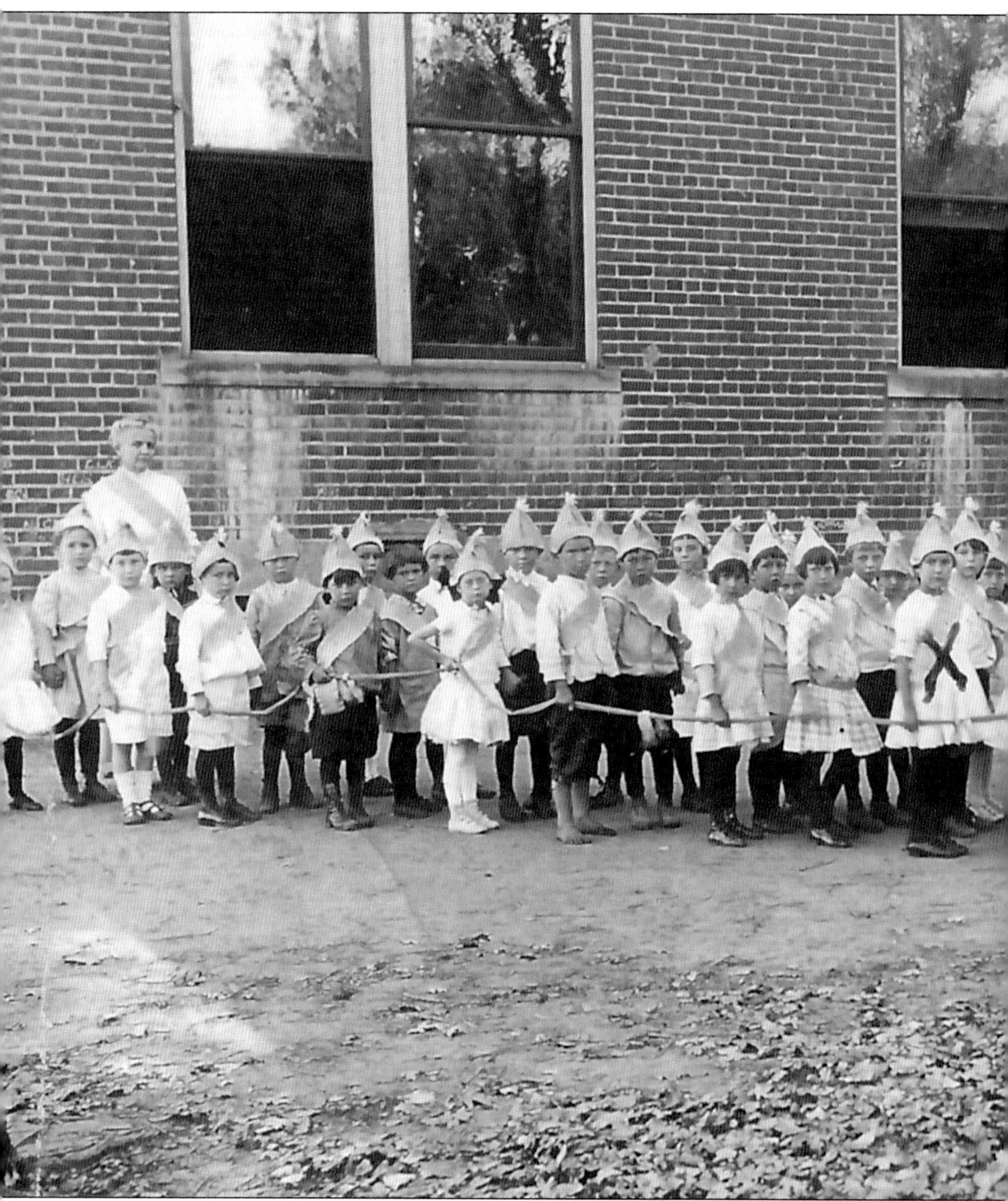

Pictured here in the 1920s are students of the elementary school at the east end of the former Main Street School wearing hats and nice clothes as they prepare to celebrate May Day. Also seen is long-time first-grade teacher Mattie Pierson (left), who taught from 1894 to 1921. While May Day celebrations are more common in Europe, they are still found in the United States from

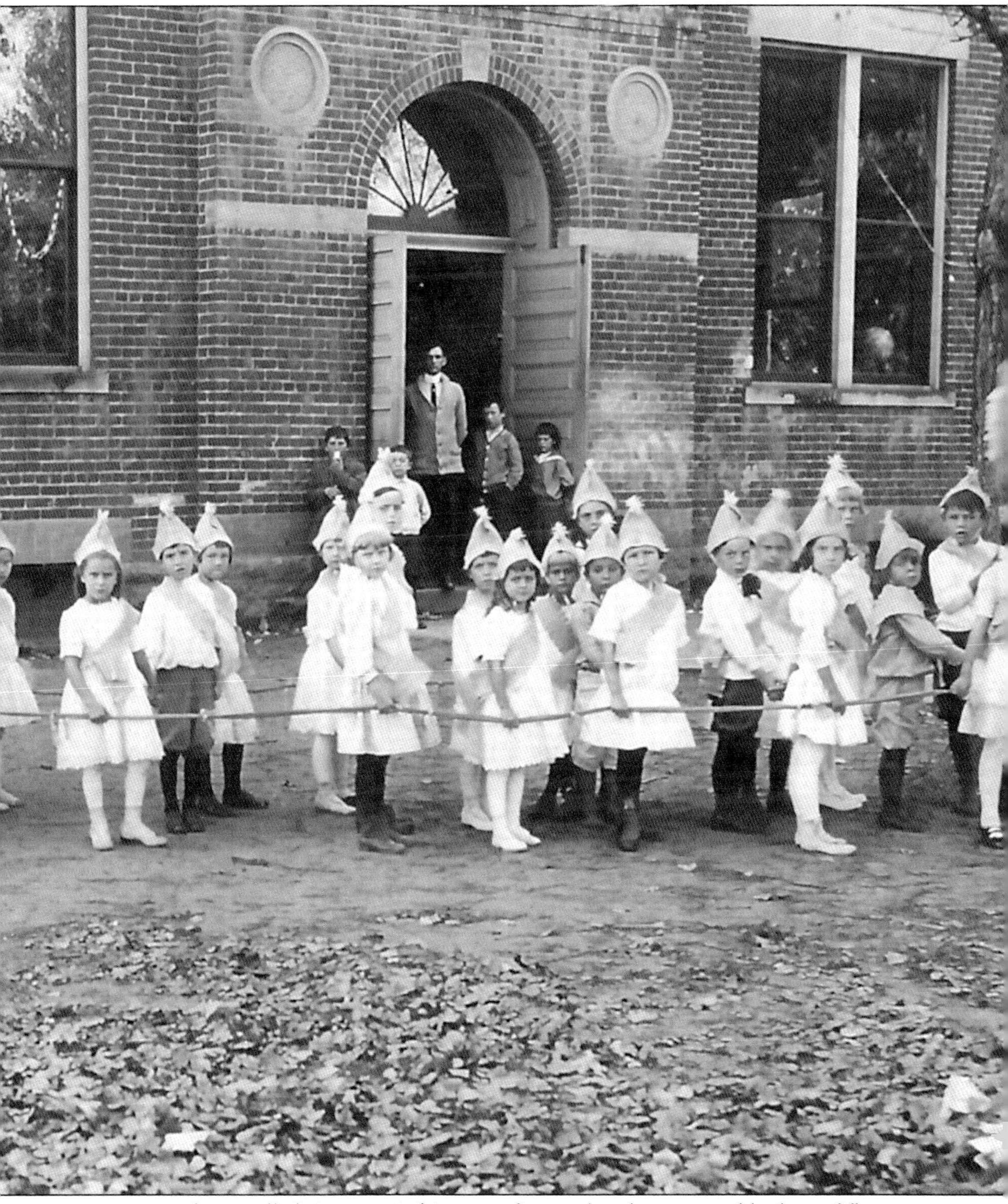

time to time and generally bring to mind images of maypoles, dancing, and baskets of flowers. Despite the implied fun of the image, it is amusing to see the flat faces of several of the students, who look less than pleased to be lined up wearing their little white hats.

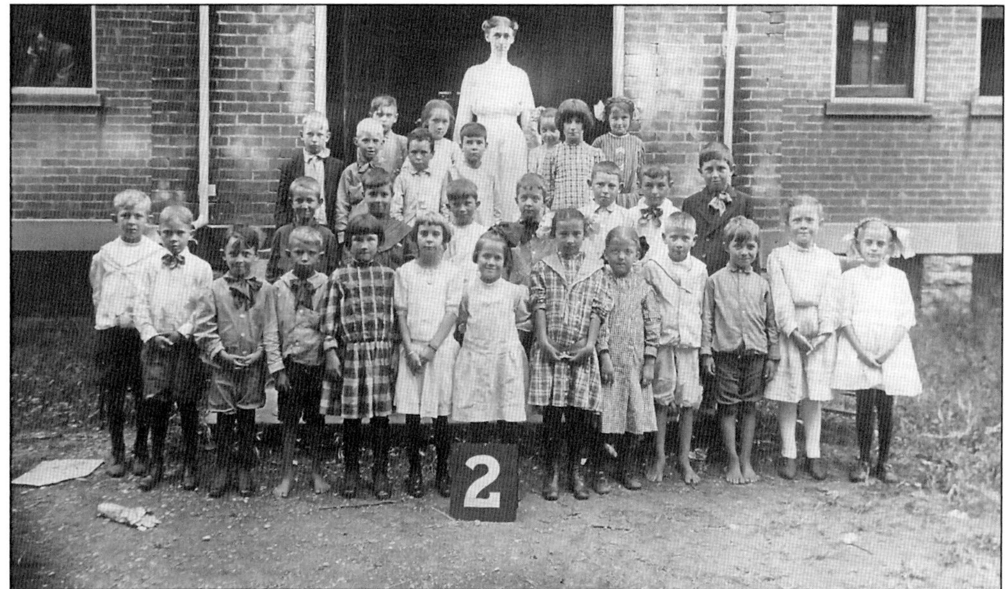

Pictured here is the entire second-grade class of the elementary school. Probably taken in the 1920s, this photograph shows the students, their instructor, and the east end of the building, which housed the elementary school, while the west end of the building held the high school students.

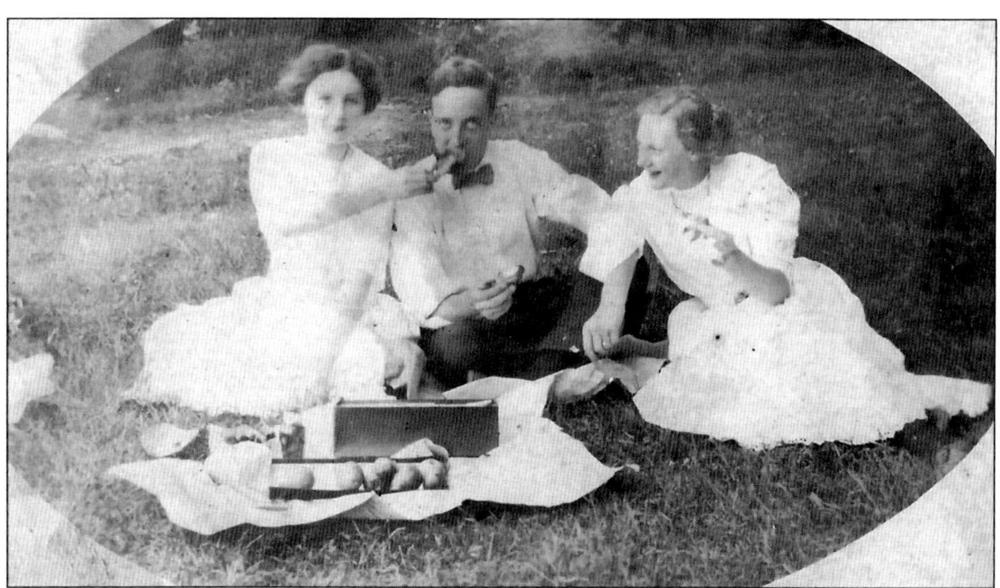

Photographs like this make it clear why so many graduating students ended up marrying their classmates. Pictured here is a friendly picnic being enjoyed by three unidentified Blanchester High School students in 1909. It was not all about studying; strong social bonds were also formed during the school years.

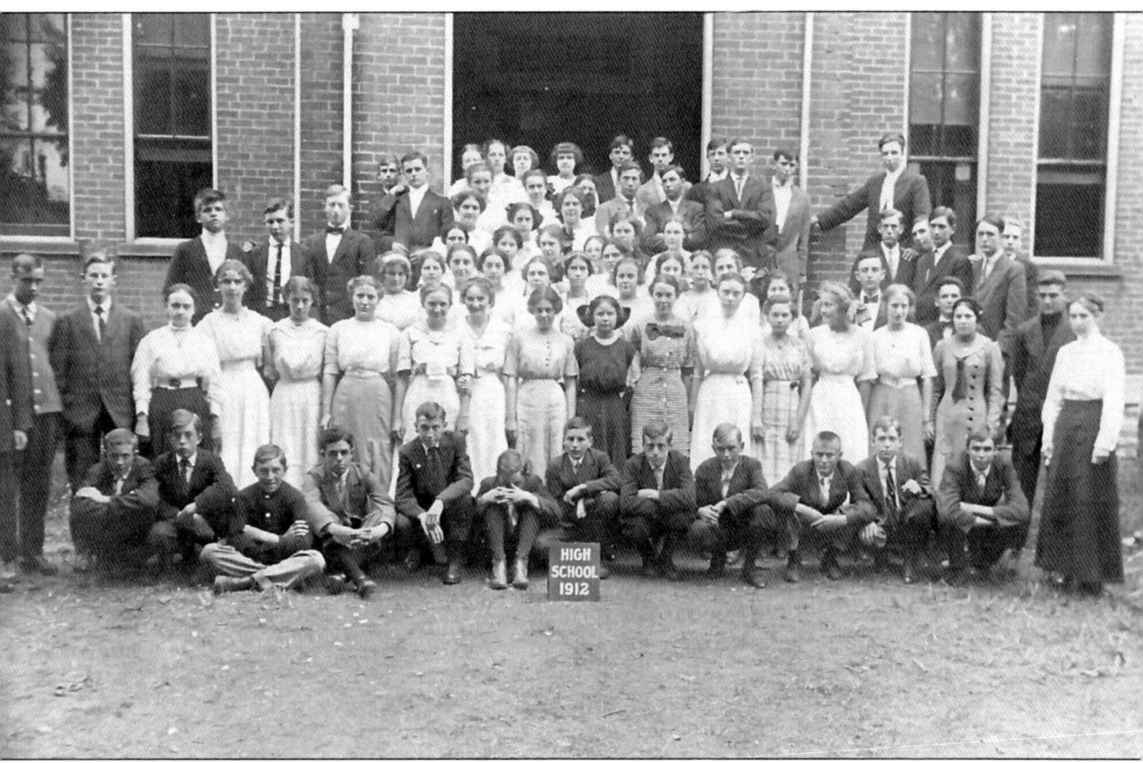

This photograph, taken in 1912 at the east end of the Main Street School, captures the entire high school student body. Looking at the size of the group, it is hard to believe that only one student made up the high school graduating class in 1883, less than 30 years prior. Adding students from the surrounding area and increasing the focus on education in the village made the number of students pursuing higher education grow exponentially. It is notable that this was during the school years of Clarence J. Brown Sr., who went on to become a congressman and publisher, starting his career not long after his graduation. He is still one of the most notable people to come out of the area. Obviously, the education provided at the Main Street School worked well for him.

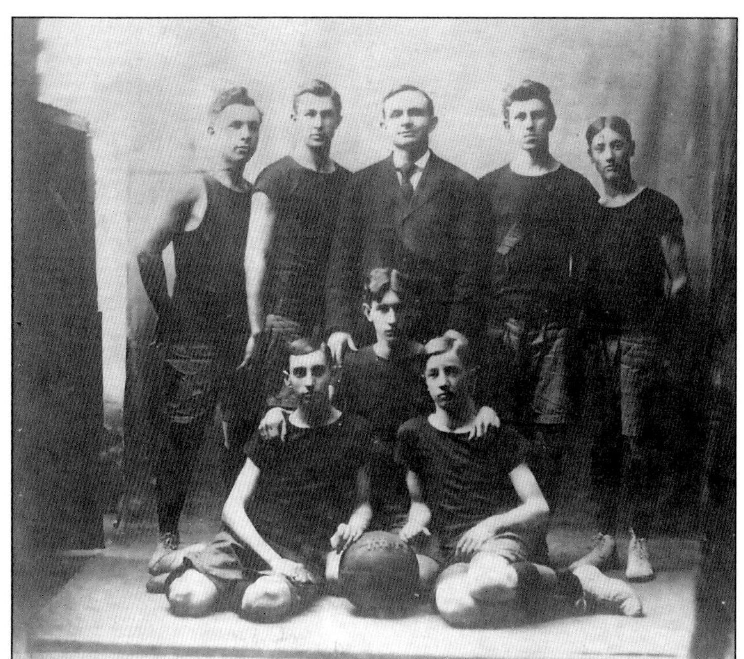

This photograph depicts one of the high school basketball teams, though the exact year and players' names are unknown. The team was most likely active from 1910 to 1920. Blanchester High School had some success with its basketball teams in the area over the years.

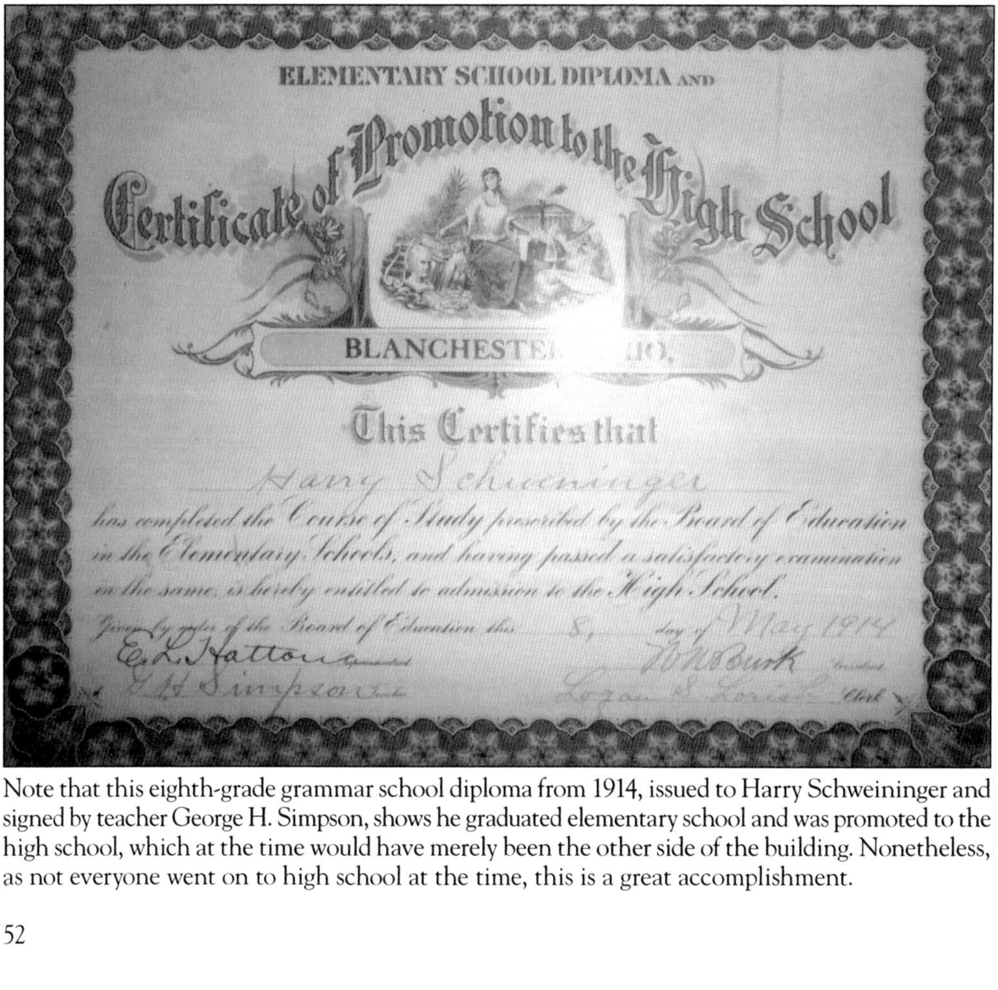

ELEMENTARY SCHOOL DIPLOMA AND

Certificate of Promotion to the High School

BLANCHESTE… HIO.

This Certifies that

has completed the Course of Study prescribed by the Board of Education in the Elementary Schools, and having passed a satisfactory examination in the same, is hereby entitled to admission to the High School.

Given by order of the Board of Education this day of

Note that this eighth-grade grammar school diploma from 1914, issued to Harry Schweininger and signed by teacher George H. Simpson, shows he graduated elementary school and was promoted to the high school, which at the time would have merely been the other side of the building. Nonetheless, as not everyone went on to high school at the time, this is a great accomplishment.

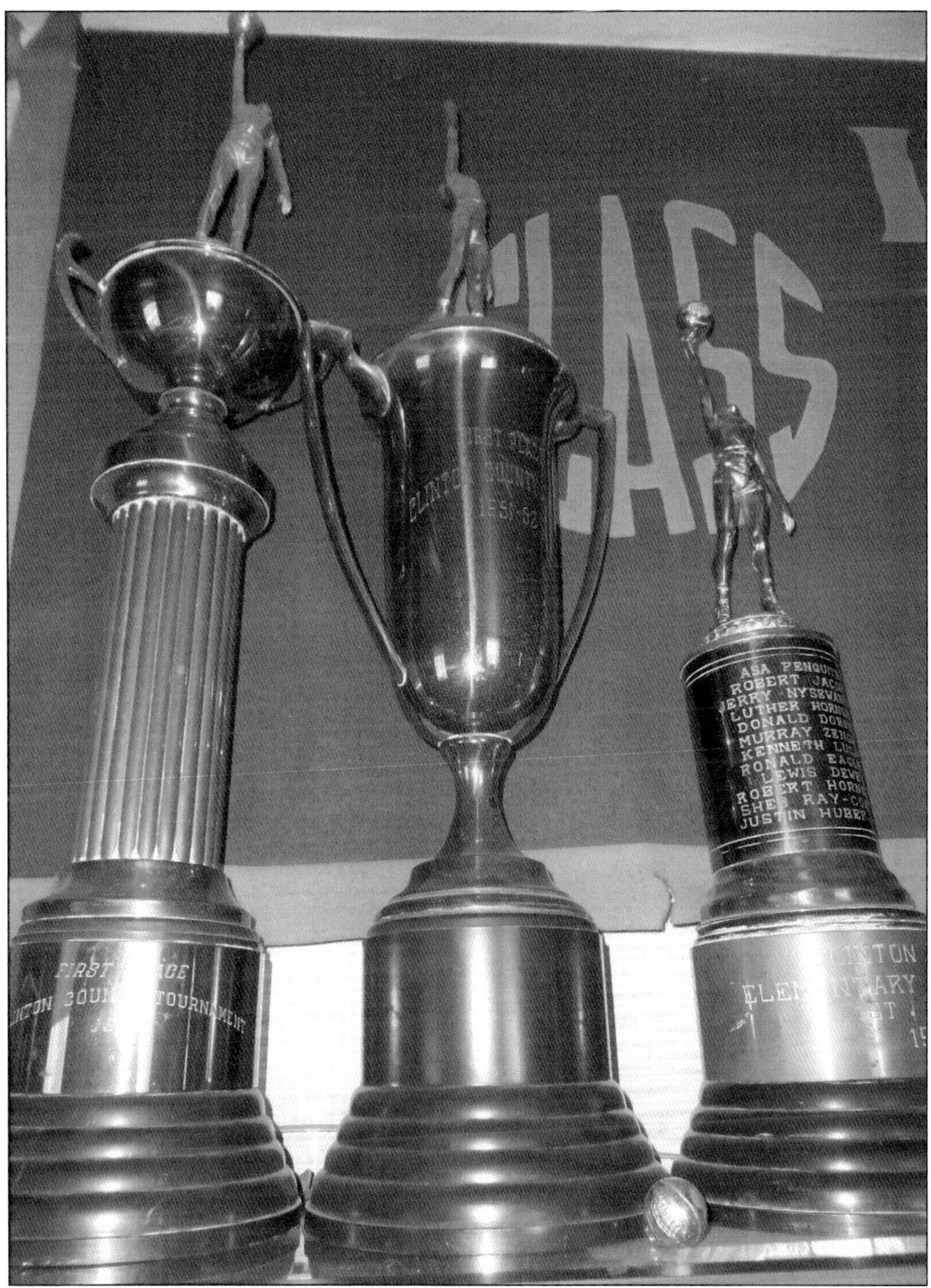

These three trophies represent the same basketball team that came out of the Blanchester High School. They represent increasing victories spanning the 1948–1952 school years. Initially, they won the elementary tournament in 1948. The next victory for the team took place when they won first place in their division of the Clinton County League. Finally, they won first place in the entire Clinton County Tournament. The trophies are now proudly displayed at the Blanchester Area Historical Society Museum. Surely this was a feat of which the whole town was proud of. It is likely that, given the size of the team and the town, nearly everyone in Blanchester was personally affected by their victories, knowing one of the players or his family. One of the joys of a small town is sharing in the triumphs. (Photograph by the author.)

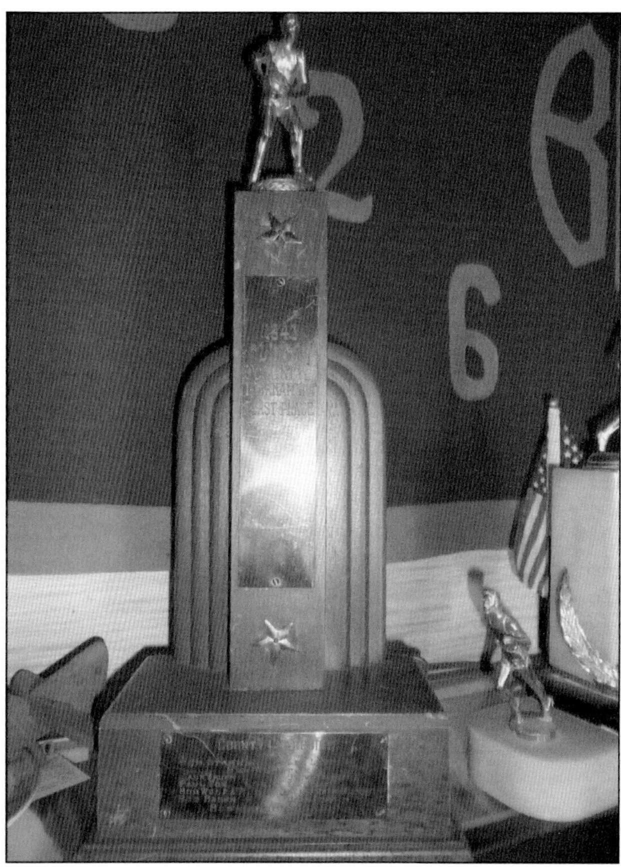

This trophy commemorates the victory of the 1943 Blanchester High School basketball team. It won the title of county champions for the year. Four of its senior players were drafted to serve in World War II, leaving only one senior for the next season starting team. Note that during the war, the trophies were wood rather than metal, but this victory served the town as a bright spot during the war years. (Photograph by the author.)

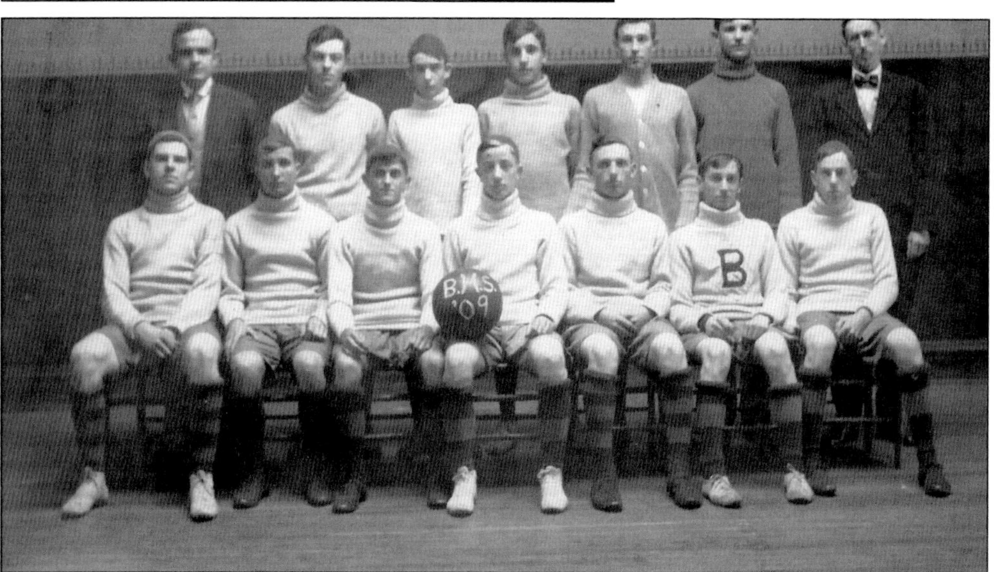

This is a photograph of the 1909 Blanchester High School basketball team, one of the earliest in the school's history. In the early days, the players did not have anywhere to practice in the school itself and had to find outside locations at other area buildings. The school had no gymnasium or auditorium.

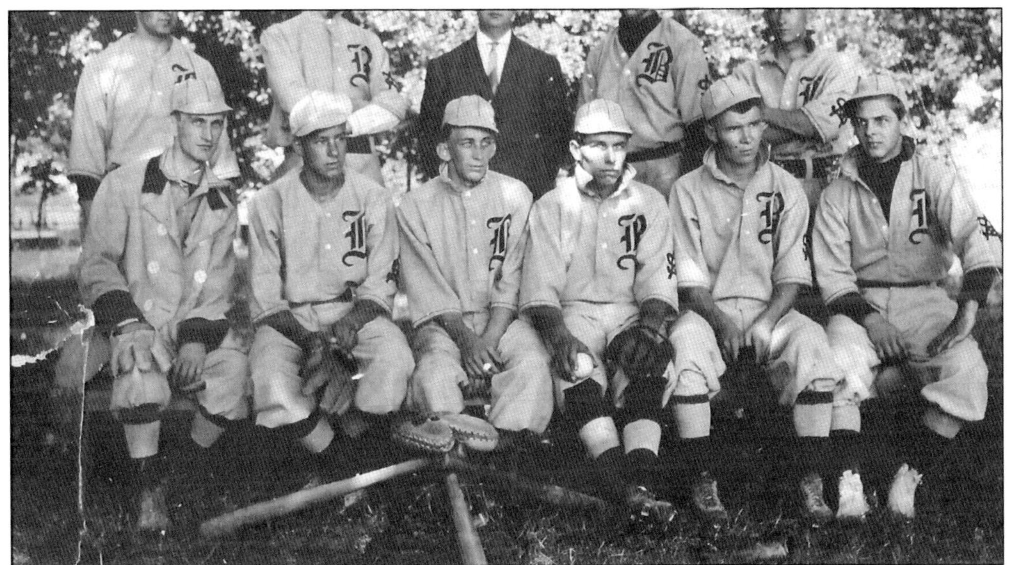

Basketball was not the only sport appreciated in Blanchester. This image shows a local baseball team from the 1920s. Their upscale uniforms and solemn faces make it clear that they were not high school students, but merely using the school grounds as a location for the team photograph and games.

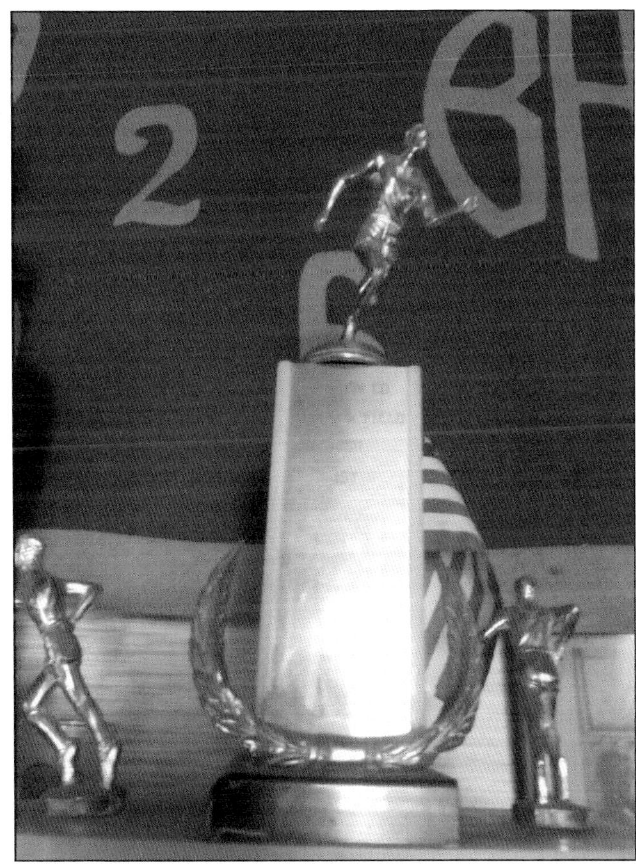

This track and field trophy is from 1958 and celebrates the first-place prize in the Clinton County track meet. It is especially notable, as this victory broke the four-year winning streak of nearby Jefferson High School, which closed in 1960 and consolidated into Blanchester. (Photograph by the author.)

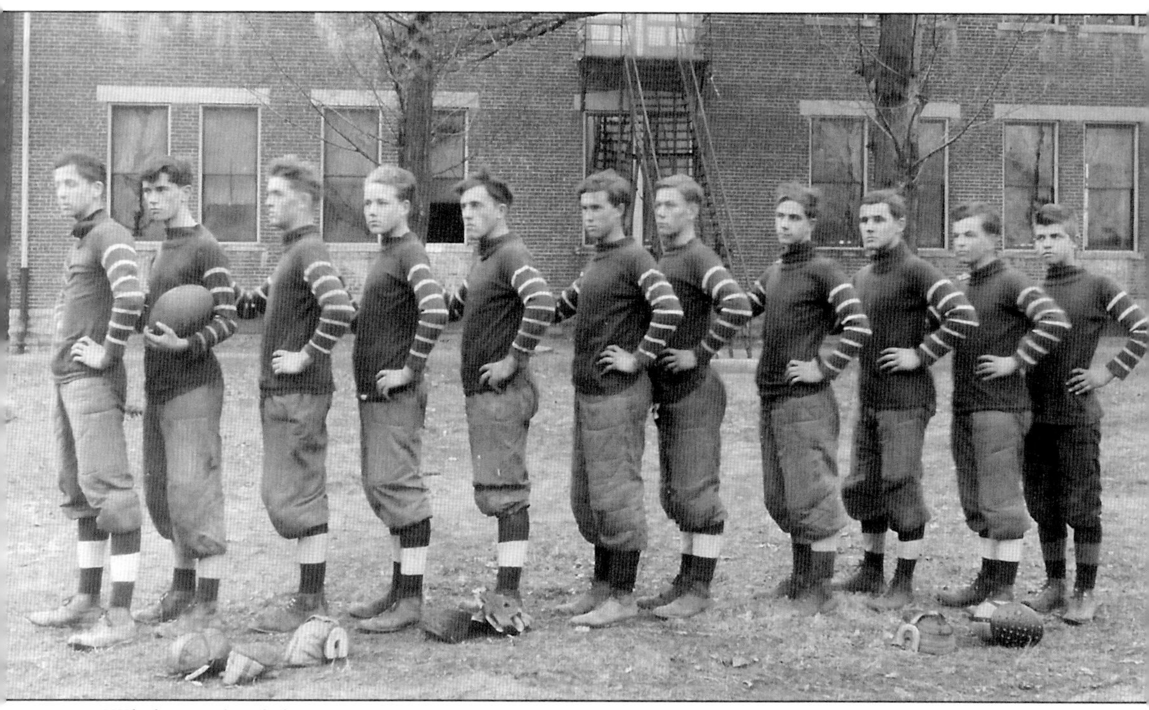

While much of the country is enraptured by football now, it was not always the case. This is a photograph of the 1912 Blanchester High School football team, one of the first the school produced. It was also the football team that Clarence J. Brown Sr. played on during his years at the high school. Shortly after graduating, he would marry classmate Ethel McKinney and start working in the Ohio Secretary of State's office, which would launch his political career. He would later start his work as a publisher. Graduation obviously left him inspired and eager to prove himself. Some of that fierce drive he surely learned while playing on the football field with the rest of his team.

Six

Touched by War

No city or village has been untouched by all of the wars that this country has faced—Blanchester is no exception. Many of the sons and daughters of the town have served their country or helped with the war effort at home, and Blanchester is proud of their contributions.

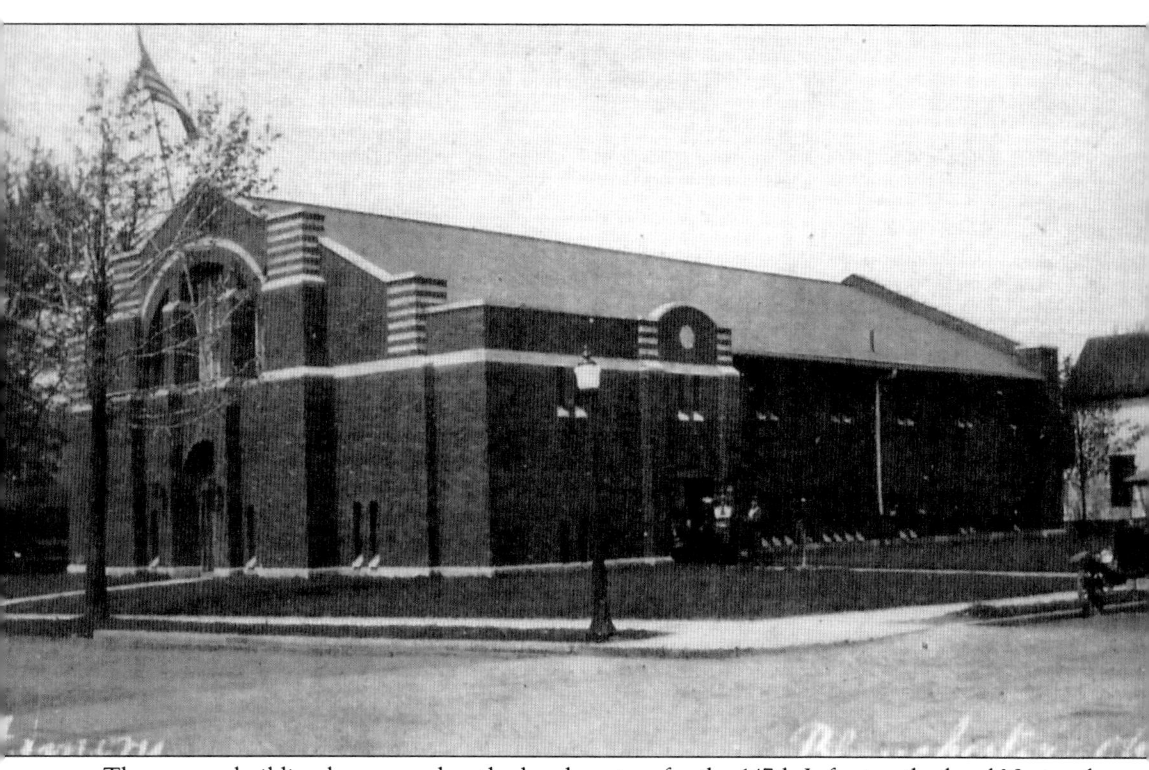

The armory building long served as the headquarters for the 147th Infantry, the local National Guard unit in Blanchester. It was under construction from 1924 to 1926 and was one of the many local buildings constructed by the Dewey brothers, who also built the Main Street School. For a time, the Dewey brothers used it as their business headquarters. The local guard unit called the building home until it closed in 1993. It has gone through many hands since that time, and members of the Blanchester Area Historical Society hope to some day make it their headquarters. Around the 1940s, the armory displayed a service honor roll monument out front, honoring the local sons and daughters who had participated in the fighting, along with a cannon taken from battle in World War I, which was later taken and turned into scrap during the World War II era.

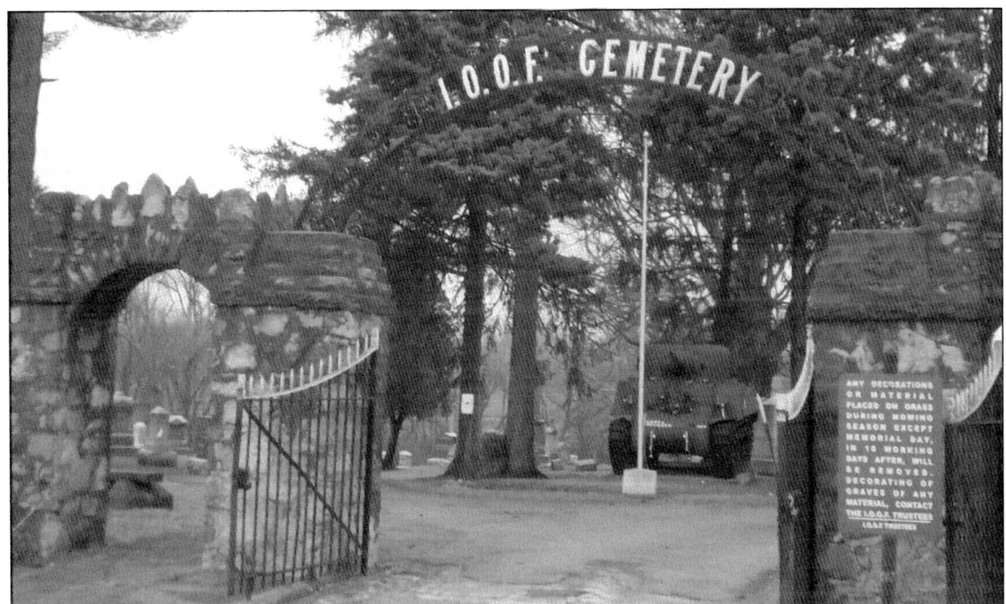

The International Order of Odd Fellows founded its cemetery in Blanchester in 1869 as a place to remember those lost in war. Blanchester men served in the Civil War, and to honor them a cannon from the Battle of Chickamauga was sent to Blanchester from the Rock Island Arsenal in Illinois by an act of Congress in 1915. It was made in Cincinnati and resided in the cemetery as a monument until it was stolen in 1985; it was never recovered. (Photograph by the author.)

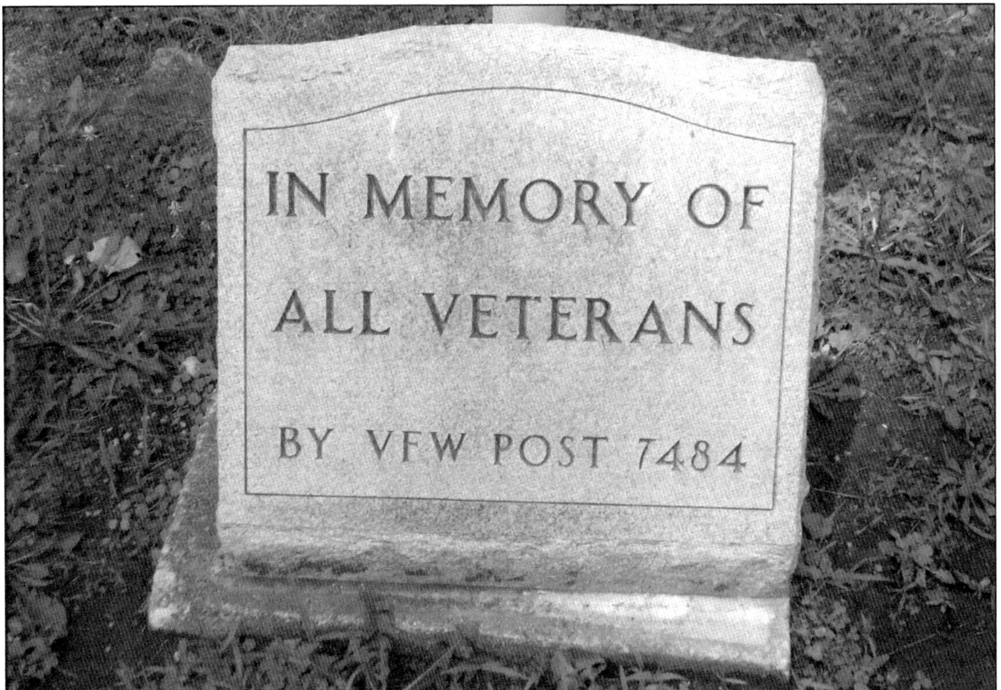

Just inside the gates of the Blanchester IOOF Cemetery stands this monument under an American flag in memory all of the veterans of the area who gave the ultimate sacrifice and were buried in the cemetery. It is a gentle reminder of what so many paid for freedom. (Photograph by the author.)

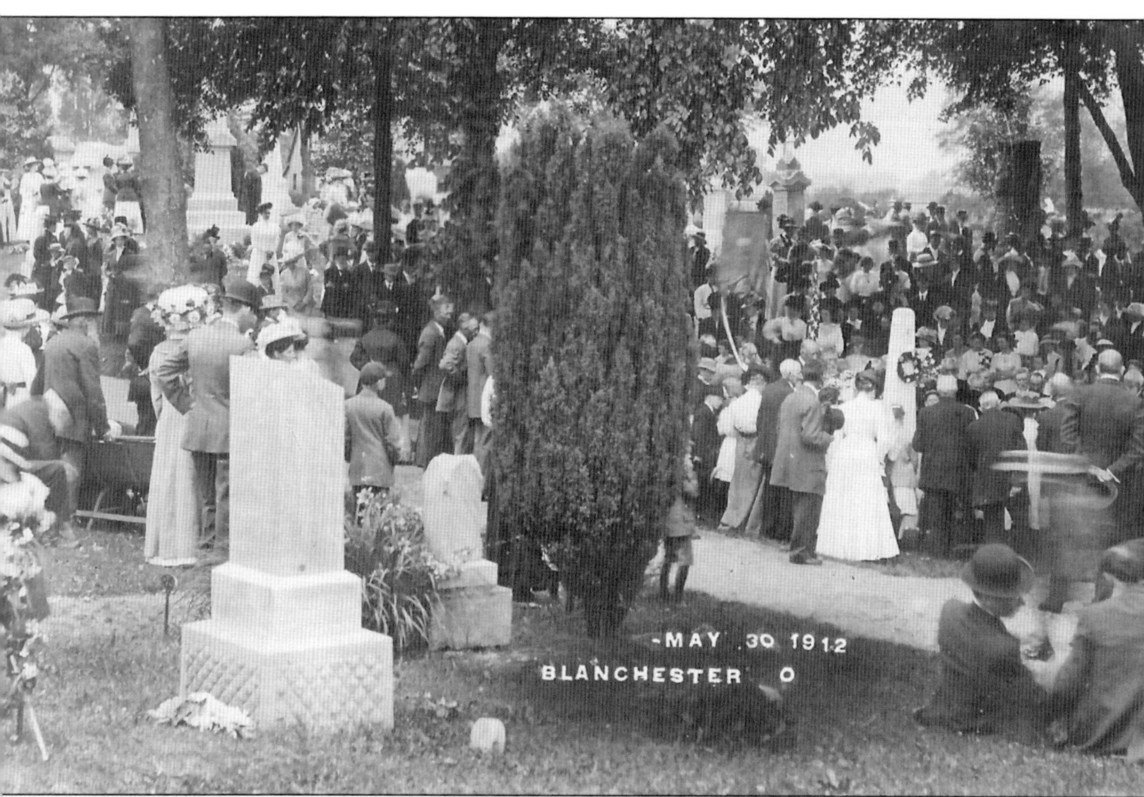

Every year, citizens come to pay their respects to the soldiers buried in the cemetery, those who gave their lives for their country, and those who served. Pictured here is Memorial Day in 1912, when flower decorations were hung on a wooden construction in the heart of the cemetery. Even today, if one were to walk around the graves, those of the soldiers are immediately obvious, marked with small emblematic flag holders that grab visitors' attention. Blanchester was and is proud of those local sons and daughters who served their country. Given the number of memorials scattered throughout the cemetery, there are a lot of souls of which to be proud.

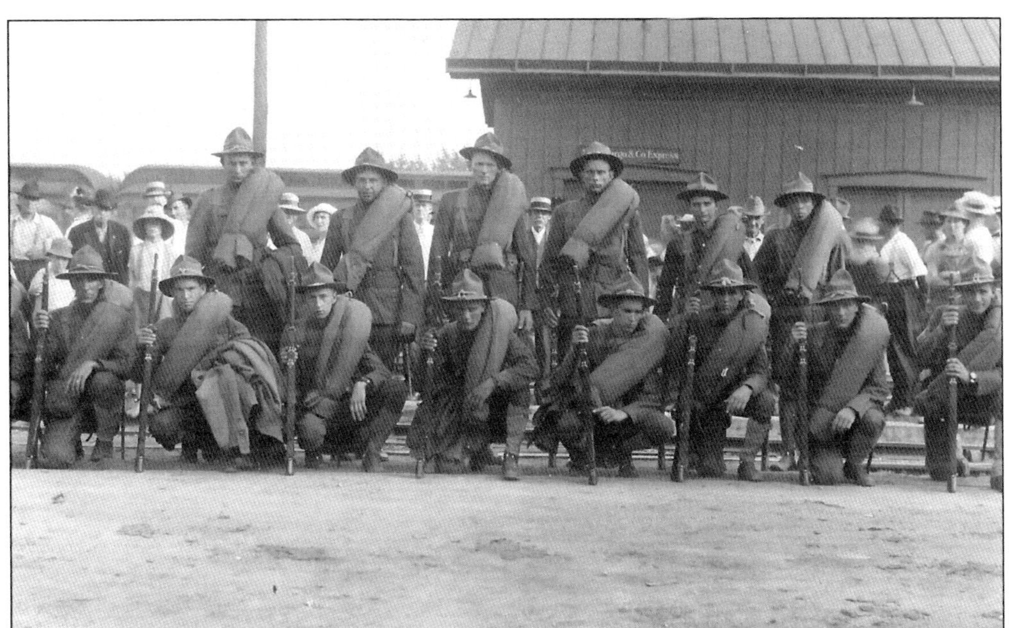

Members of the 147th Infantry, 37th Division, of the National Guard are shown here with their bedrolls and gear, waiting for the train at the Blanchester Depot. These brave young men, all clad in their new uniforms, would soon be shipped off to fight in World War I. Behind them, friends and family wait to say their good-byes.

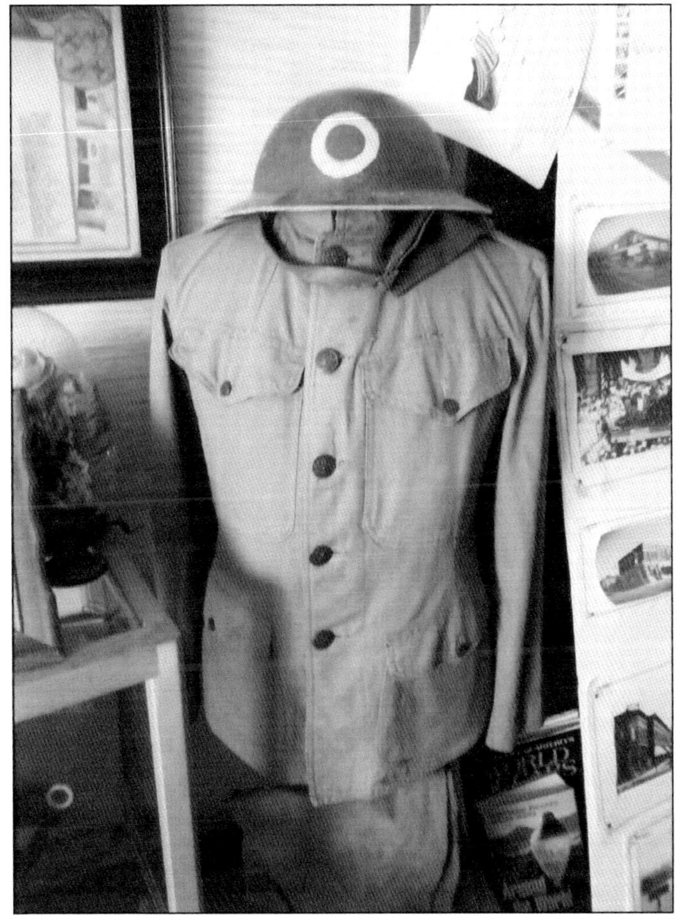

This uniform belonged to Volley Edinger of the 37th "Buckeye" Division. He was a Blanchester local and served in World War I. His complete uniform as well as Clyde Leffler's mess kit and field compass are on display at the Blanchester Area Historical Museum. (Photograph by the author.)

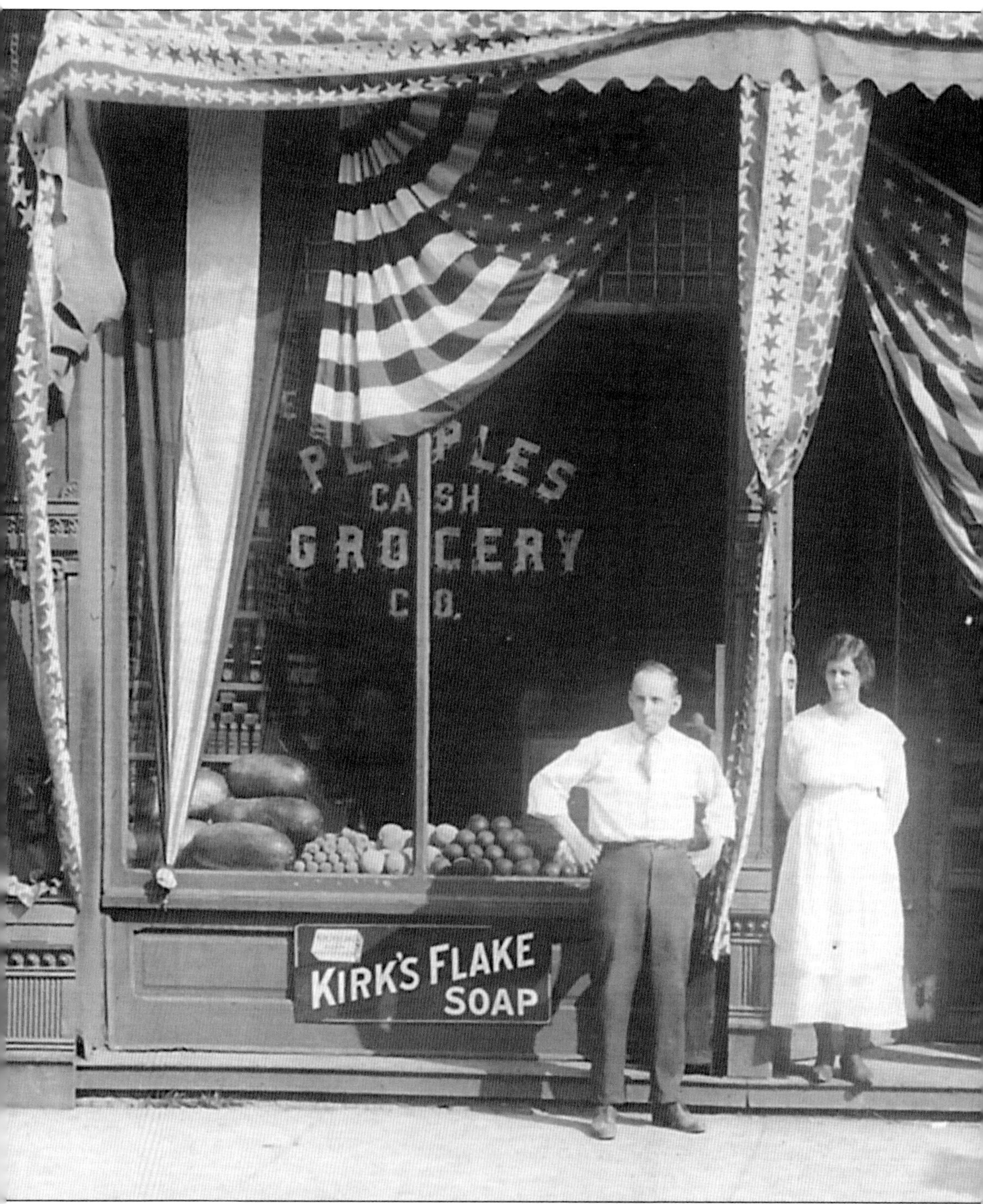

The People's Cash Grocery store was owned and operated by the Hunter brothers, who were well-known businessmen in Blanchester, even leaving their names on the buildings that still stand. Pictured from left to right are Amos Hunter, Violet Ross Simpson, George Hunter, F. Trovillo, and Virgil P. Hunter (son of Amos and who started Coffee by Hunter). The shop is decorated to show support for the troops who were away fighting in World War I. While not everyone in Blanchester

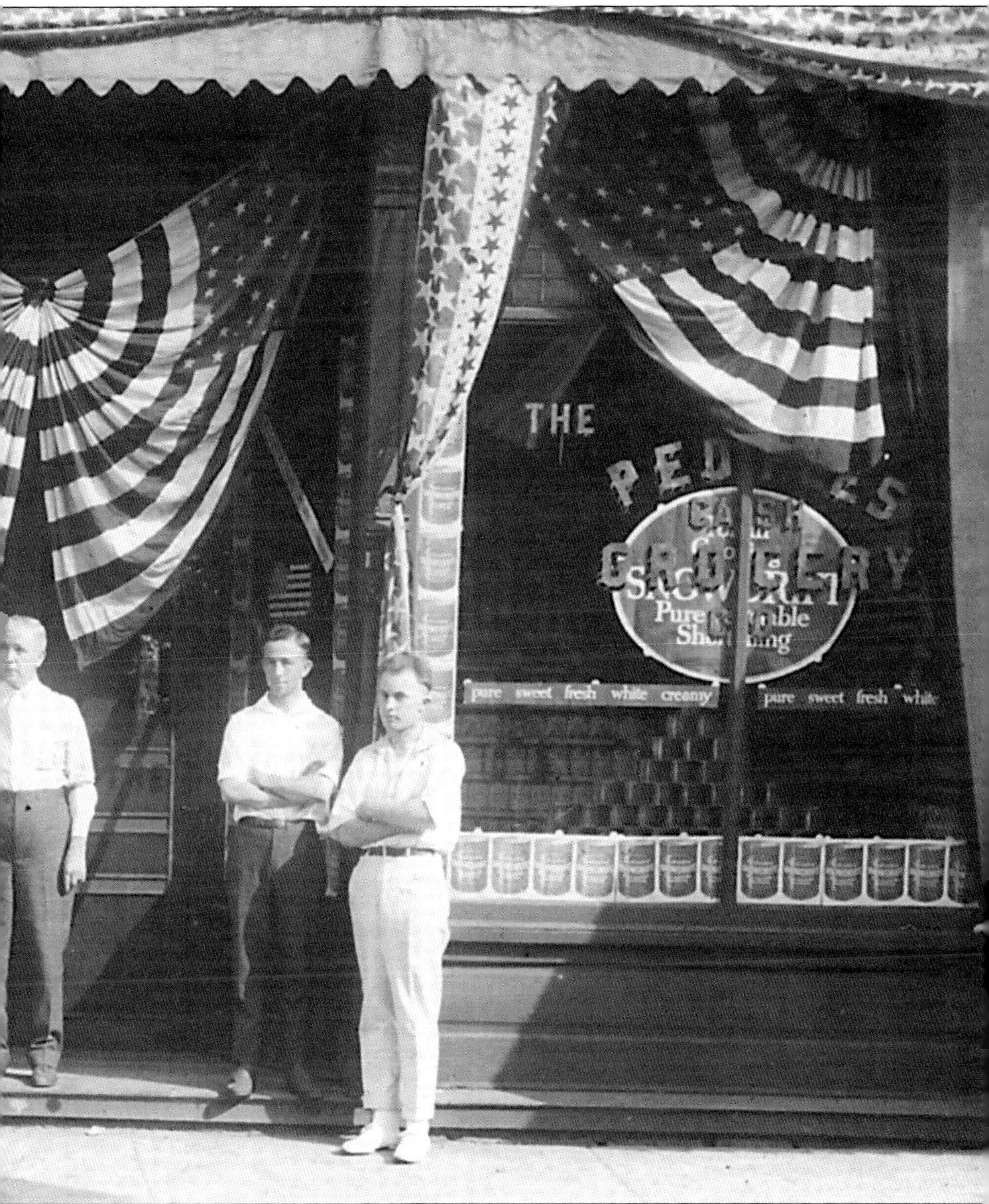

saw action, those who remained behind showed their support for the war by rationing, collecting scrap, and helping the war effort in any way they could. Truly, the war effected everyone in the country, especially in small towns where those who were lost were most noticeable.

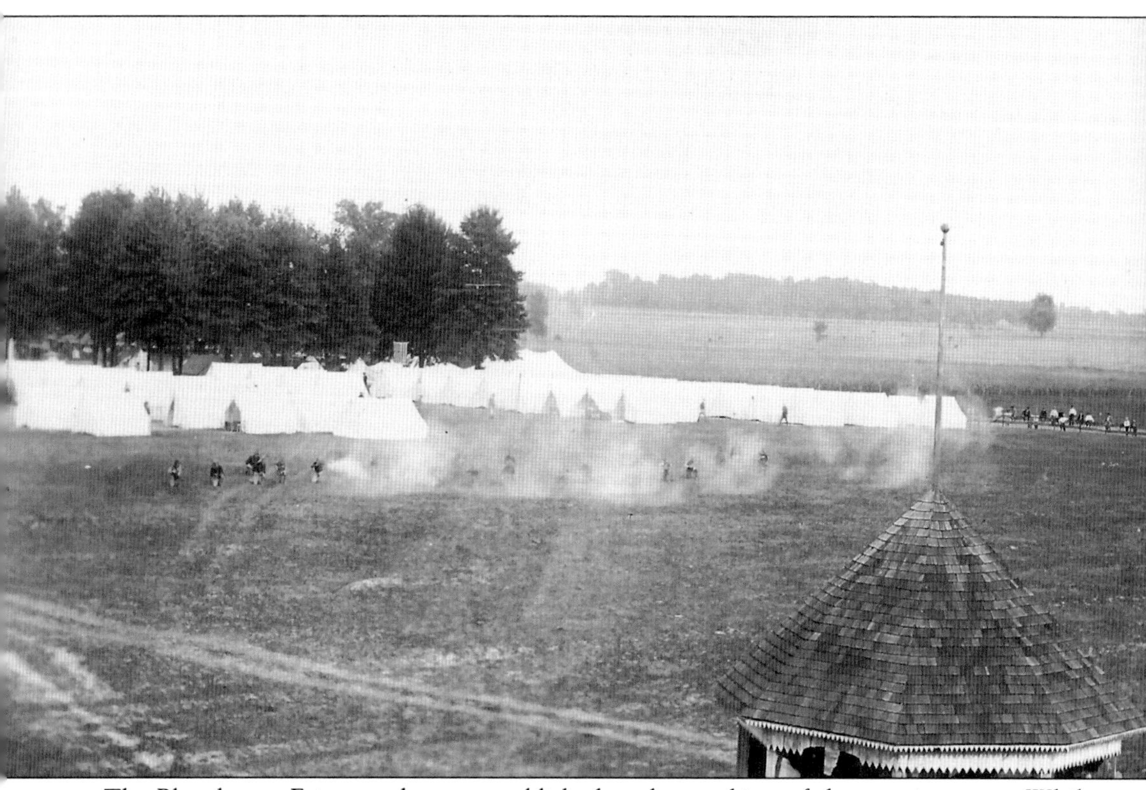

The Blanchester Fairgrounds were established at the outskirts of the growing town. While generally used for social occasions such as fairs and sporting events, they were also used for more serious purposes when the need demanded. This photograph shows the fairgrounds during the World War I era. Soldiers of the 147th Infantry National Guard unit pitched their tents on the grounds and used the space to train and drill before going to the depot to be shipped out to join in the war effort abroad.

Seven

A Sense of Community

The first and most pervasive thing an outsider might notice about Blanchester is the sense of community. In the stores and restaurants, everyone seems to know one another. Just walking down the streets in the business district makes it seem as if the locals firmly belong where they are, as if they are secure in their home and their heritage. When encountering someone from Blanchester outside of the town, eyes will light up if one is familiar with their home. There seem to be churches on every corner, and for such a small population there are a huge number of social clubs. Friendship and community are vastly important in Blanchester and have been throughout the history of the town.

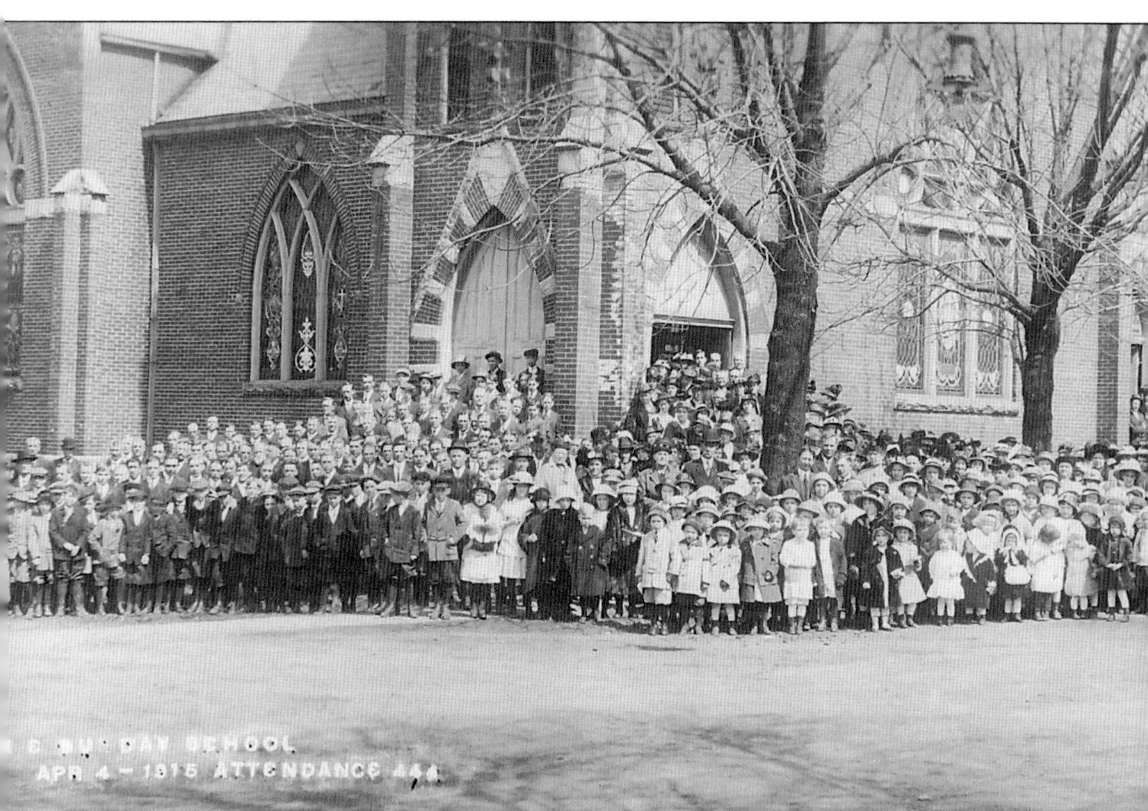

This photograph was taken after the Easter service of the Methodist Episcopal Church on April 4, 1915. That day, the Sunday school had an attendance of 444, which would have made it incredibly crowded. This was prior to the building of the basement in 1933 and the fellowship hall in 1959. Seeing the size of the crowd, it is easy to understand why the building would have to be expanded upon. The image is especially interesting for the variety of Sunday hats being worn by the children and the beautiful stained-glass windows in the building itself.

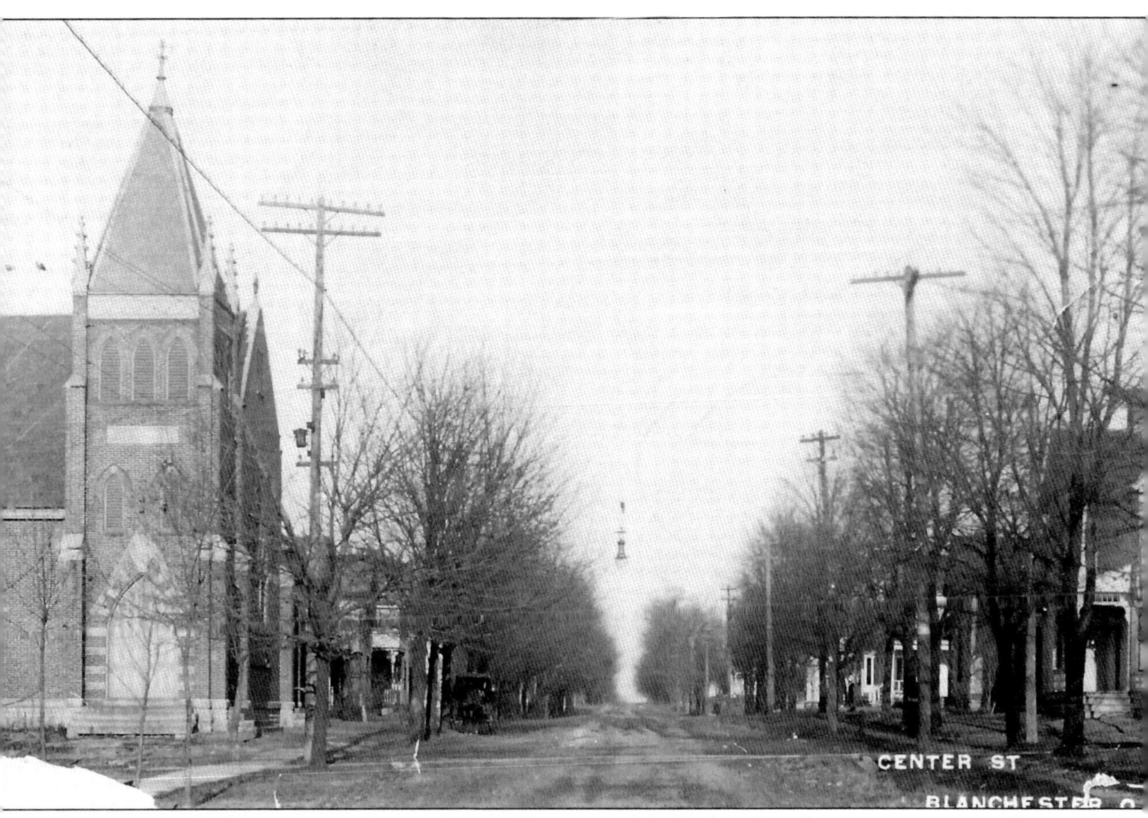

This is a view looking east on Center Street. The iconic Methodist church is easy to spot on the left side of the street, displaying the beautiful stained-glass windows seen in the previous image. The date on the bell tower of the church is 1896, presented in Roman numerals. It is meant as a reminder of the rebuilding after the conflagration of 1895, and the stonework was done by the local Acton Artistic Monument Company. On the right side of the street are private residences.

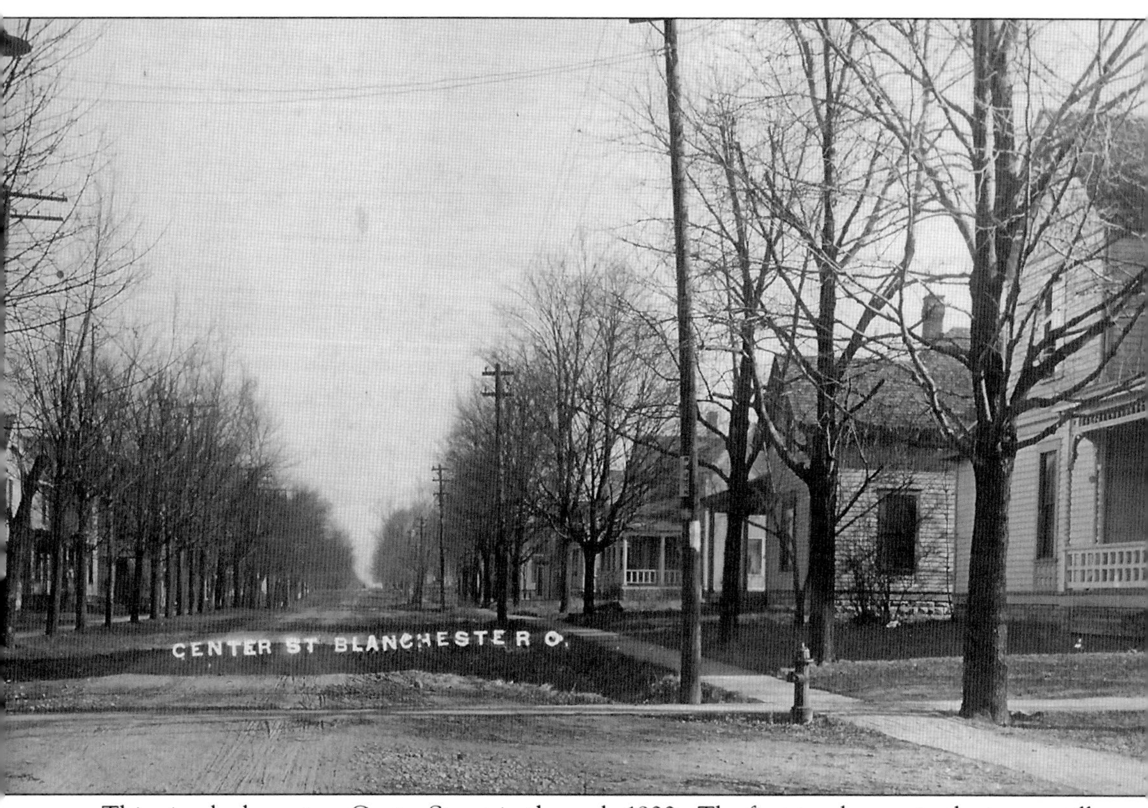

This view looks east on Center Street in the early 1900s. The first two houses in the image still exist and serve as private residences.

The Holy Name Catholic Church building was constructed in 1873. A new Catholic Church was constructed in 1958 on Bourbon Street, and it is currently part of the Wilmington Diocese.

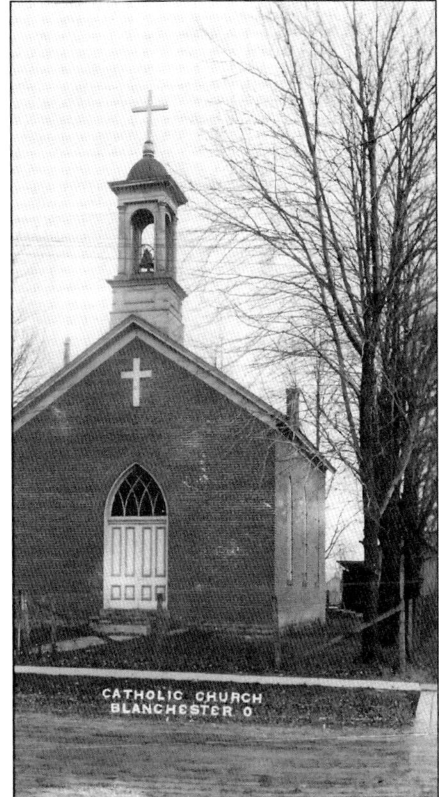

The original building of the Second Creek Church of the Evangelical United Brethren is shown here. That original frame structure was destroyed by fire and replaced with a brick building in 1885 and is still in use today with the addition of a fellowship hall. In 1968, the church was merged with the Methodist church.

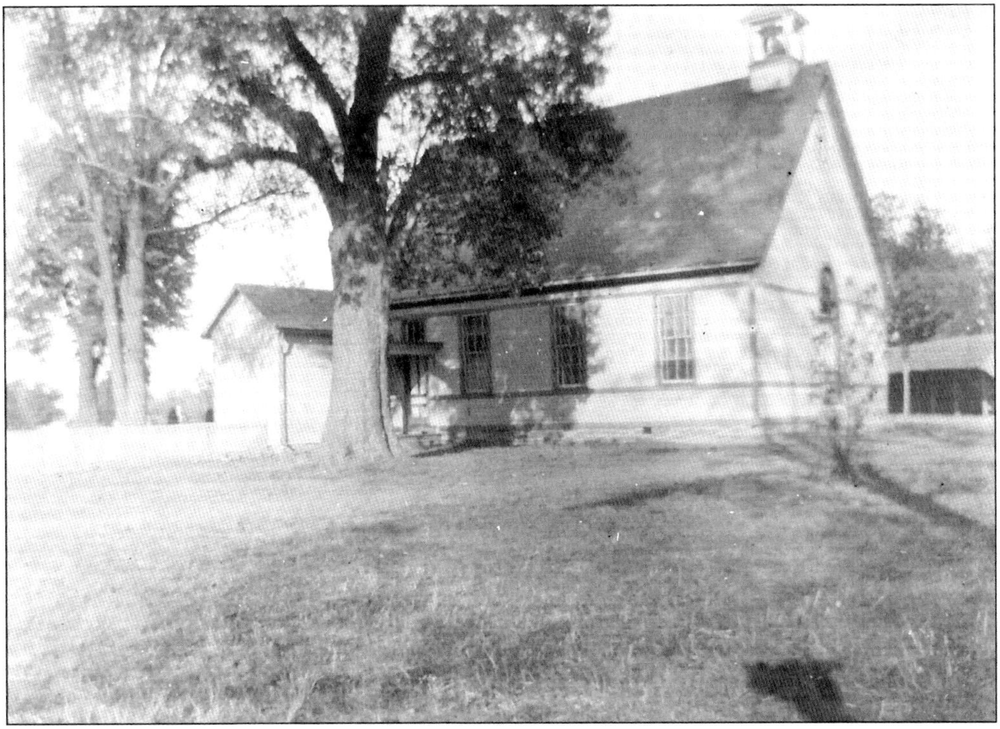

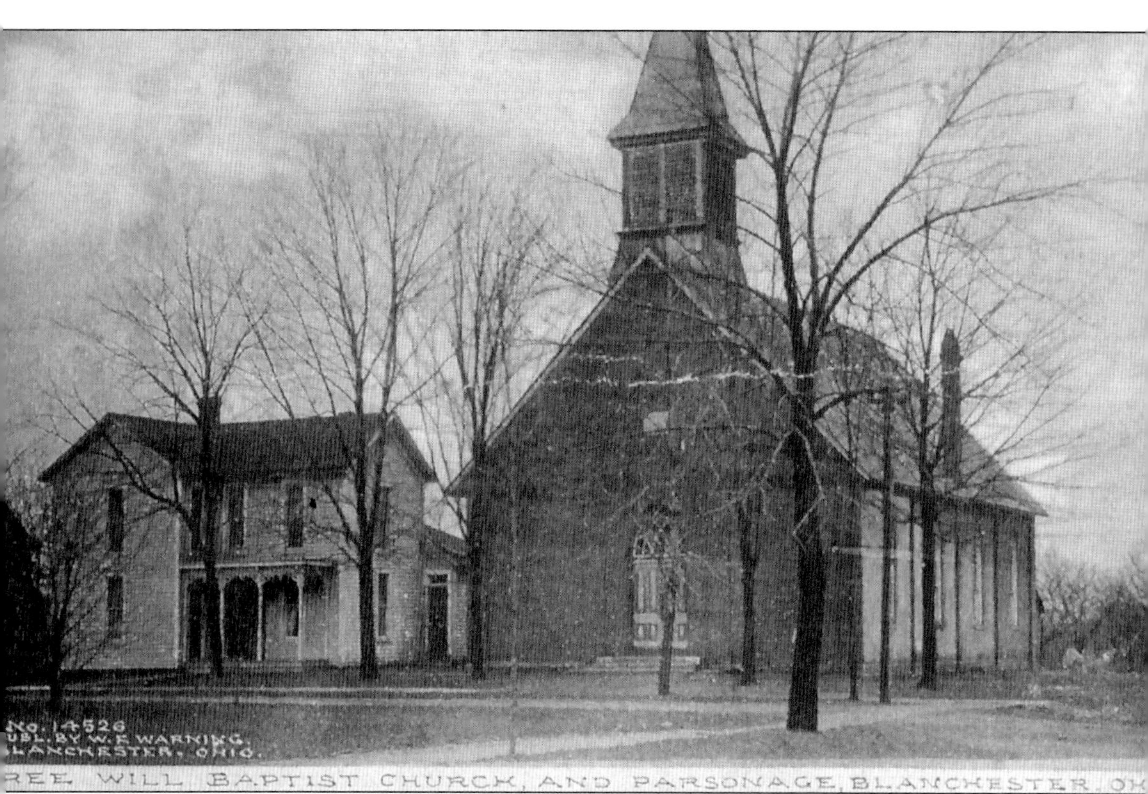

Pictured here is the Free Will Baptist Church and adjacent parsonage, located on West Center Street. It was built in 1852. While there were many churches constructed in the growing community, many of which are still standing and serve their original purpose, the Baptist church is especially notable, as it was the first church in Blanchester with a bell. The bell tower proudly stands over the building and would have brought pleasure to those hearing the chimes on Sunday morning, Baptist or not. An addition for offices and classrooms was added to the rear of the original church, plus basement classrooms for youths. The AWANA Building was constructed in 1991 for fellowship meetings and functions as a gymnasium and assembly room.

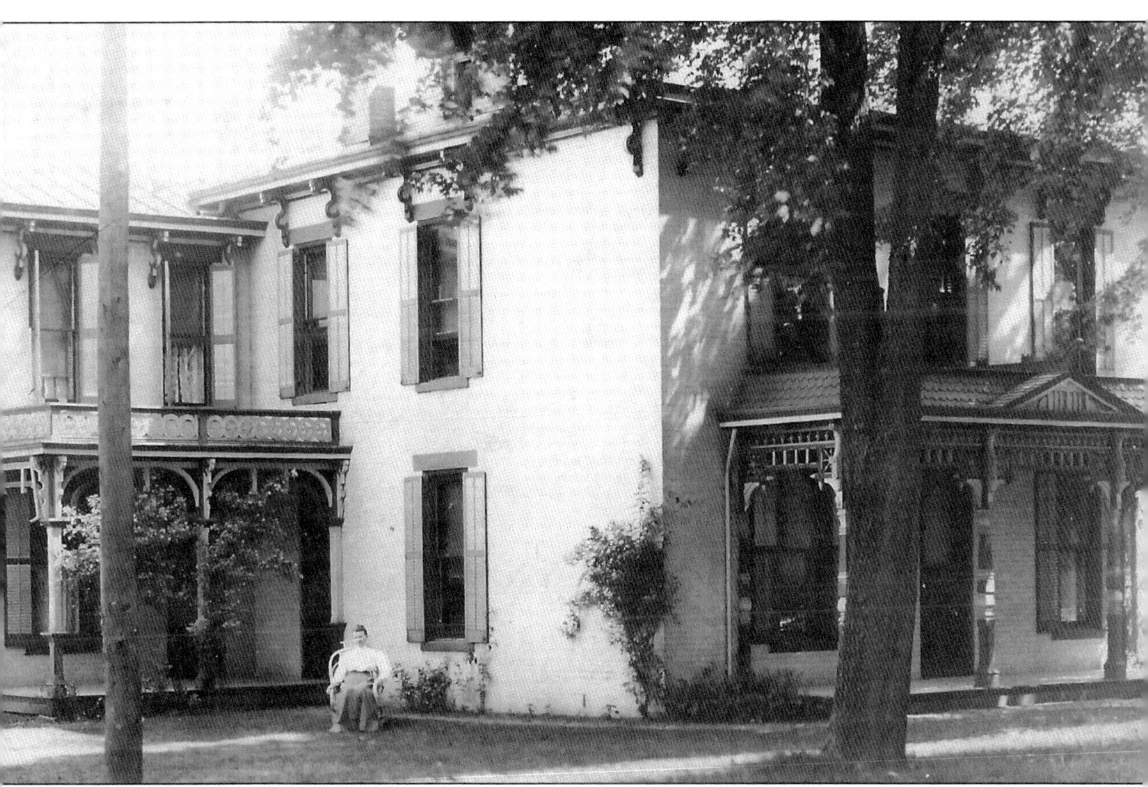

An unidentified resident of the community sits in front of a house on West Main Street. This was the old Baldwin house, and it still exists, though it no longer has the beautiful trim or front porch, which were removed over the years as they became difficult to clean and maintain.

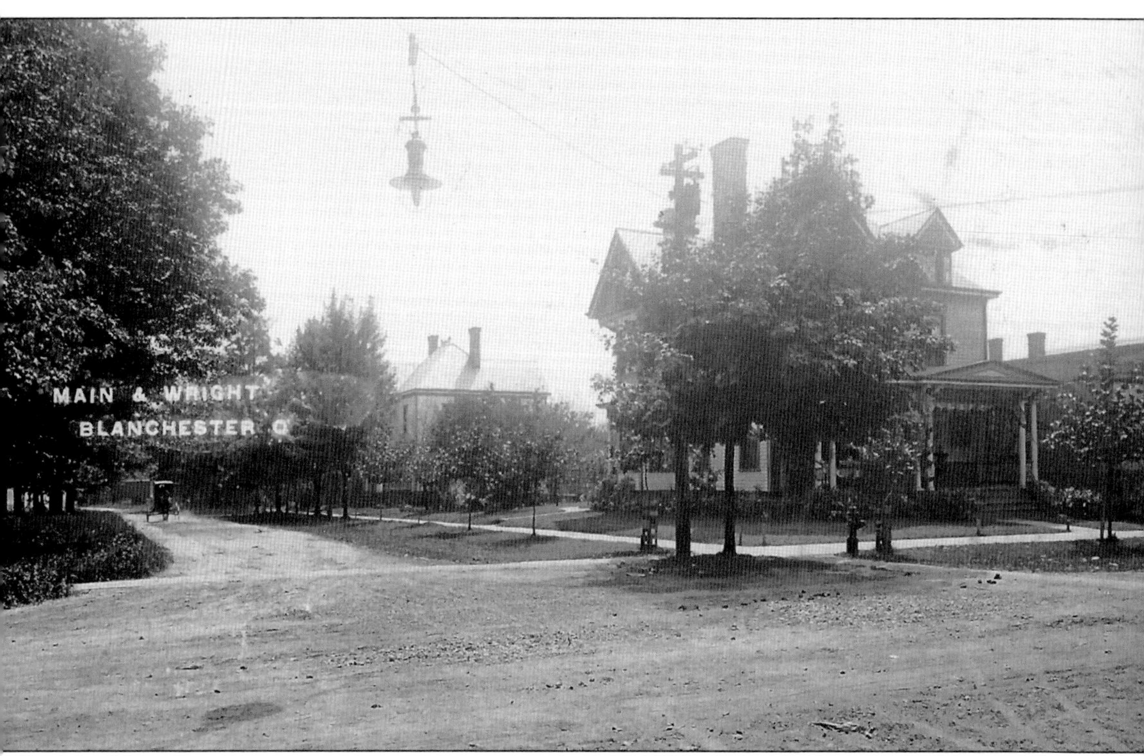

This is a 1926 photograph of the intersection of Wright and Main Streets. Hidden behind the trees is the old Warning house. The house itself was purchased that year by Clarence J. Brown but was later removed and replaced with a parking lot for the automotive shop at the end of the 20th century.

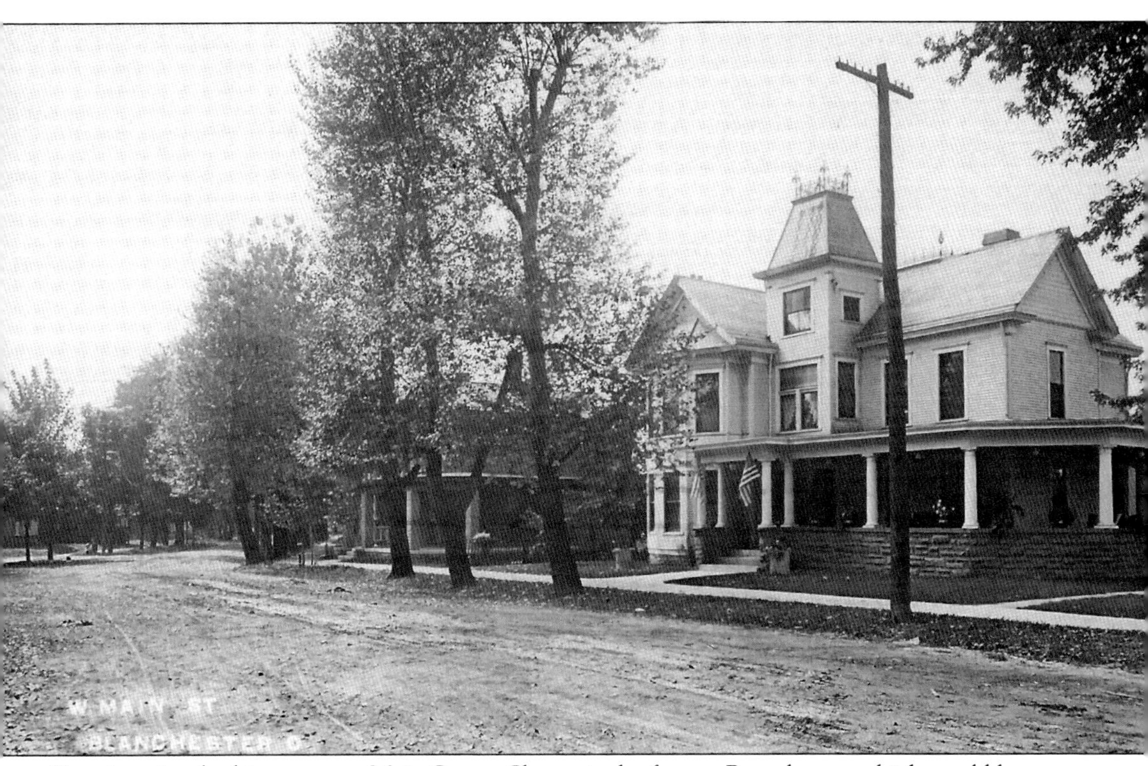

Here is a view looking west on Main Street. Shown is the former Bates house, which would later become the Hannah Funeral Home in 1915. There are many buildings surrounding it now, but it is still a striking structure.

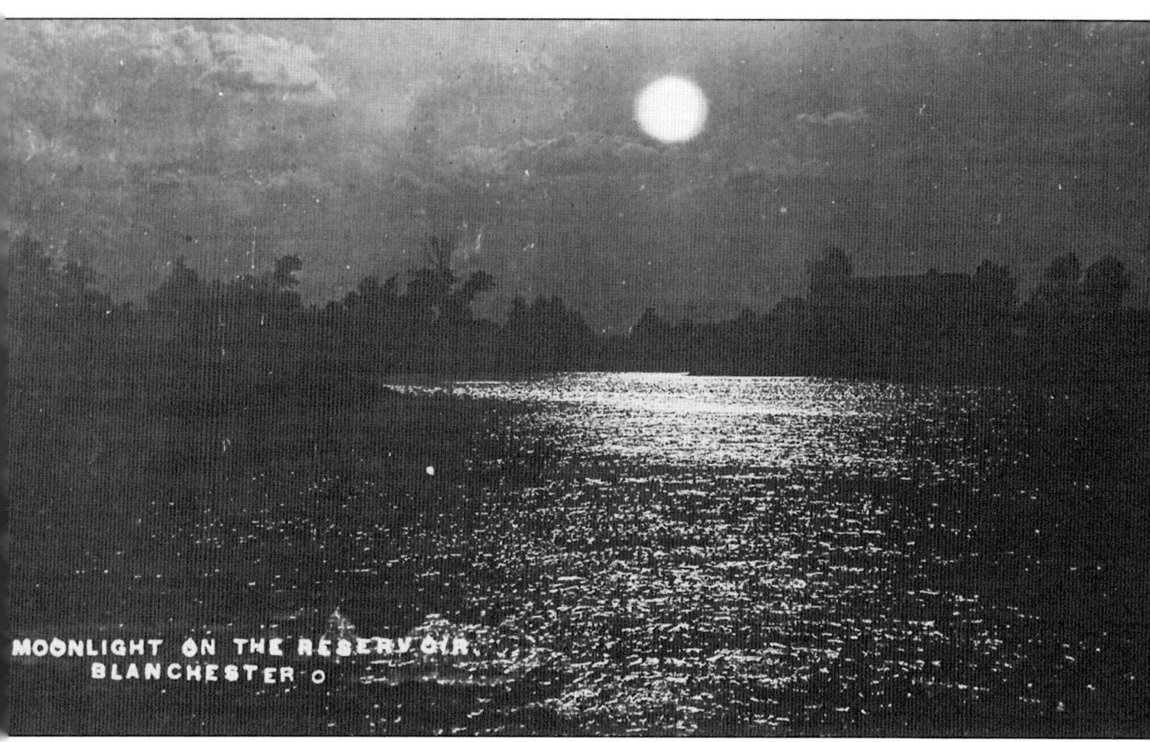

The moonlight glistens on the Blanchester Reservoir, part of the Blanchester Waterworks. An adjacent house stored ice cuttings in the cold-weather months. Once, the town was small enough for just one reservoir to serve residents, but since this photograph was taken there have been an additional five reservoirs added. It was a romantic view and surely a good place for courting couples to go on an evening date.

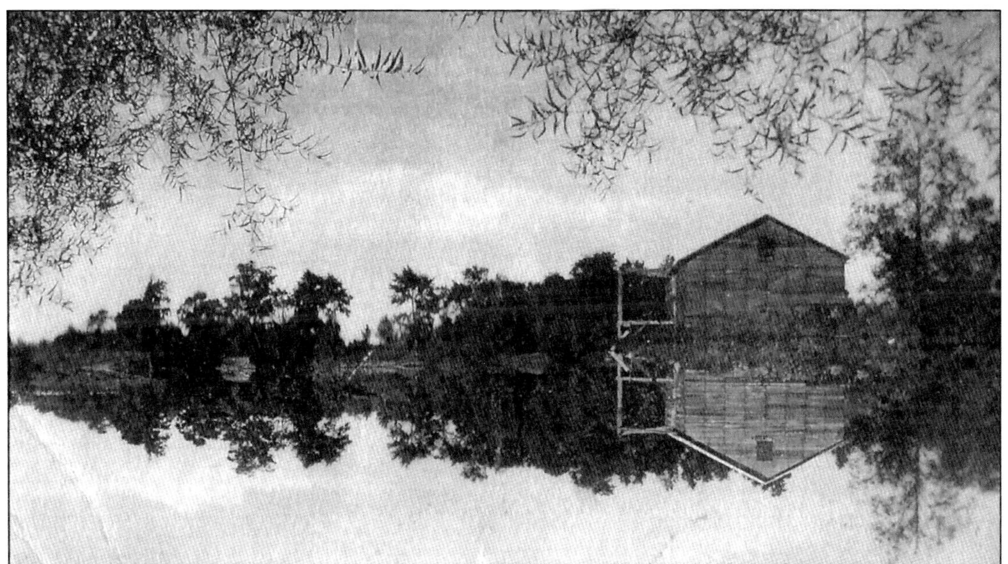

This is a daylight view of the Blanchester Reservoir when it was the only one in the area. Here, the ice-cutting house is clearly visible through the line of trees surrounding the water—a perfect place for a summer picnic with the family.

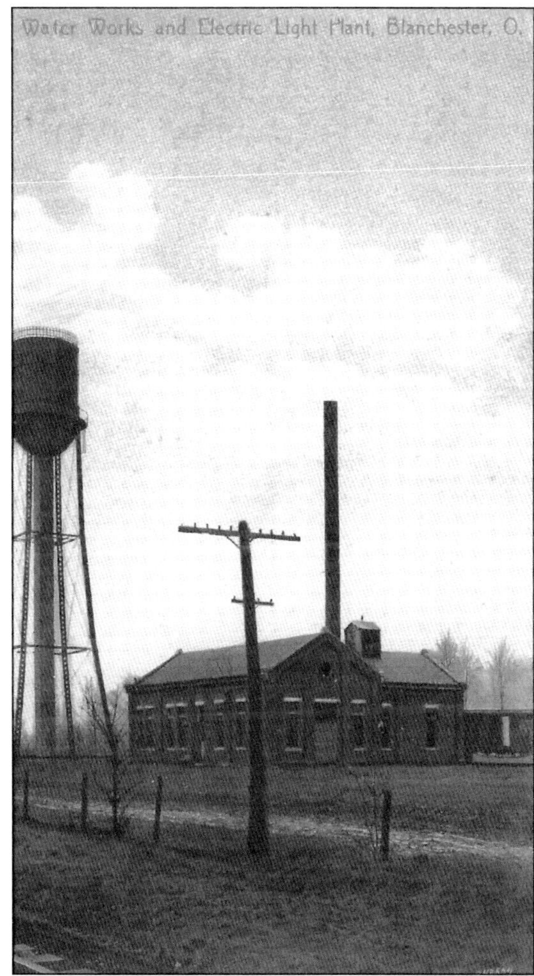

The Blanchester Waterworks was built in 1896, the year after the devastating fire that nearly destroyed the growing village. This photograph shows the wooden water tower, which was later replaced by a metal one with more capacity, in front of the water-purification plant.

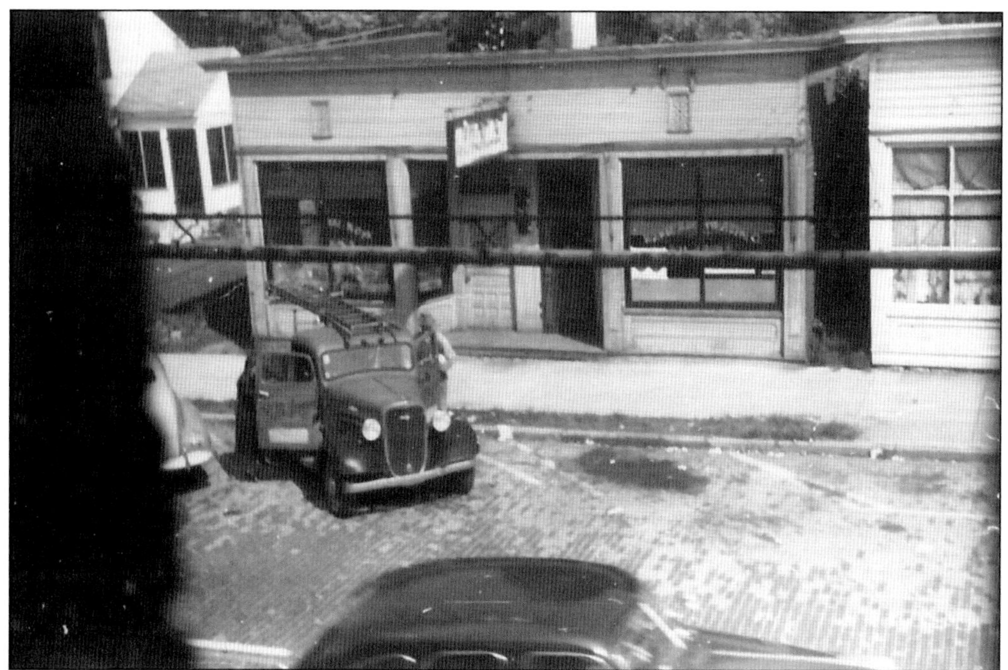

Velma Chaney was a well-known figure in Blanchester, especially for her participation in the Blanchester Area Historical Society. The photograph above was taken from the window of her home in the Bates building by John Simpson, overlooking the street and the future location of the public library. At the time, the building across the street was a tin shop. She was also responsible for organizing the Blanchester contribution to the bicentennial celebration of the nation. Sadly, she passed away in September 2011, prior to her 105th birthday in October, but her legacy is remembered. The bicentennial capsule seen below is buried near the stone entrance to the Blanchester IOOF Cemetery. (Below, photograph by the author.)

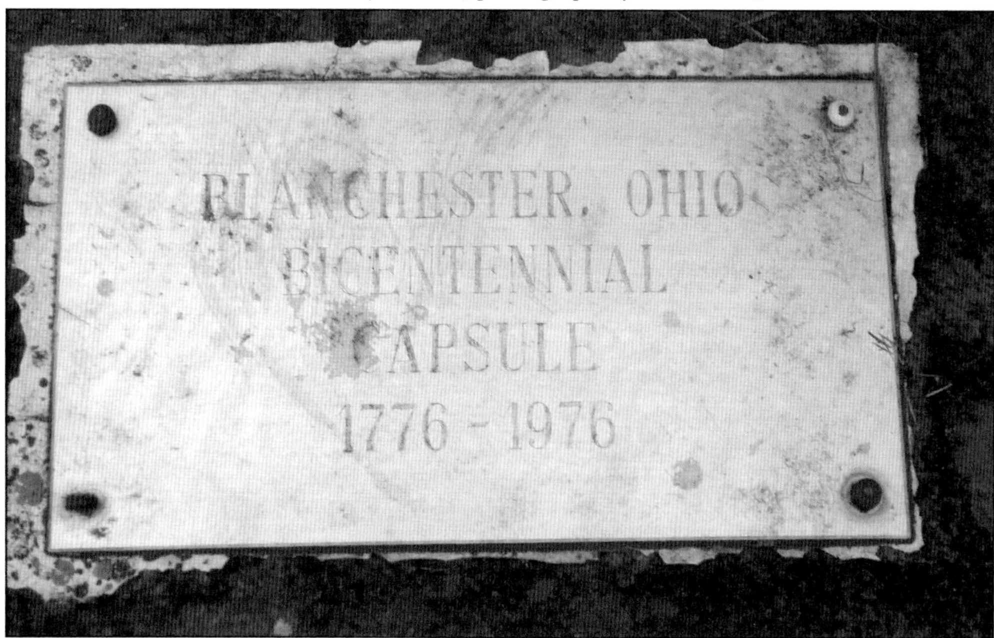

While residents have only had one centennial celebration so far, they also celebrated their sesquicentennial, or first 150 years, in 1982. Designed by J.W. Simpson and produced at the local Allen Co., these memorial tiles ordered for the occasion show popular landmarks, some lost and some still in existence (the Bindley Block is all that remains today), as citizens remembered their history and the years that have passed. The celebration was marked by a festival very similar to the centennial celebration 50 years prior, with parades, street fairs, and performers. The town celebrated for a week. (Photographs by the author.)

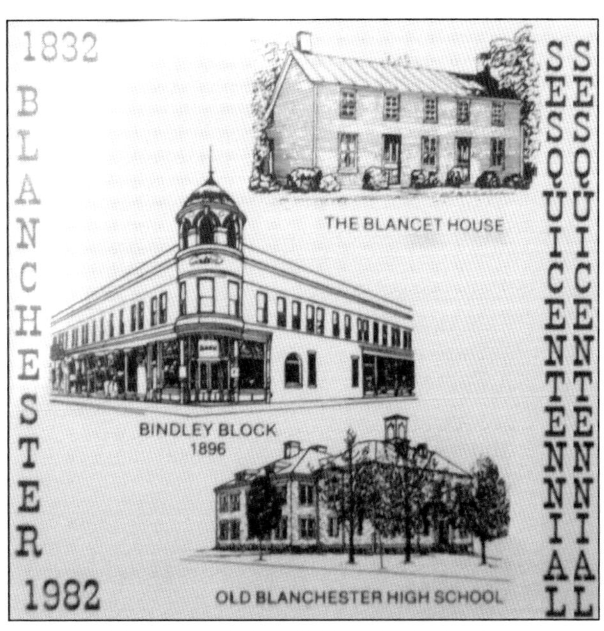

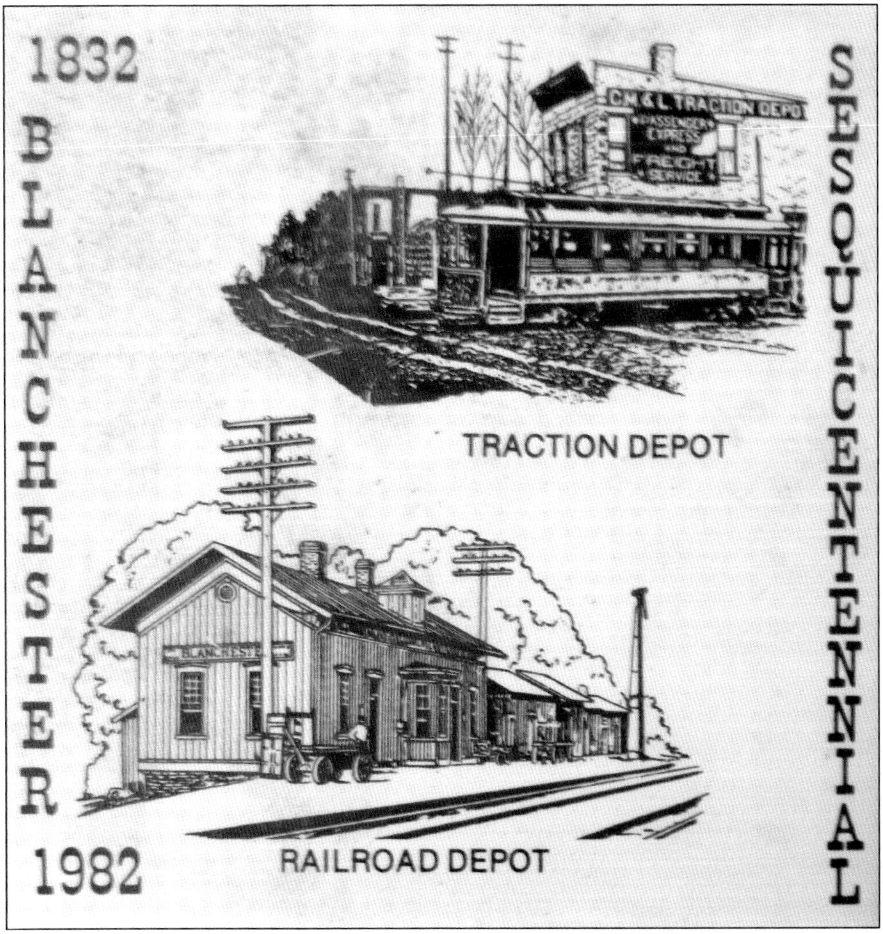

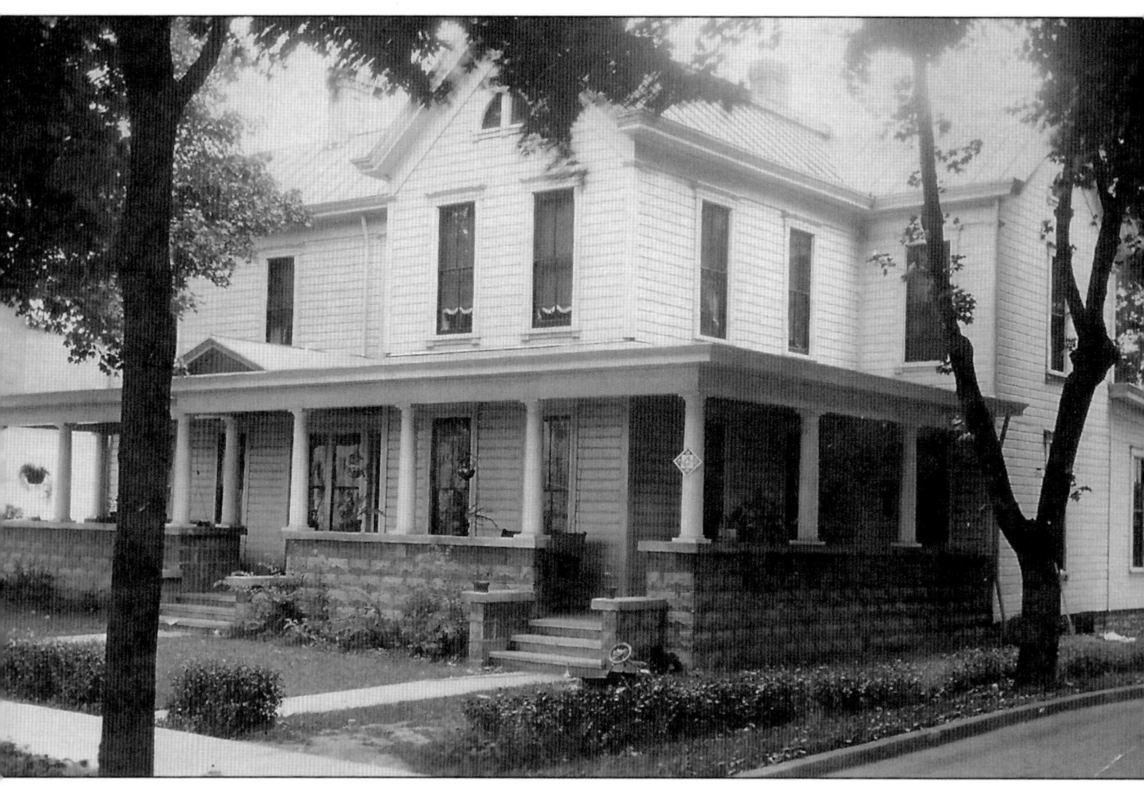

This large and gorgeous building was originally a hotel on Bourbon Street. It was torn down and is now the site of a local fencing company. It was also a delicatessen, an automobile agency, and a hardware store at different times.

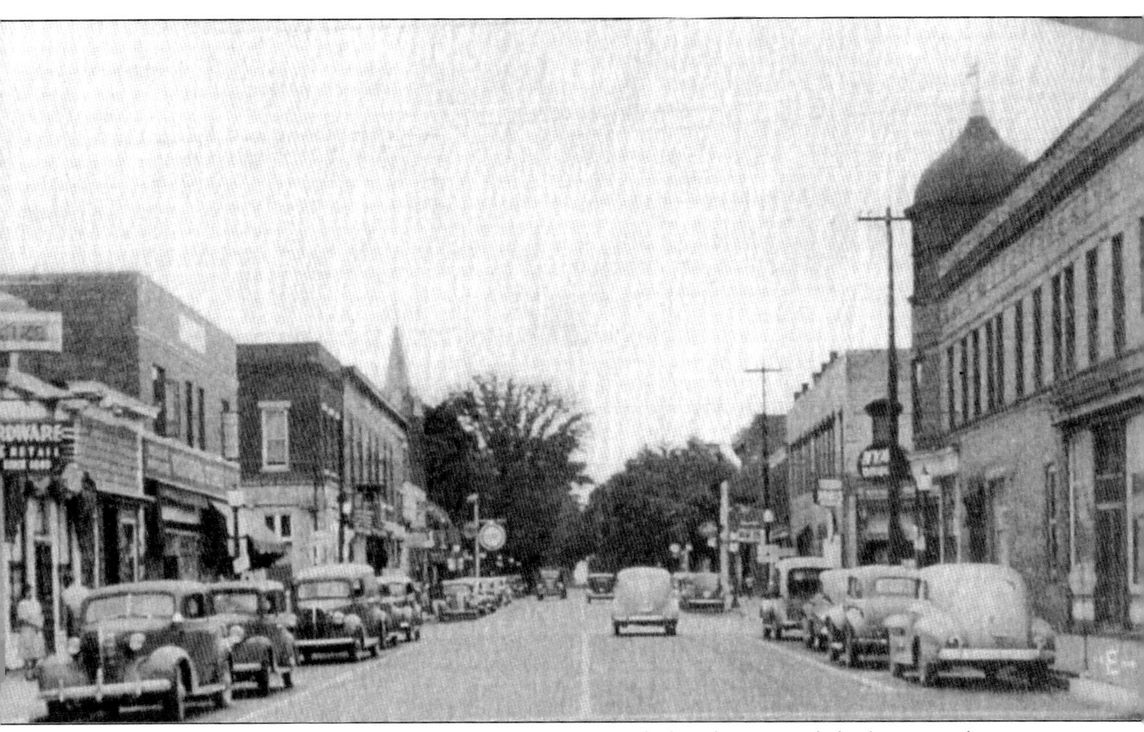

Here is a view looking east on Main Street in the heart of Blanchester and the business district. The photographer was standing on Wall Street, and the image clearly shows the beautiful Bindley Block on the corner, with the distinctive cupola and its "M & F" weather vane atop the Merchant and Farmers building, which closed in 1928. The business district is in many ways the heart of the Blanchester community.

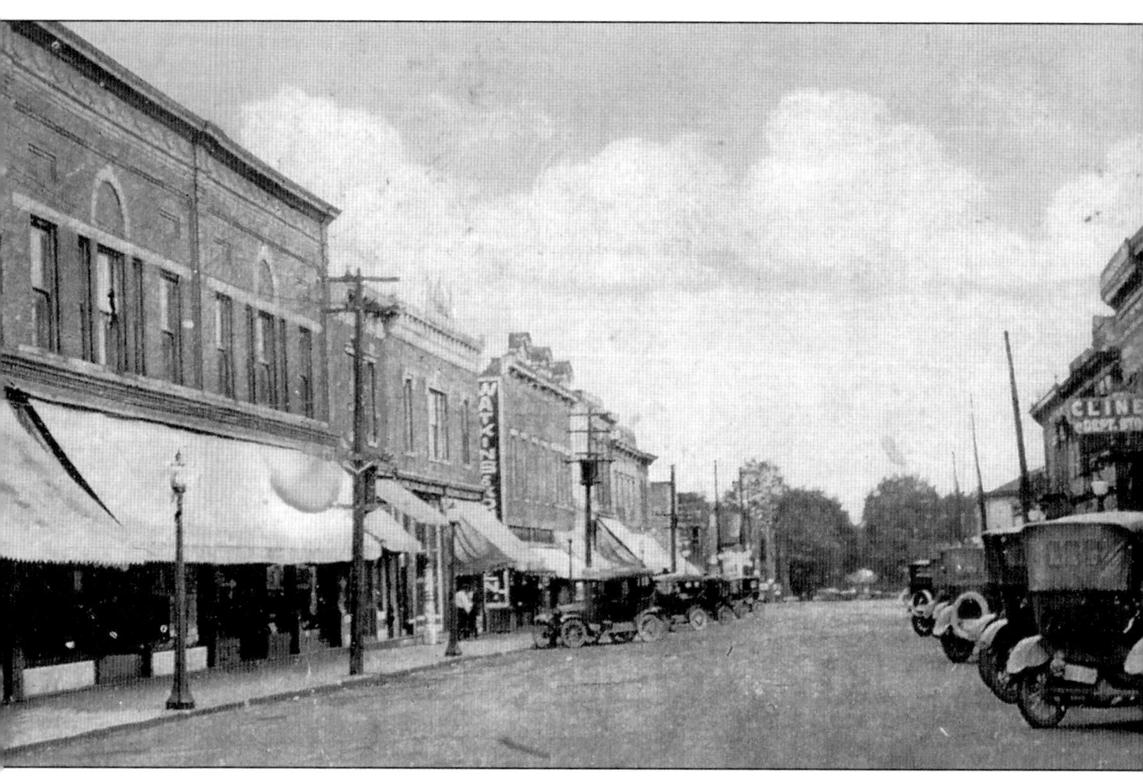

This view looks south on Broadway Street. While the original pediments over the buildings were gone by the time this photograph was taken, the stonework and windows are still present, making it clear that this was the former Rice Building. Of note is the diagonal parking of the vintage automobiles, establishing this scene as the pre–World War I era.

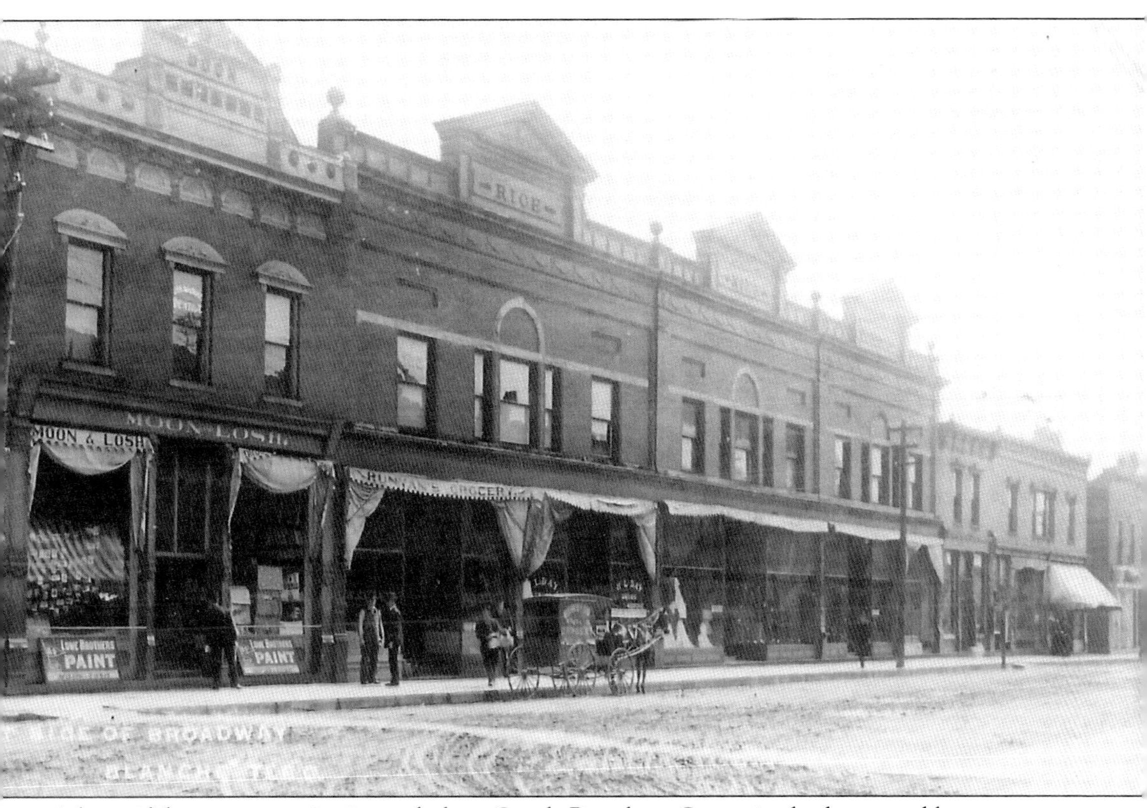

A beautiful street scene is pictured along South Broadway Street in the horse-and-buggy era. Clearly seen are the Moon and Rice Buildings, holding Moon and Losh Drugstore and Runyan's Grocery. The gorgeous pediments and awnings no longer remain, and only about one third of the buildings themselves are still standing because of fire and demolition that house stores many residents can easily walk to on a nice day.

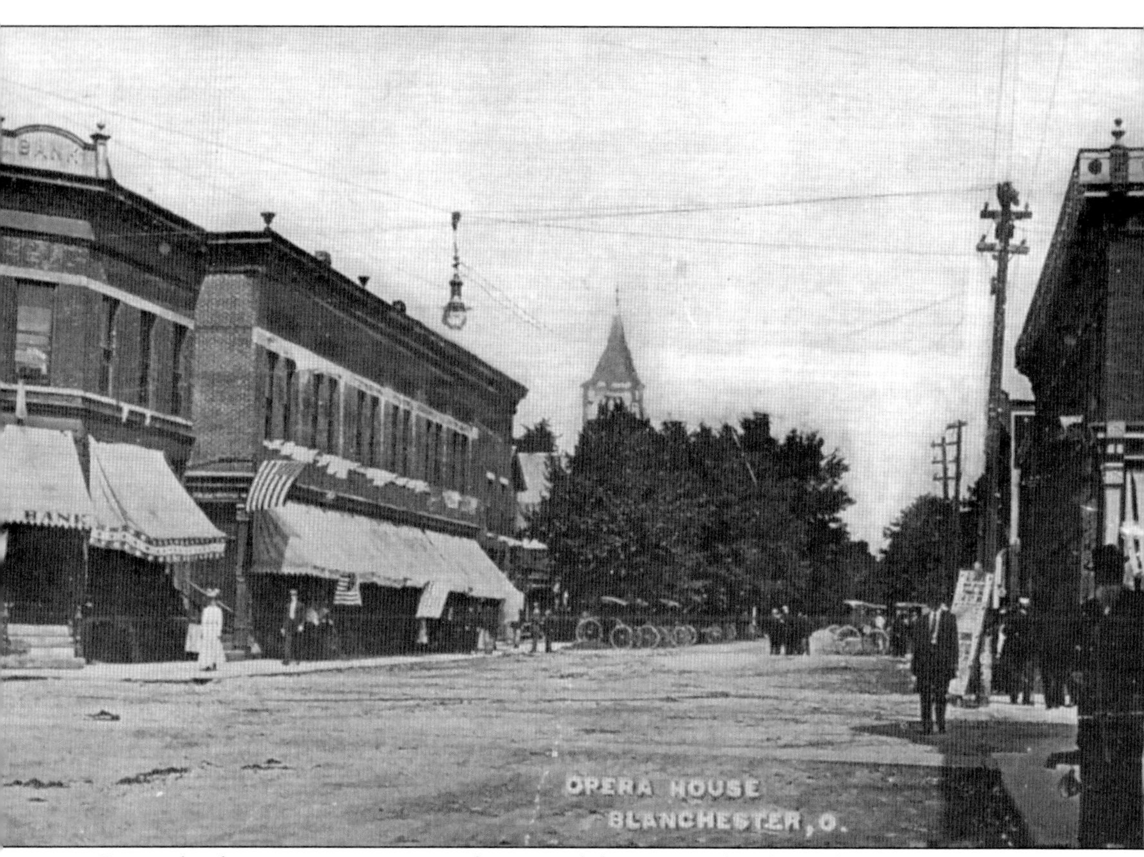

Pictured is the main intersection in the original downtown Blanchester business district, looking east on Main Street, in the World War I era. At left are stairs going to the second-floor opera house and awnings for local shops. In the background is the impressive spire of the Universalist church, which was located where the First National Bank would later be placed in 1967. The bank building was remodeled in 2007 for its 100th anniversary.

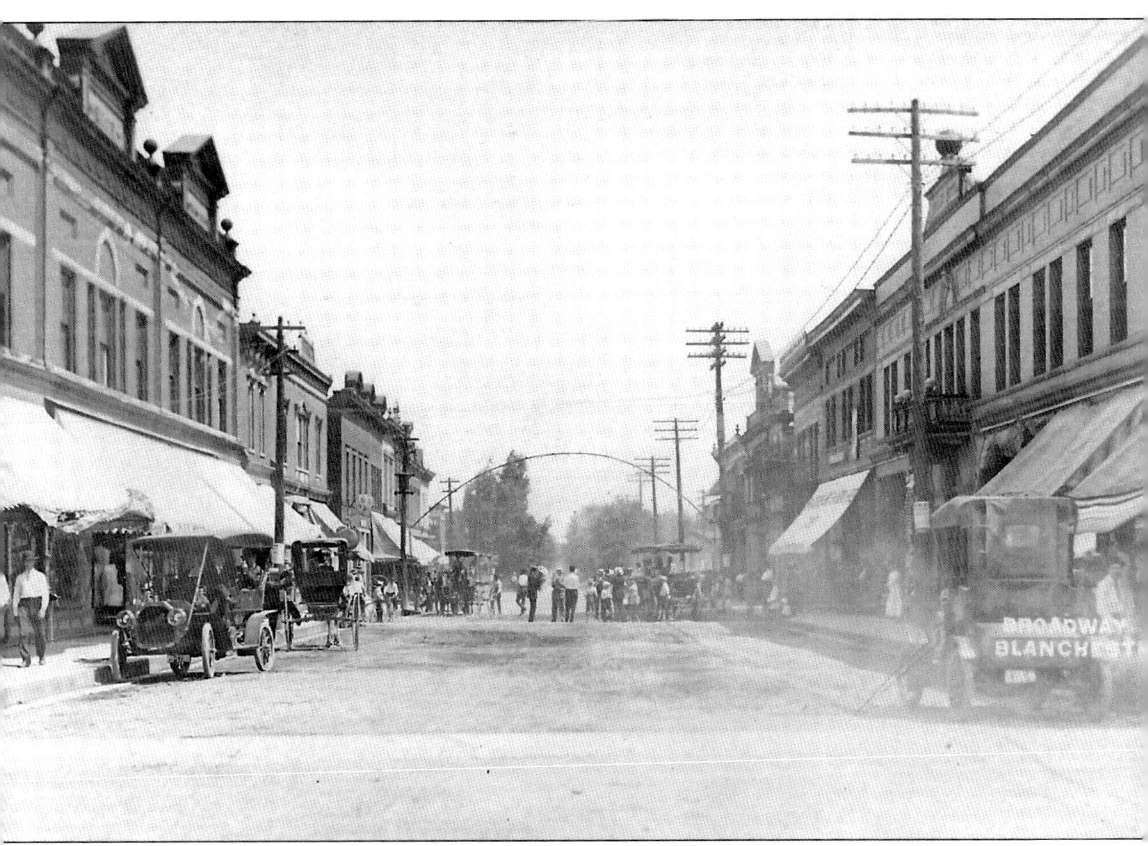

This is a similar view but shows parallel parking, awnings, and people going about their daily lives in the business district. The arch of lights was very well known to locals during the years it was standing, and on Thursday evenings in the summers from 1921 to 1941, a band concert would be held there. Local merchants and residents performed, including area musicians from Westboro, Clarksville, Martinsville, and Wilmington, as well as high school students.

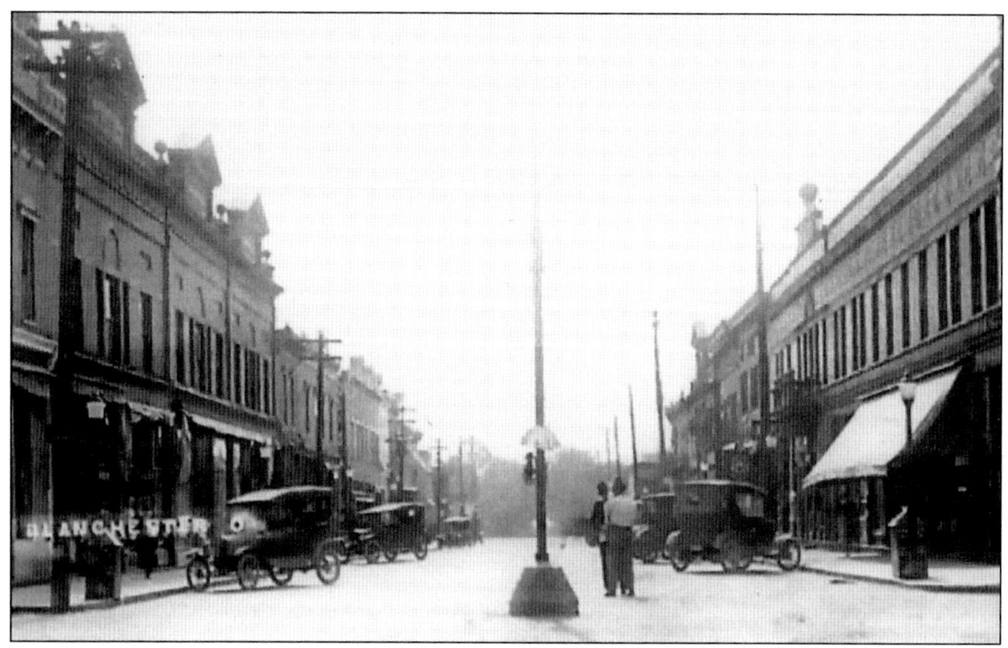

Shown here is the main intersection of the business district, with the traffic light positioned in the center of the intersection. Along the sides are the diagonal parking of beautiful old cars.

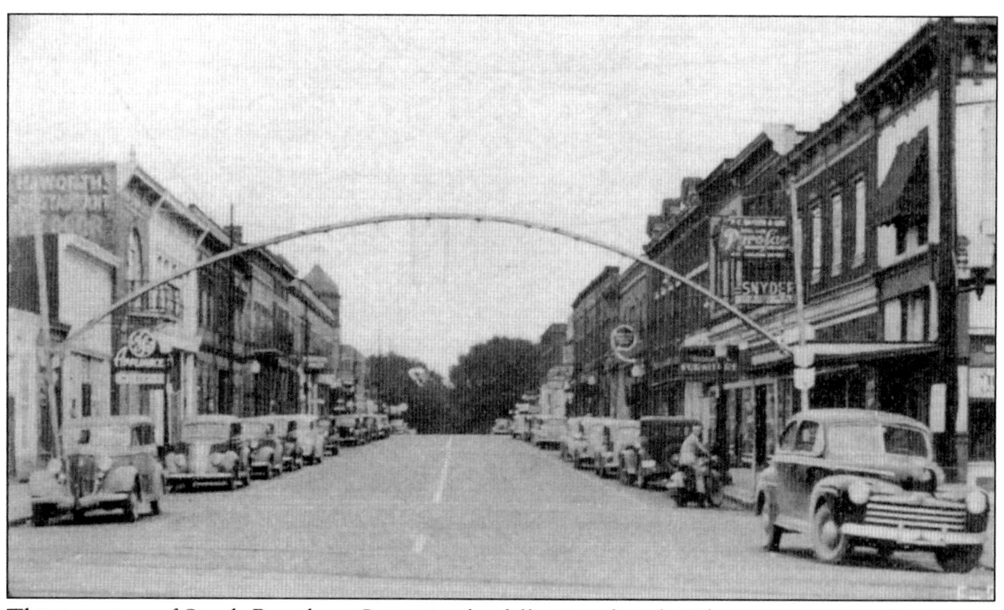

This is a view of South Broadway Street in the following decade. The cars are more familiar to what is seen today, and the signs for the various shops now stand out from the buildings rather than being proclaimed on the awnings.

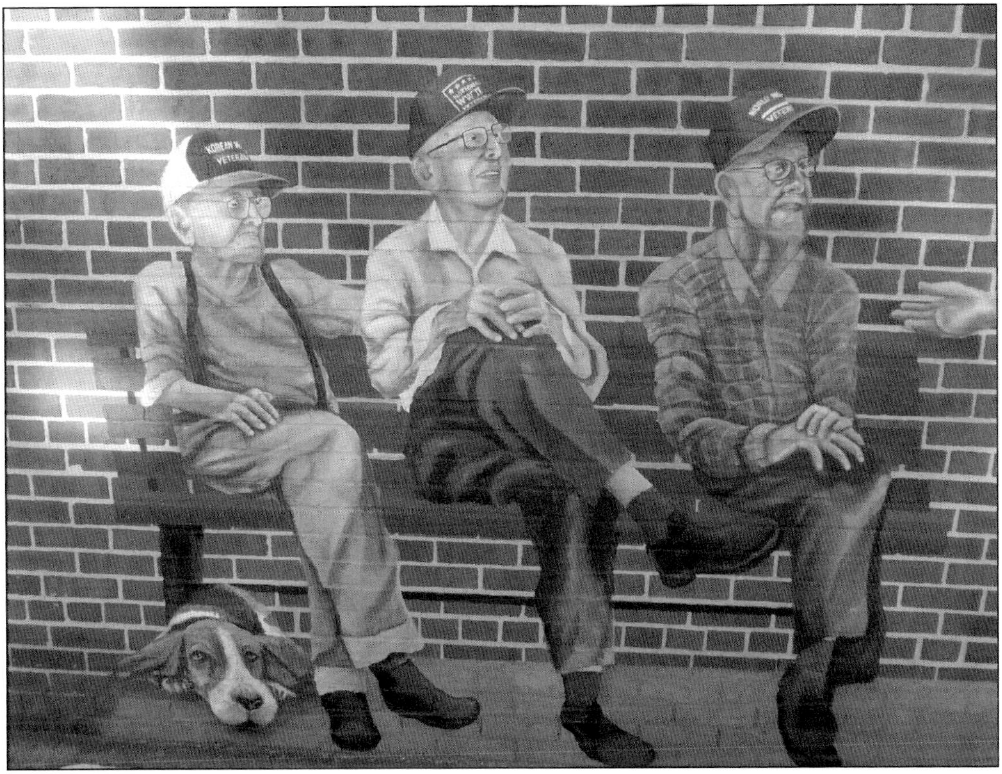

While the pediments and awnings of the business district may be a thing of the past, residents still have pride in the heart of their town. This mural was painted in July 2012 on North Broadway Street on the side of the current Main Street Mall by Ronald D. Keith and is called *Chewing the Fat*. It depicts three local veterans, former mayor Lee Miller, Chester Wilson, and Jim Flemming sitting on the bench, with Lee Miller's dog underneath. Chatting with them is J.W. Simpson, a local historian and curator of the Blanchester Area Historical Society Museum.

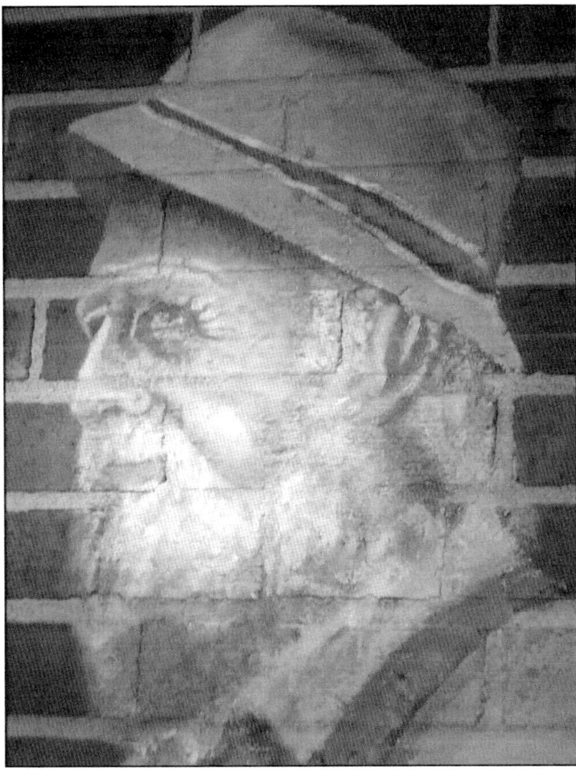

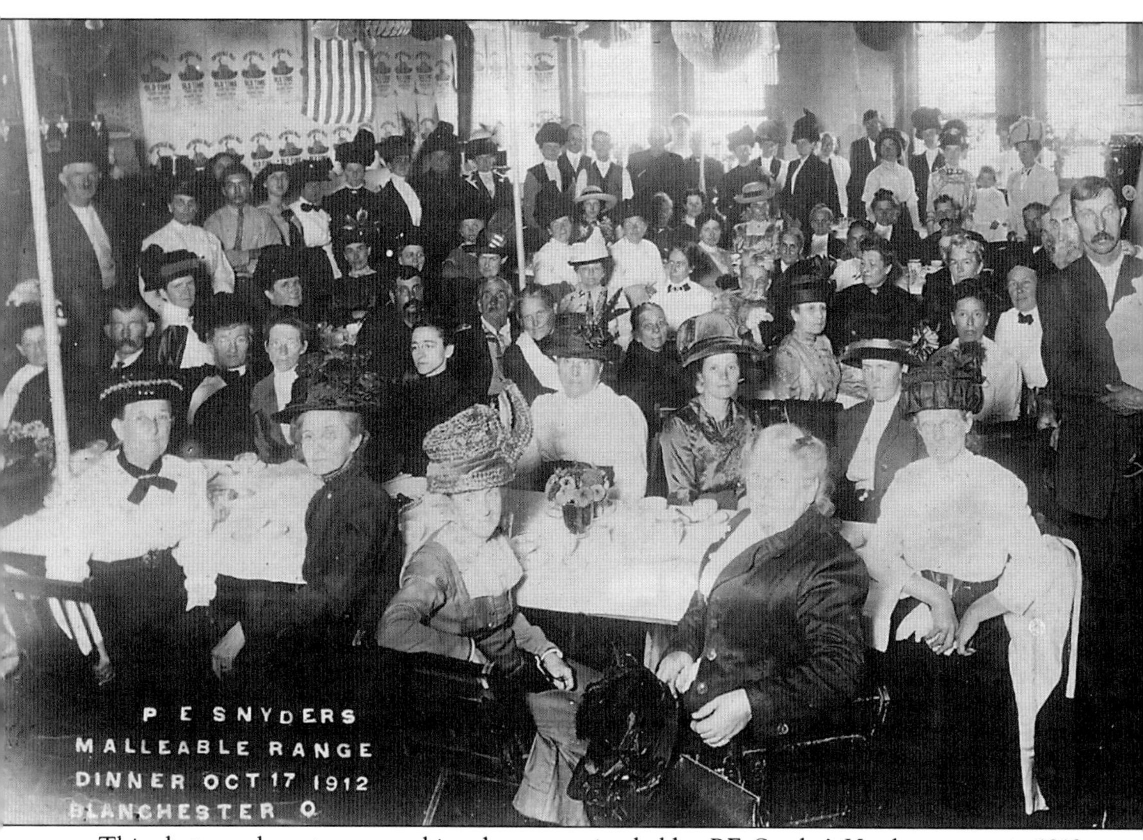

This photograph captures a cooking demonstration held at P.E. Snyder's Hardware store in 1912. The attendees, who came dressed nicely in family groups, were shown the uses of a malleable range in the hopes that they would buy one for their own homes.

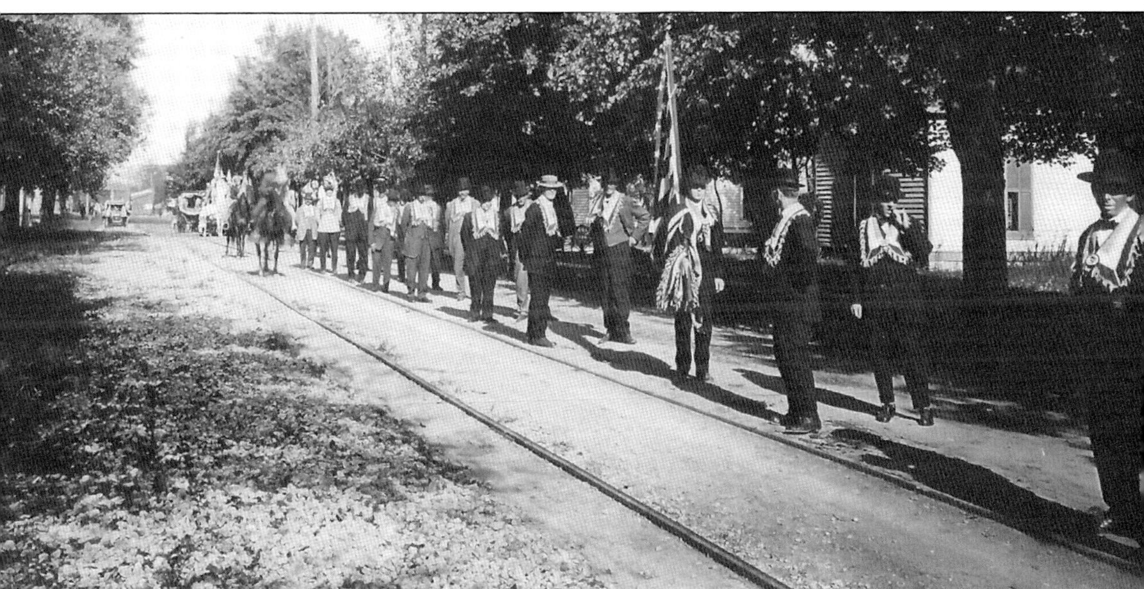

The Junior Order, known also as JROUAM, is shown here participating in festivities. It was founded in 1901. Its building was constructed in 1915 and celebrated its centennial in 2015. A fraternal organization, its recreation room has a card table, billiard table, and ping-pong table and was once a stage for vaudeville shows and Bartone medicine shows and melodramas.

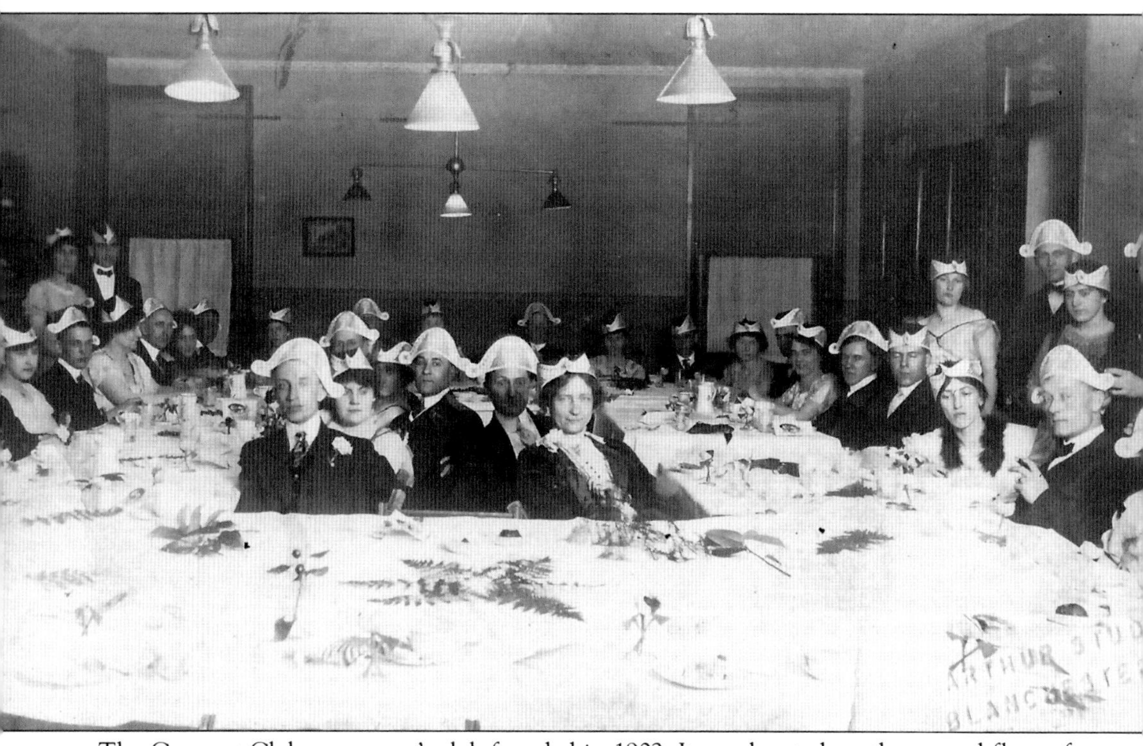

The Crescent Club was a men's club founded in 1902. It was located on the second floor of a building on South Broadway Street but moved across the street. This image shows a guest night for the club, where members brought their wives in for dinner. Their activities over the years have been social and entertaining in nature. The group, one of the first in the state of Ohio, organized formal dinners, banquets, balls, minstrel shows, and plays. Originally there were 25 members, but by 1948 it had risen to 55. Sadly, the club disbanded in the 1970s.

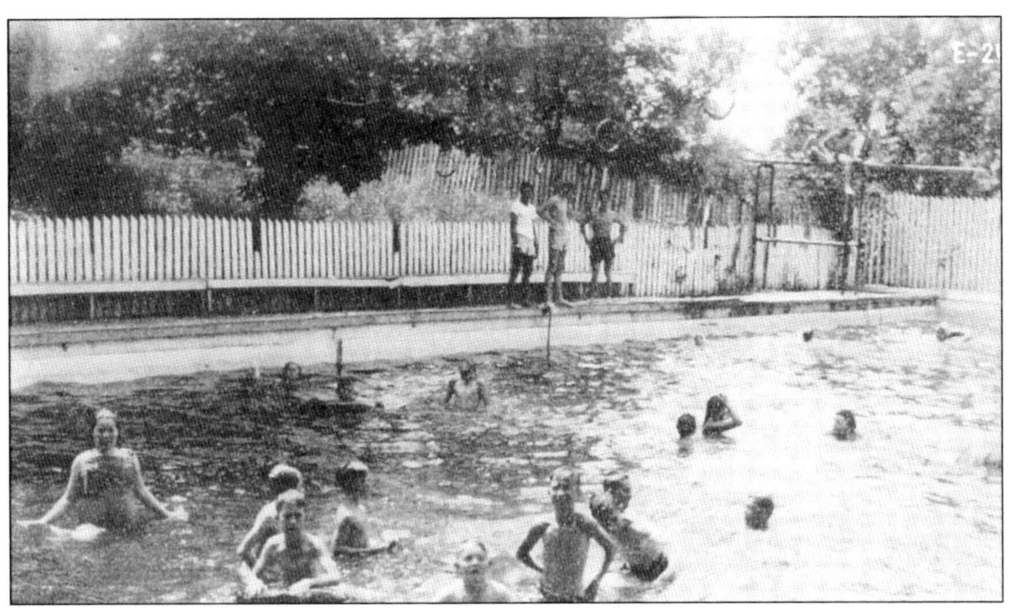

The local watering hole, the Merry Dale Swimming Pool, was opened in 1931 and operated by J.C. Spence, DVM. Later, his son Ross Spence, also a veterinarian, took over ownership and operation of the pool. While it is no longer in that location, or owned by the Spence family, hot summer days can still be spent at the membership-only pool owned by the Blanchester Swim Club, located on East Center Street. The swim club also hosts local swim meets.

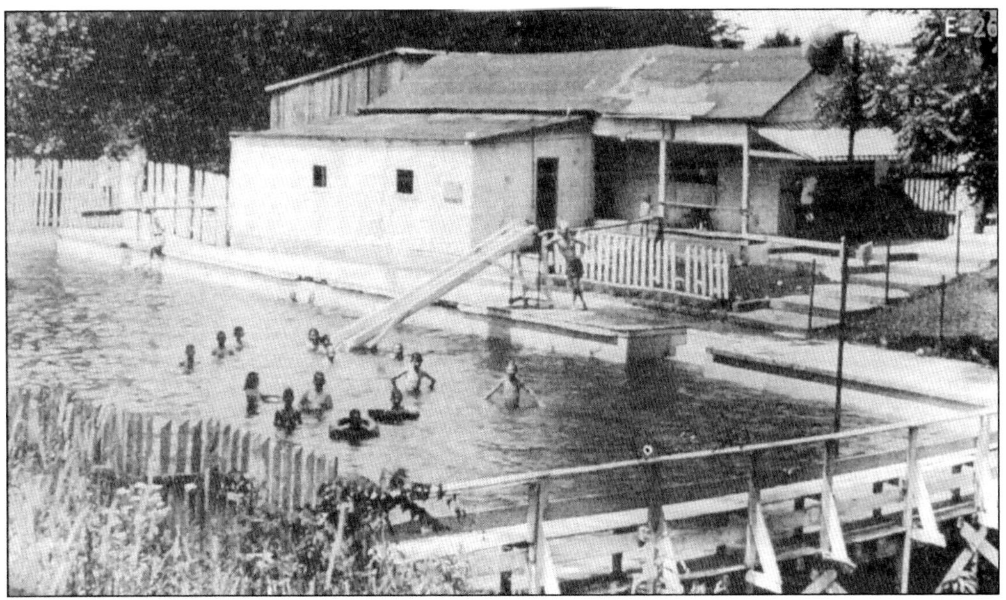

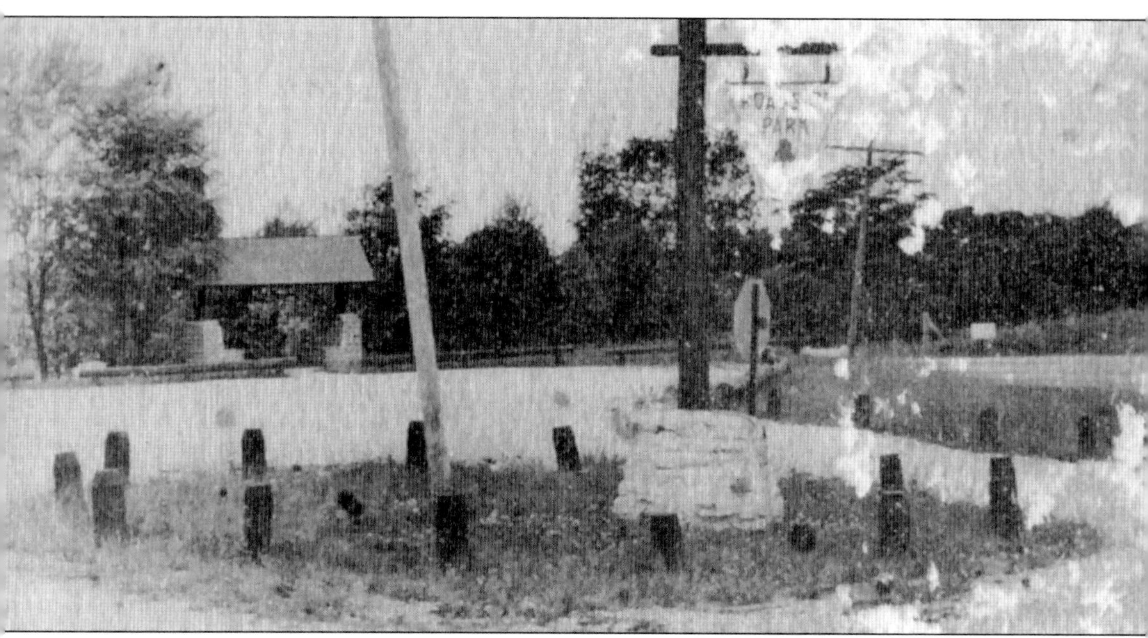

Roadside Park was designed for the early days of automobiles, in the 1930s and 1940s, when people would regularly take their cars out for short trips just to enjoy driving. It was located at the southwest edge of the community and closed in 1970; however, it was later reopened by the local Rotary club. The water pump and shelter have been replaced by a bubble fountain and there are new lighted, flush facilities. It is maintained by the local village park department.

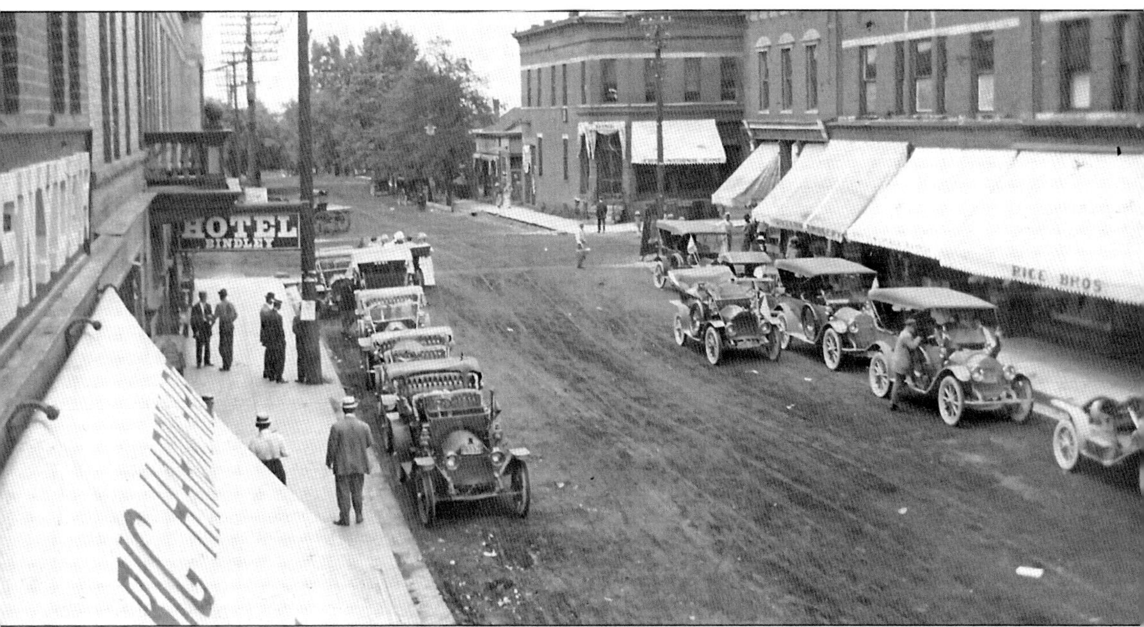

Taken in the 1920s, this image shows a collection of roadster tourist cars on South Broadway and Main Streets. The canvas awnings of the storefronts are visible along the edges, heralding in the age of the automobile.

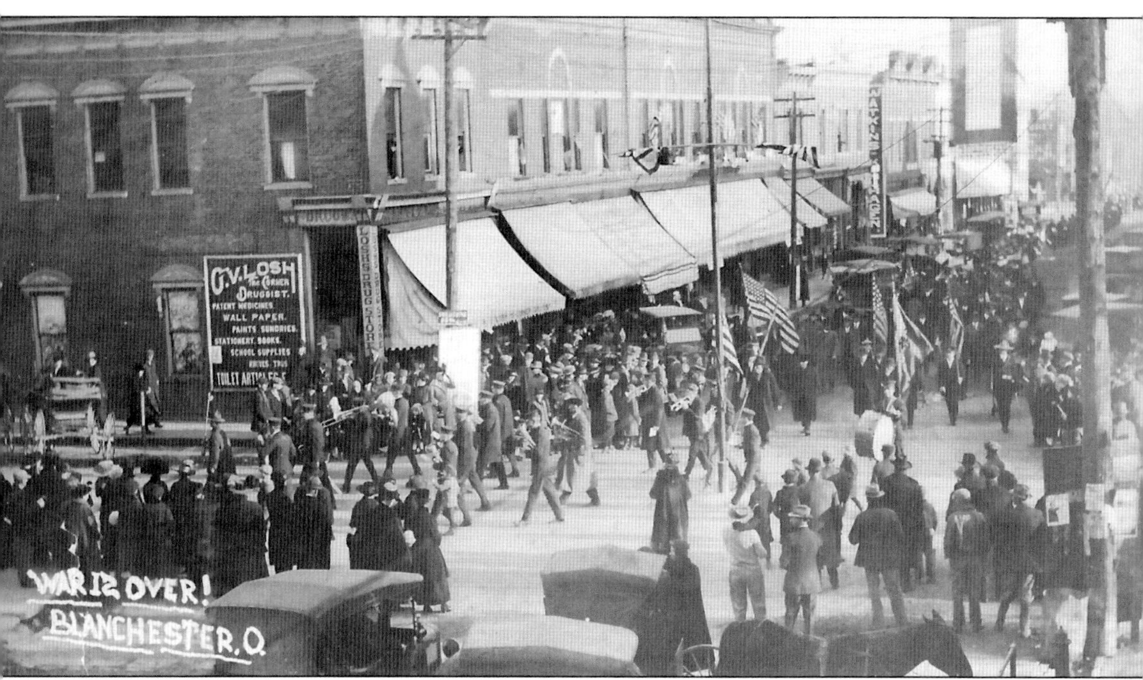

Nothing says "community" more strongly than crowds lining the streets to celebrate the return of their troops at the end of a war. This image shows a parade on Broadway Street at the end of World War I, and the troops were returning from battle after the armistice. The Service Star flag was hanging to celebrate as people cheered from the sidelines. The returning troops and the band headed east on Main Street to the bandstand for a program at the site that would later become the Basinger Building that would house the Brown Publishing Company and then the Curless Printing Company.

Eight

Business and Commerce

For a small town, Blanchester has had a lot of big business. Perhaps the most interesting thing about the majority of the businesses is the fact that most of them are centered in the same small section of town, the Bindley Block, the area that was rebuilt after the fire. Many fondly remember the businesses that have come and gone through those stately buildings, bringing wealth and prosperity as well as building a strong community. Citizens could stand and gossip outside the stores when they were preparing a sale, chat while awaiting demonstrations at the hardware store, or just marvel at the beautiful fronts of the buildings themselves, decorated for special occasions. It is the business district that is the basis of most directions given to visitors in Blanchester, and the business district is what makes the town unique, even to this day.

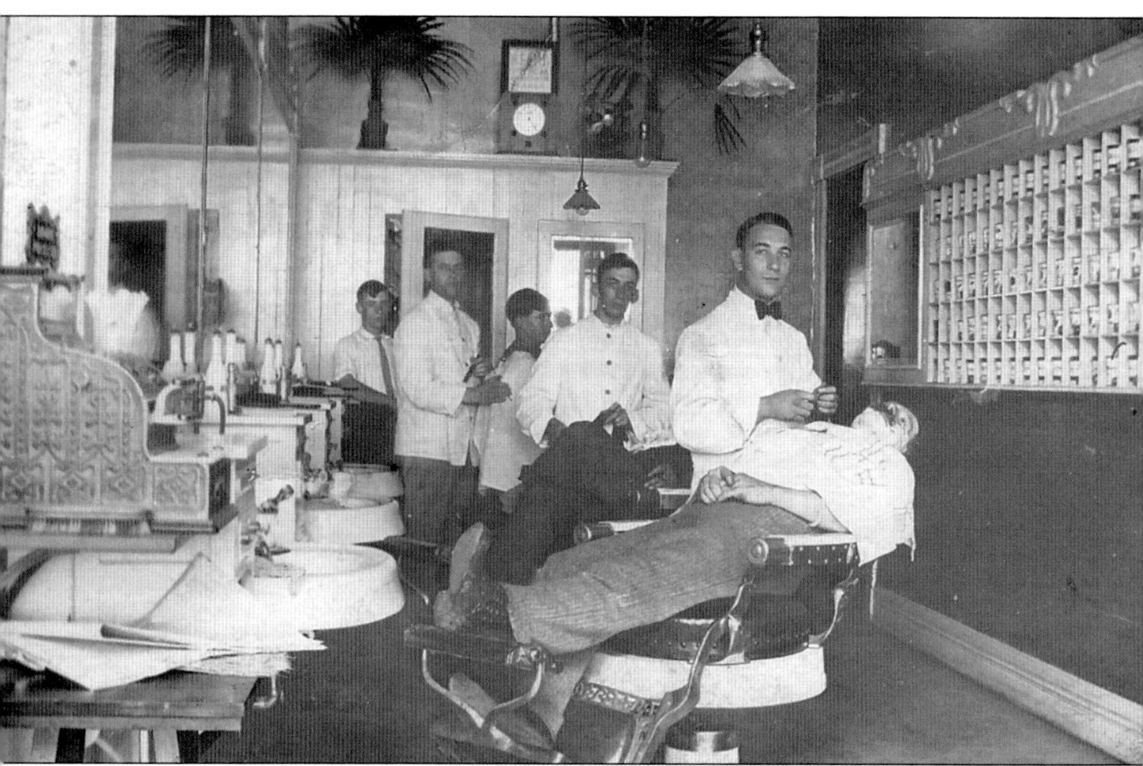

Here is the barbershop off of the Bindley Hotel Lobby. On the wall can be seen the compartments for the personal shaving mugs of patrons. The ownership has changed more than once since, but the location has always been a barbershop. Pictured here are John Trenary, Clarence Mullinex, and Rex Tutwiler.

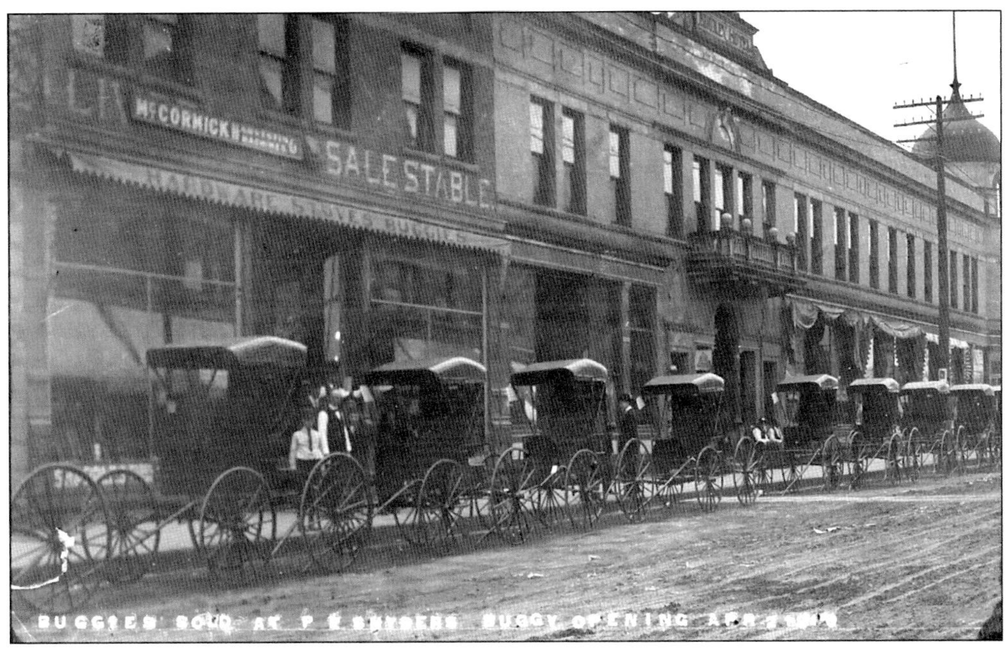

P.E. Snyder Hardware store celebrated its new stock of buggies and carriages by lining them up on the street. Usually, these items were kept on the second floor of the building and lowered for sale or use on a platform operated by ropes.

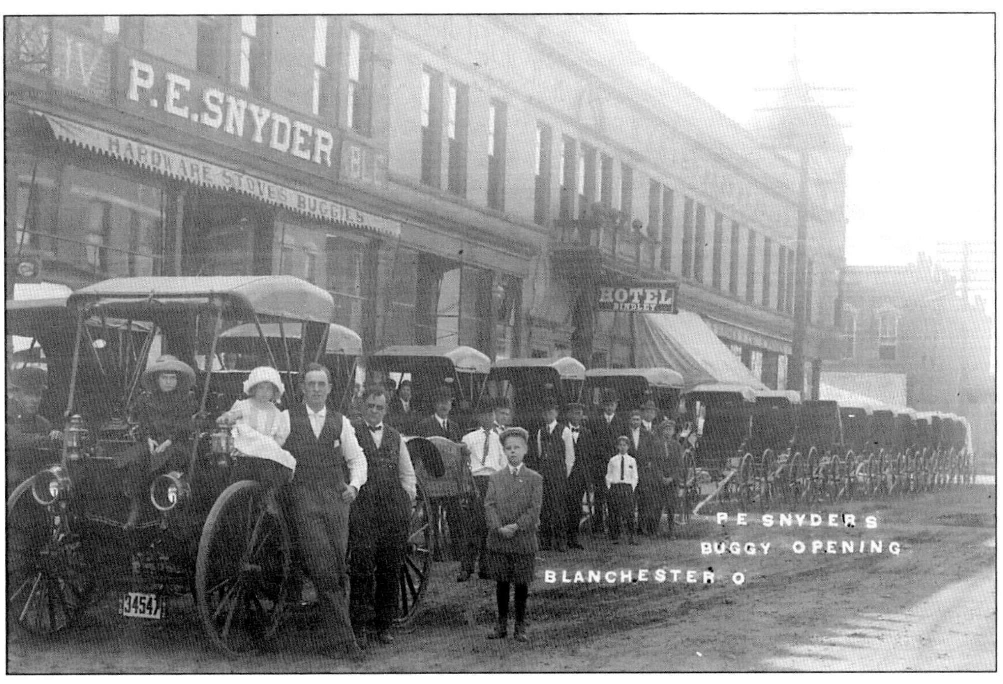

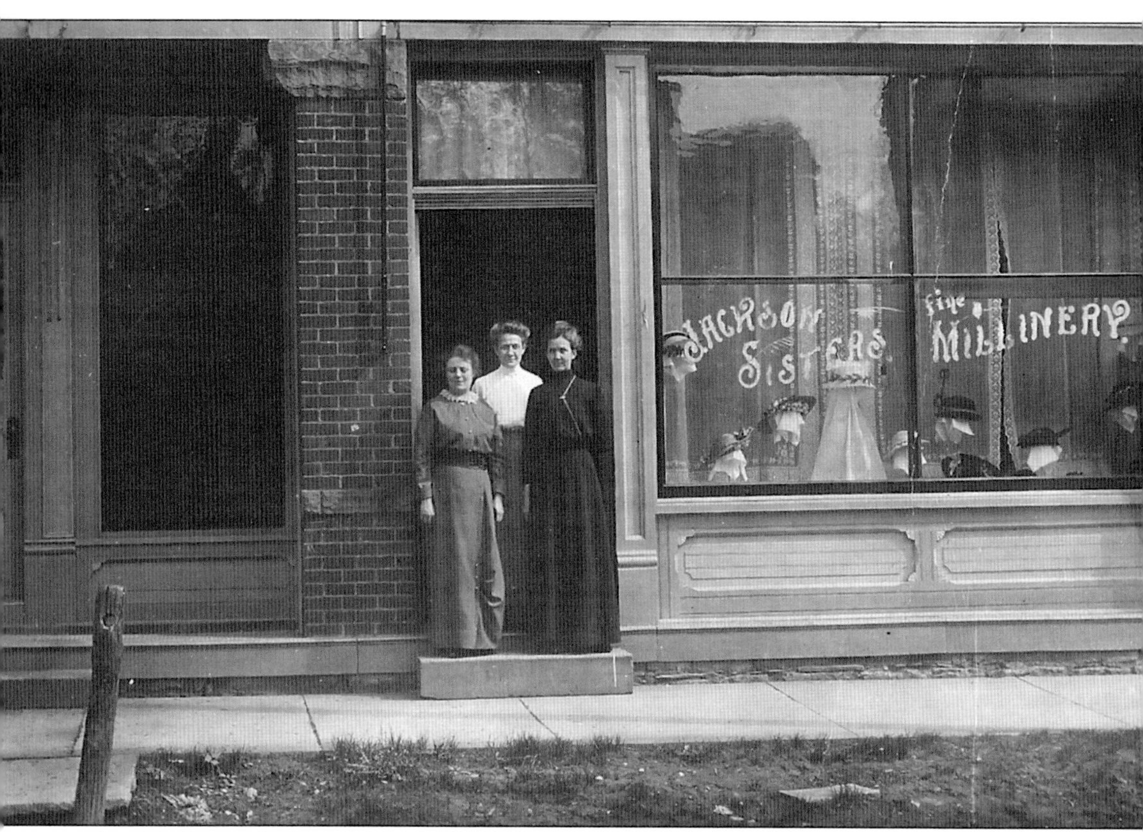

Pictured here is Jackson Sisters Millinery shop on West Main Street. This location burned down in the 1895 fire, but the business reopened at the Bates's home across the street. The site was later home of the Honeycomb Restaurant and is presently the Peoples Bank, built in 1981.

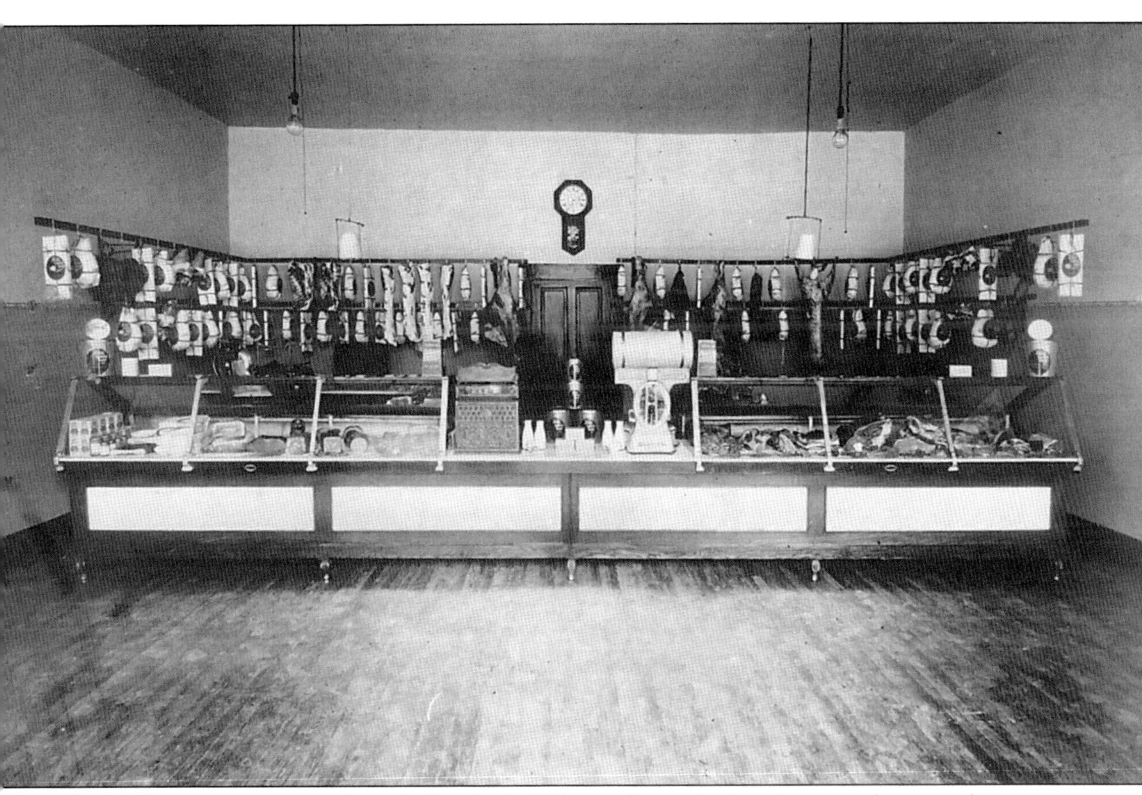

This is what the Penquite Meat Market looked like in the early days. It was in business for over 50 years in the same location. This site was later Bowman's TV, as well as McD's Diner, and it will soon open as a family recreation center.

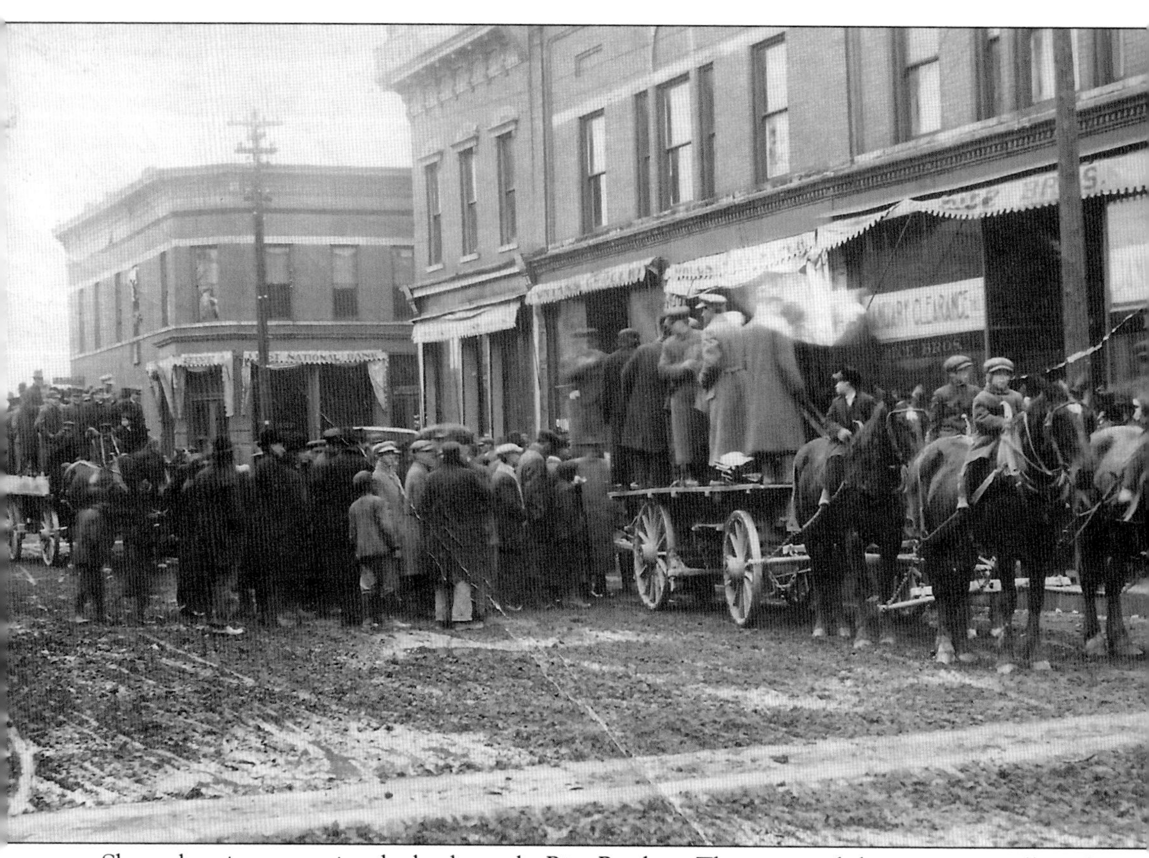

Shown here is a promotional sales day at the Rice Brothers. The mercantile business even collected customers and brought them in on a wagon so employees could more easily access the sale. Even today, Blanchester is largely surrounded by farmland.

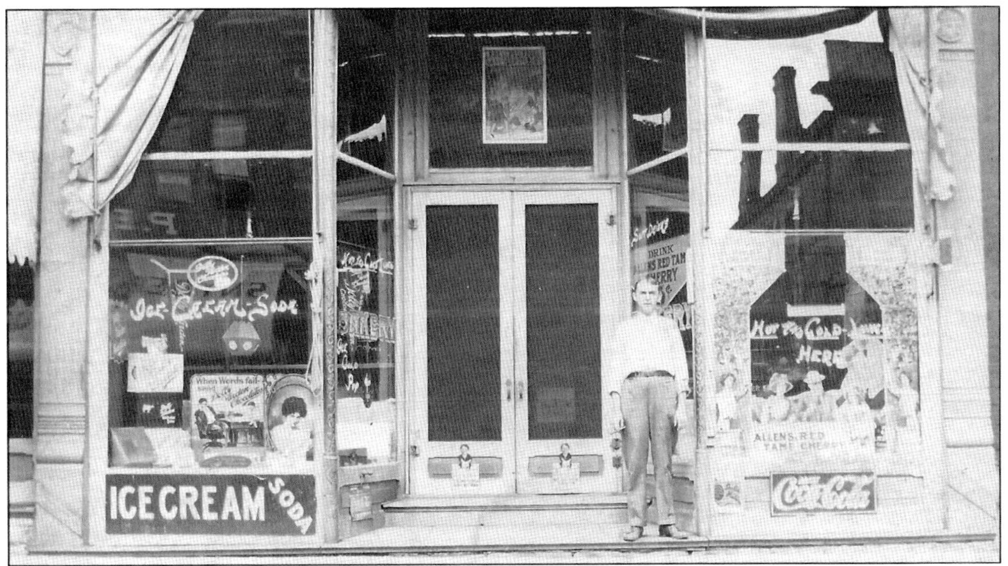

This is the William Frey Ice Cream Parlor on the east side of South Broadway Street during the World War I era.

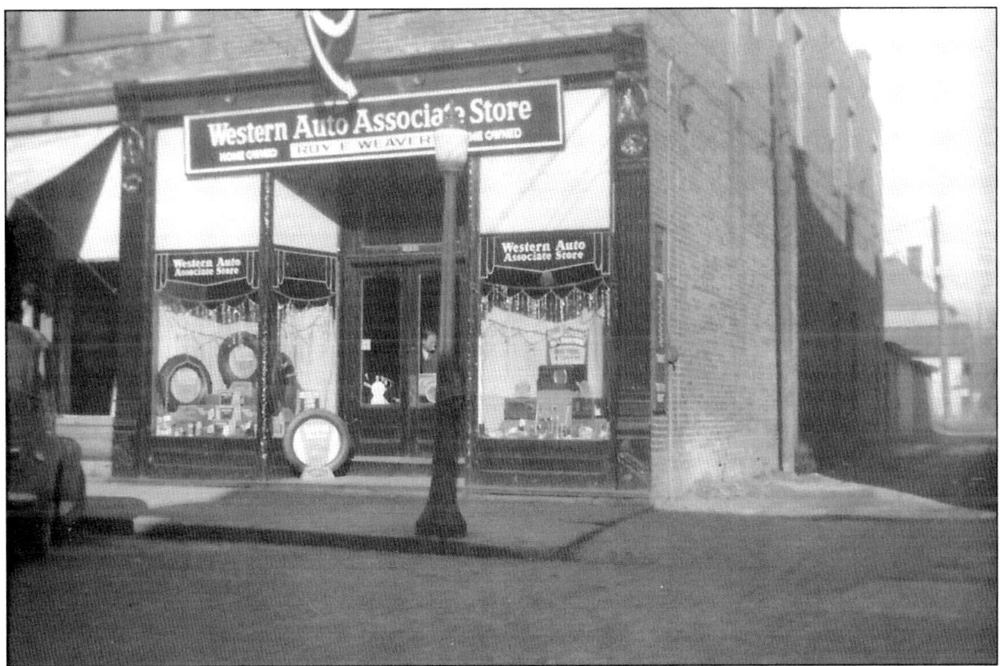

The Western Auto Associate Store, owned by Roy E. Weaver, later moved into the location that formerly housed the William Frey Ice Cream Parlor and was in operation in the 1940s and 1950s.

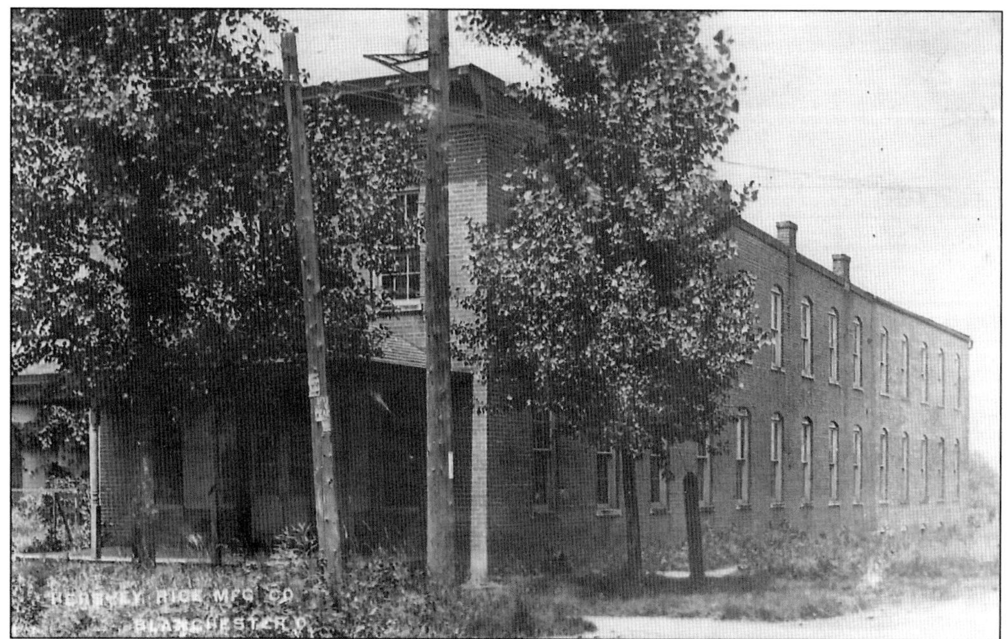

The Hershey-Rice Overall Factory was once found at the corner of Center Street. In 1913, the building was destroyed by a major fire. Employees maintained their jobs, recovering the bricks and rebuilding the structure. It operated as a clothing factory until the 1940s, when Paul Jackson developed his Fairview Hatchery, and then the Allan Company operated its cloth products unit there, producing nail aprons, barbecue aprons, and mitts. Most recently, it has been used for storage.

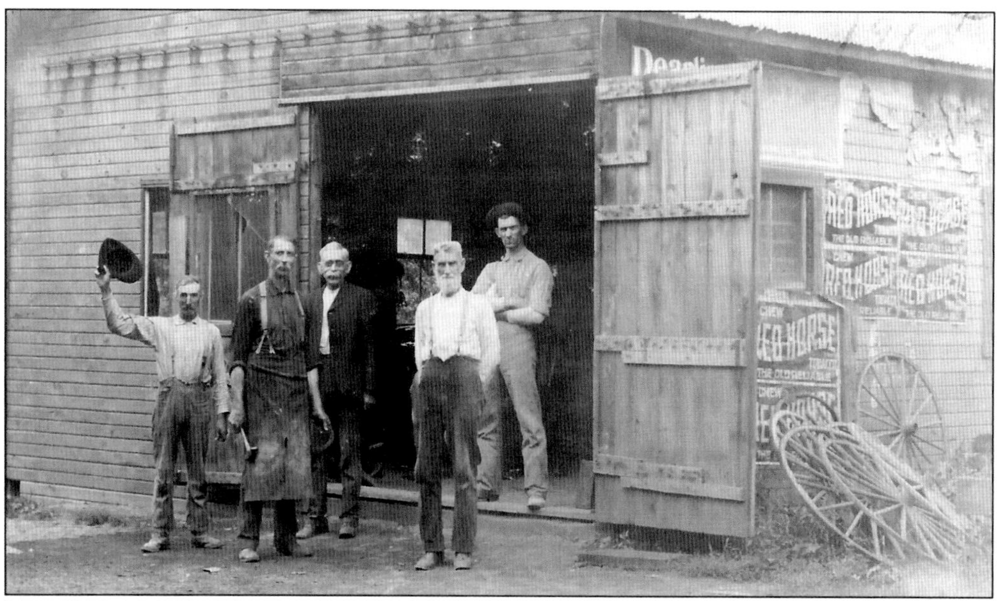

This blacksmith shop was owned by Isaac Long and located at the corner of Cherry and South Wright Streets, adjacent to the icehouse.

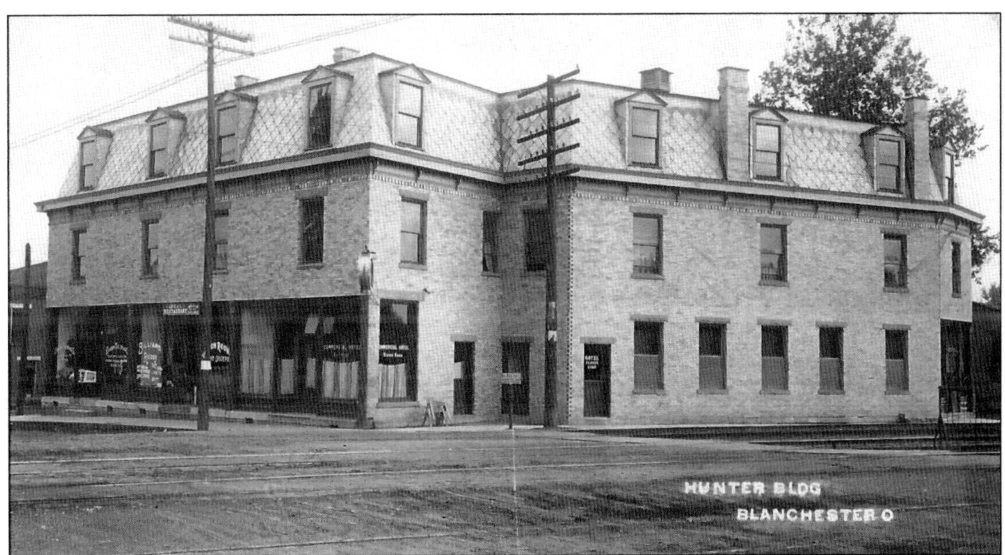

This building was originally a community hotel but became a commercial hotel at the corner of South Broadway and Bourbon Streets. It was best known as the Hunter Hotel, and it housed a bar and grill, two stores, and apartment complexes on the second and third floors.

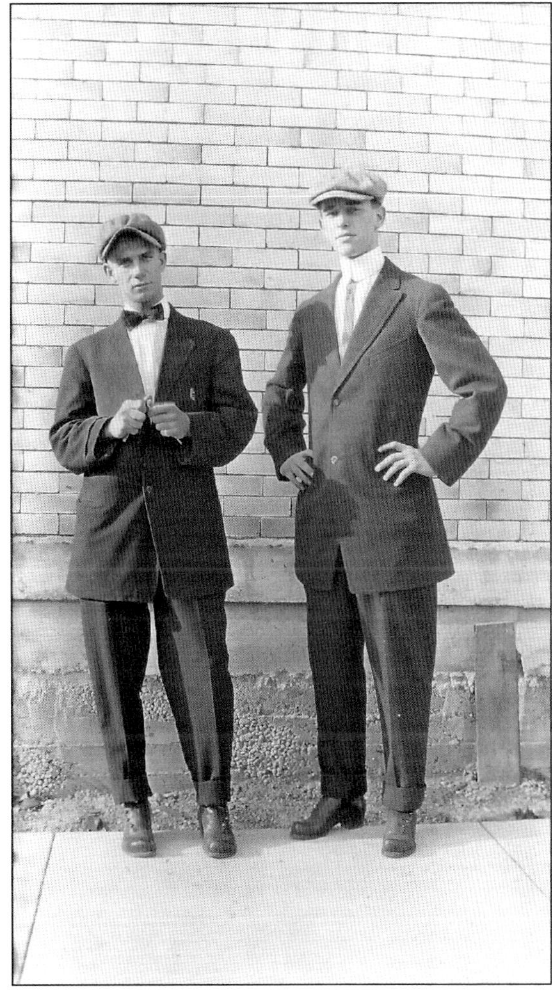

Joe Baldwin and Don McFadden are shown here outside of the Hunter Hotel around 1920, dressed in fancy suit coats.

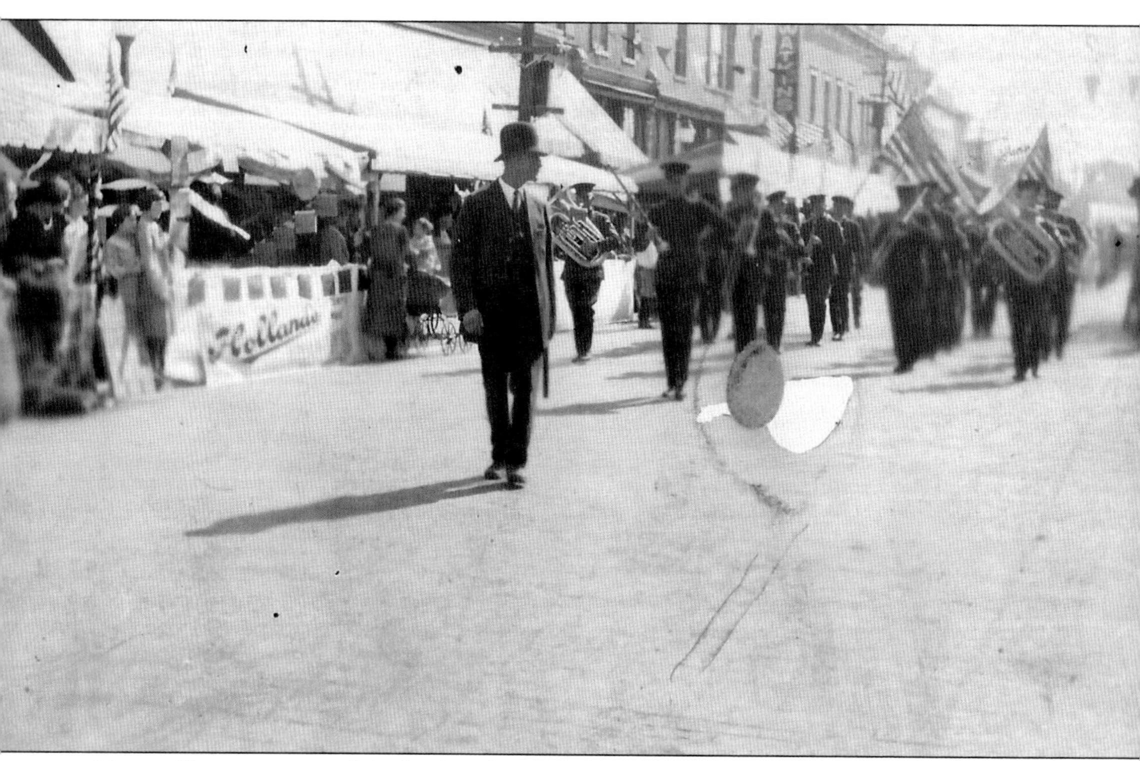

Pictured here are some of the leading businessmen of the Blanchester community. Among their number are P.E. Snyder and H.G. Bates. These were the days when the downtown business district was thronged with shoppers and visitors coming in from the surrounding area on the traction line, which deposited them conveniently within walking distance of the stores.

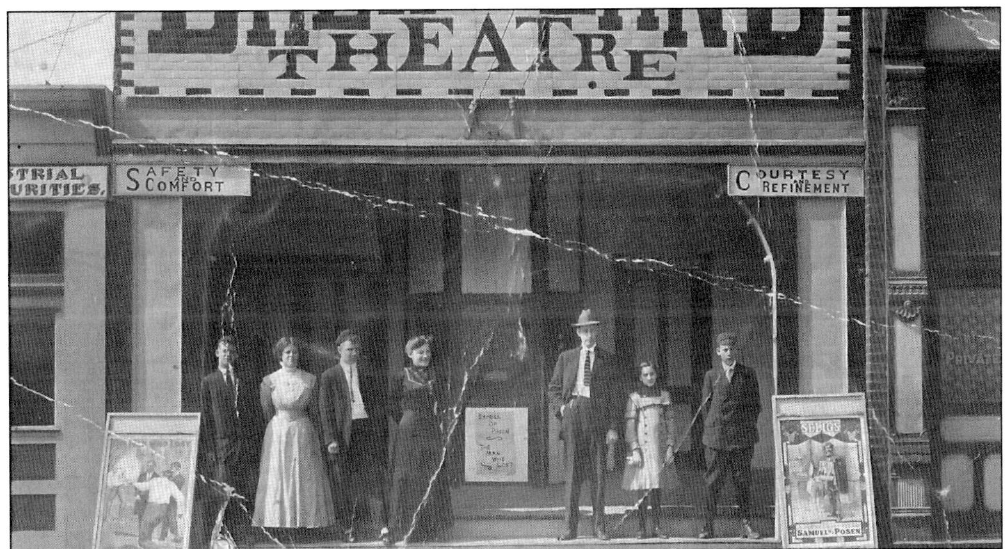

The Dreamland Theatre, on South Broadway Street, was operated by a Mr. Robertson, seen here in 1912. At the time, it only showed silent movies, which were accompanied by a local piano player. Mrs. Shawhan was one of the piano players for the theater and would provide the accompaniment with Madge Wilkin (McCoy), while Violet Ross (Simpson) was the ticket salesperson. Madge and Violet were high school classmates of Mrs. Robertson (Frances Reed). Upstairs was a band room.

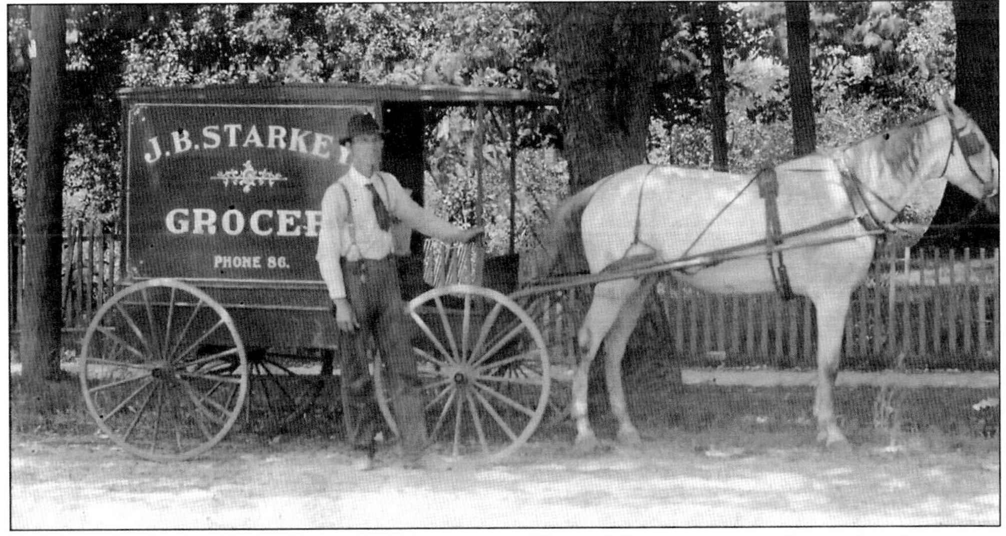

Shown here is the J.B. Starkey Grocery wagon and horse. The grocery was located at the corner of South Broadway and Bourbon Streets and later was operated by Lew Reilly and then Harold Carnahan and family until it closed and the building was demolished. The wagon, when not promoting the business during parades, was used for everyday deliveries.

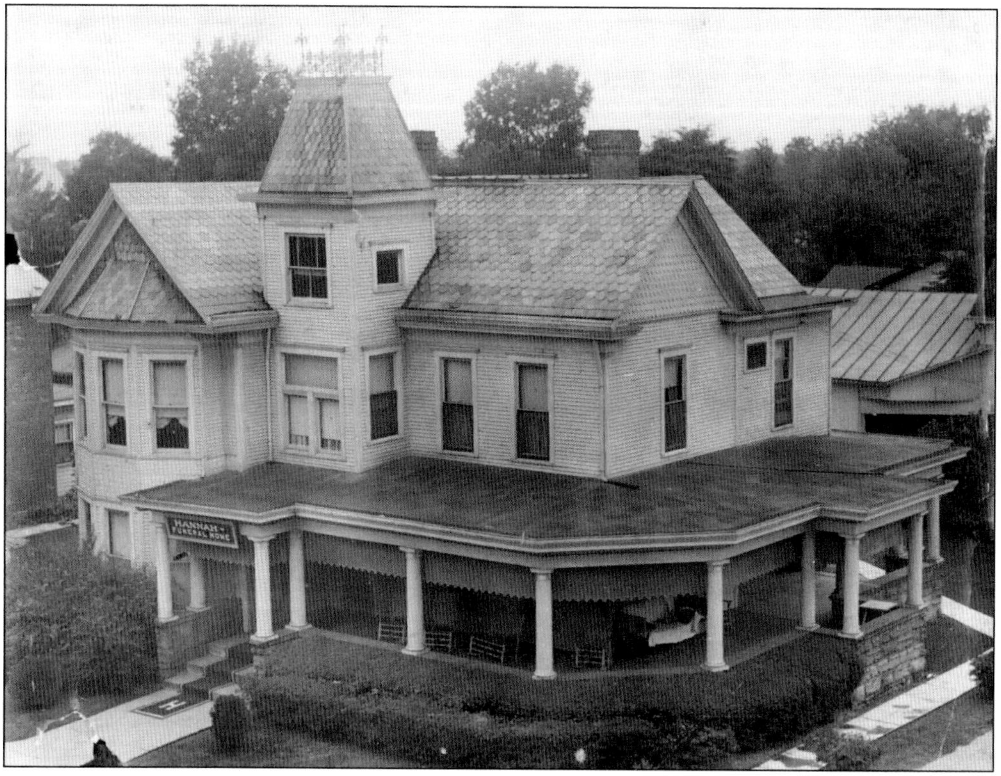

The Hannah Funeral Home was opened in the early 1900s on East Main Street. It operated for a long time before being purchased by the Tufts Schildmeyer Funeral Home, which operates in the same building today. The structure is just as beautiful and stately today, though it has been expanded upon. (Both, courtesy of Peggy Schildmeyer.)

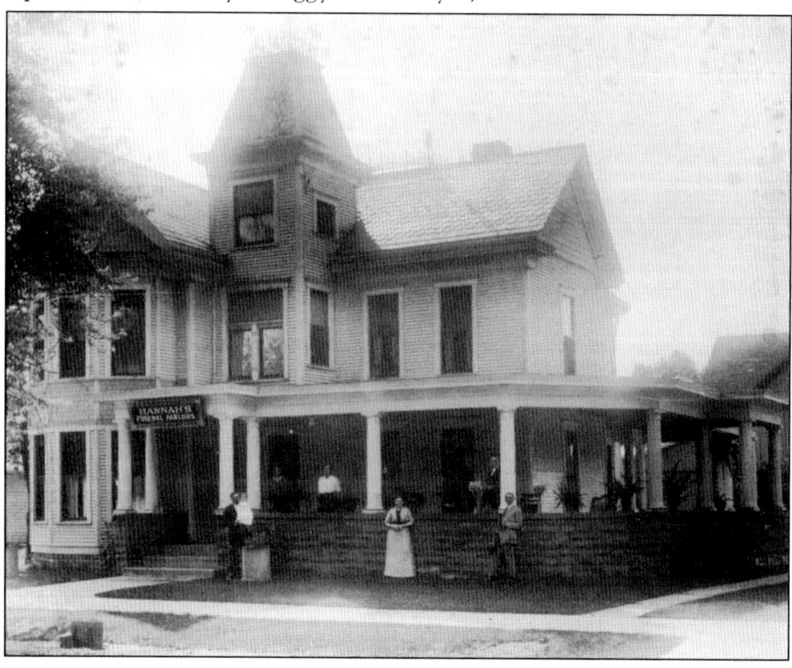

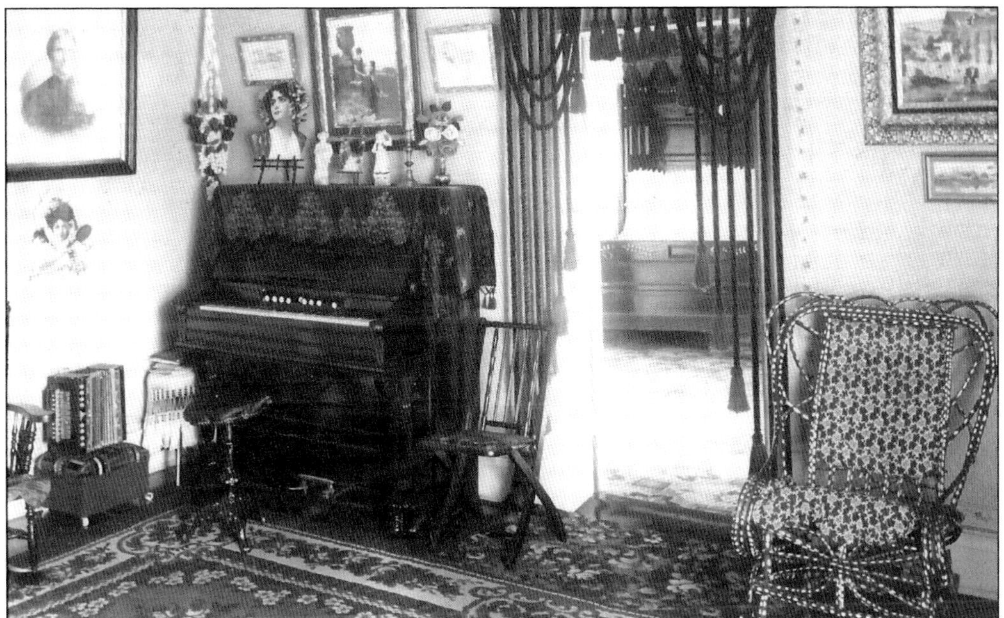

This is a view of the interior of the Hannah Funeral Home in the 1930s. Many of the portraits depicted are still hanging inside, though they are without their frames. Though a new company owns the building, the owners respect it and the area.

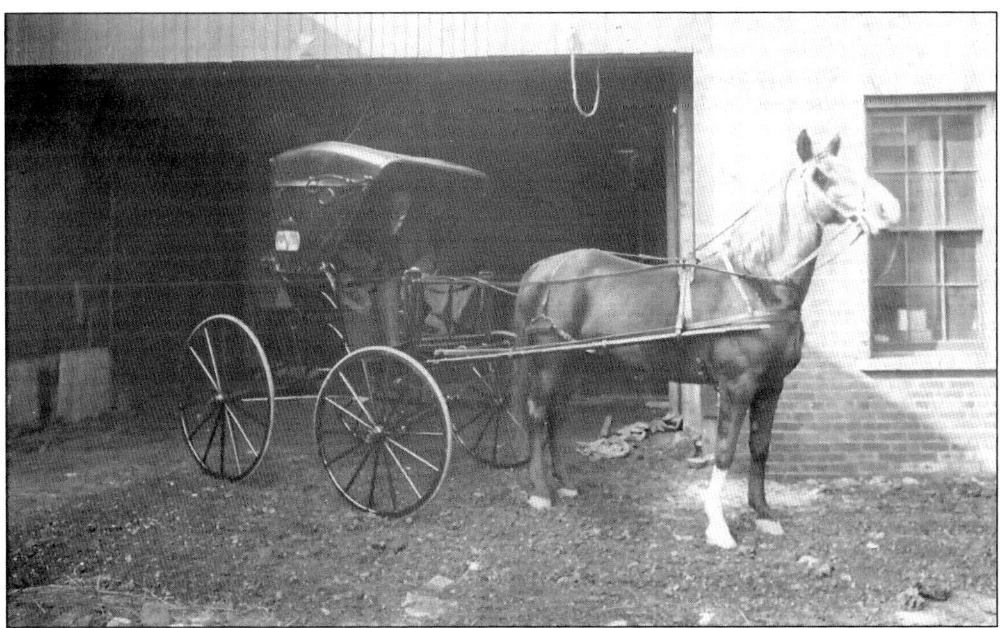

The Hannah Funeral Home buggy was used for day-to-day business but could be seen on special occasions covered in flowers for the area parades (see chapter 3).

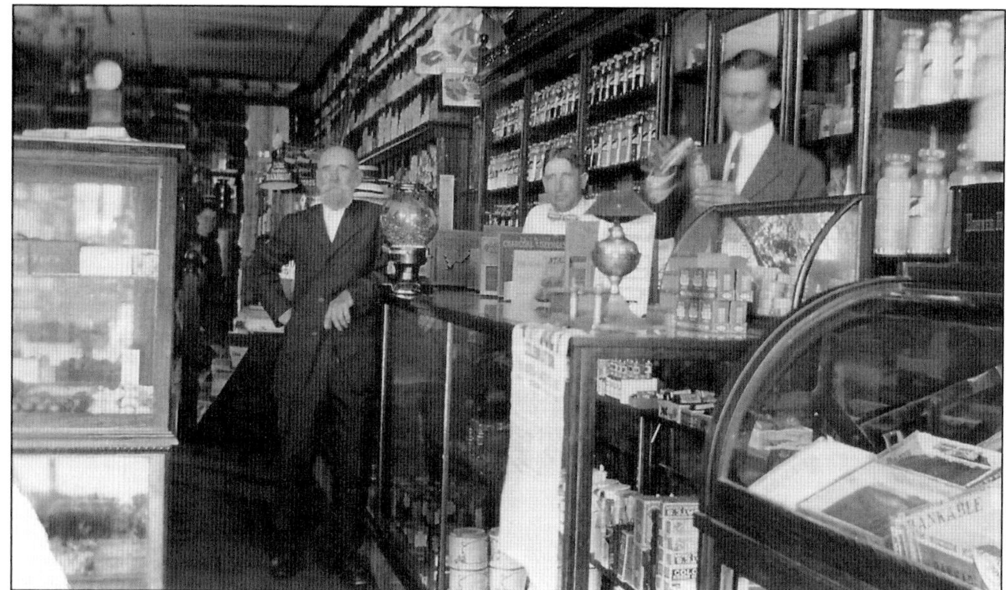

Losh Drugstore was located on East Main Street, and it is seen here in a beautiful interior shot. Later, the business became Spence's Pharmacy and relocated in 1946 to the site that originally housed the Merchant and Farmer's Bank on the Bindley Block.

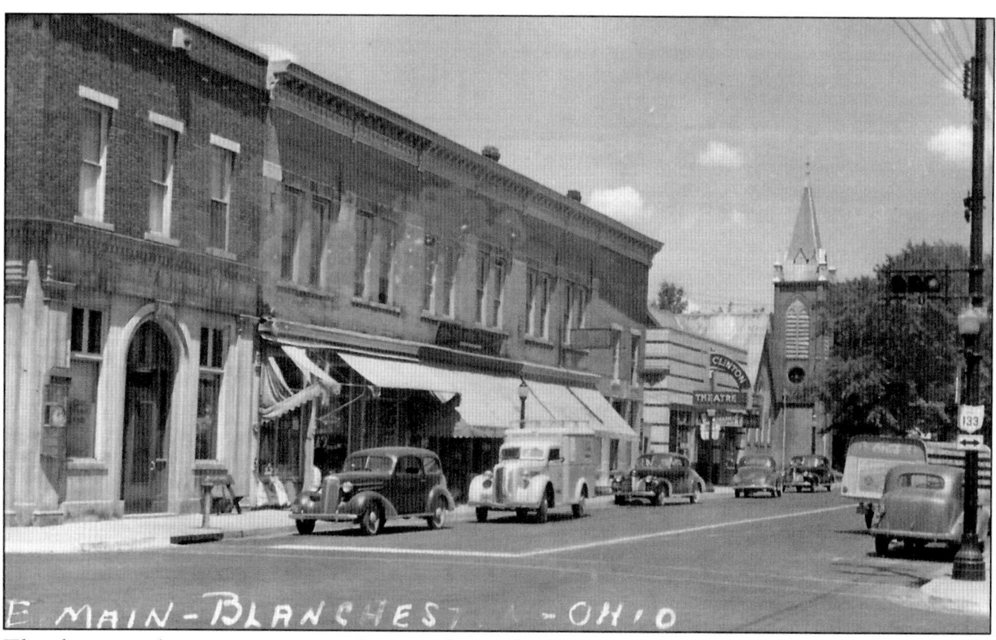

The drugstore location can again be seen here, this time from the outside, in the 1940s. Also visible are the First National Bank and the recently erected Clinton Theater, built in 1939. Also seen are some marks of beautification, the wall clock, park bench in front of the bank building, and bubbler fountain at curbside. Upstairs on the Smith Block was the Smith Opera House, located over three store spaces.

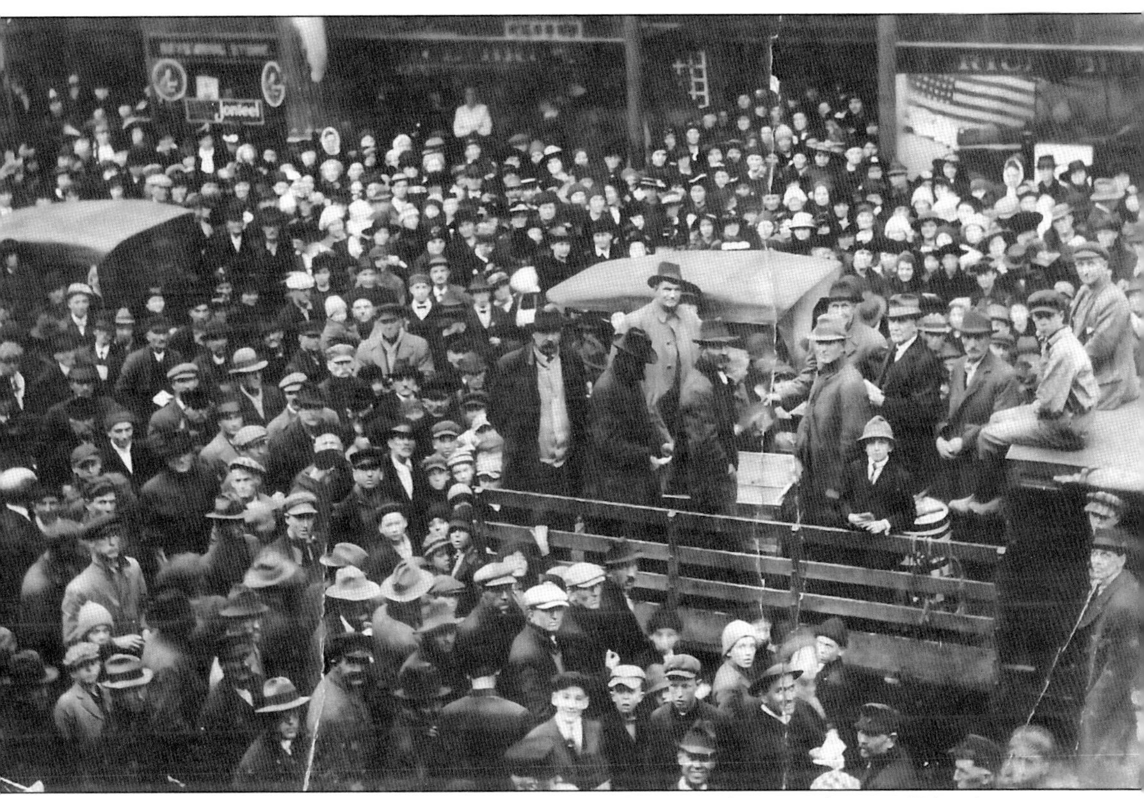

This photograph depicts a businessmen's rally held in the downtown business district of Blanchester. The street is incredibly crowded, but in the background is the Rice Brothers storefront. Modern residents may be amazed at how much commerce went on in their quiet town in the past, but it was once quite bustling.

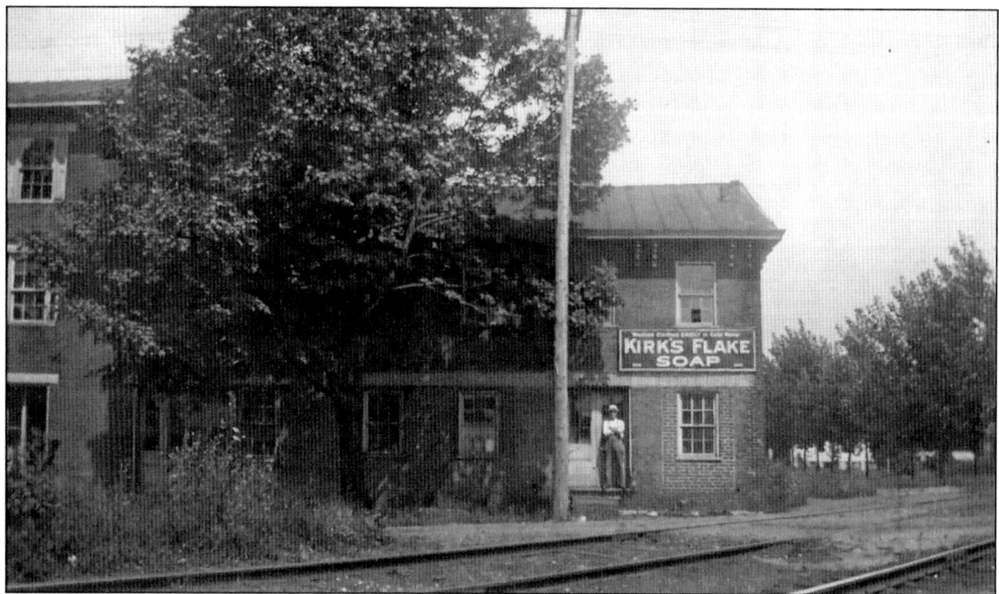

Pictured is the Kirk's Flake Soap building. The company and building no longer exist, but Hames Factory went up near the location. It produced horse-collar harnesses.

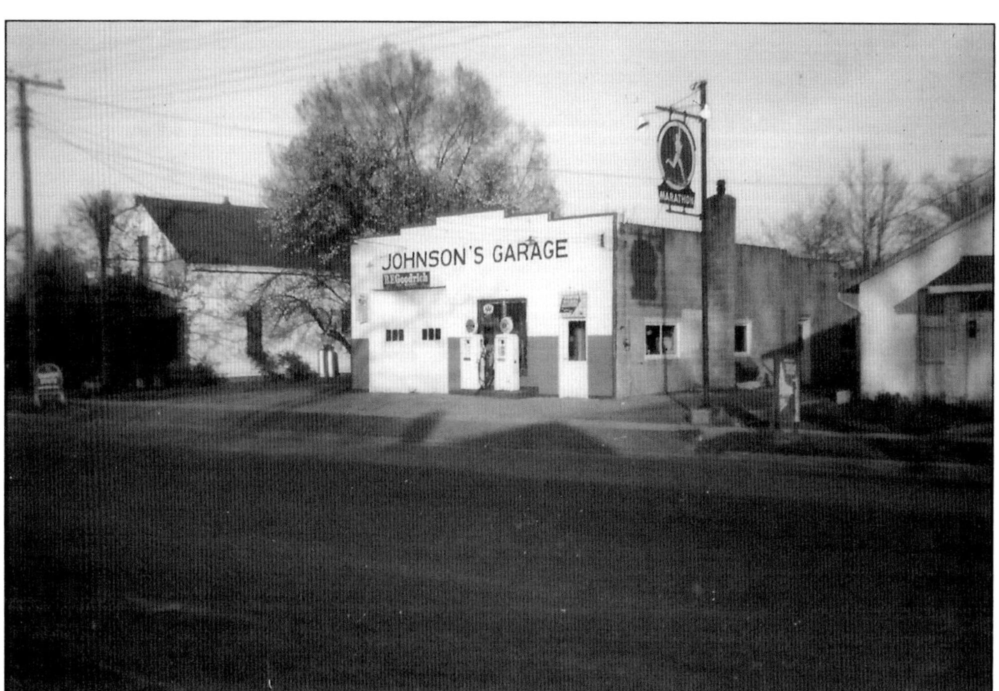

Johnson's Garage on East Main Street, past Columbus Street, was far from the heart of the business district yet still within easy walking distance. Later, it became Cook's Auto Body Shop, operated by Charles Wesley "Bob" Cook.

Wilkin's Studio, Blanchester, Ohio.

For a small town with a small population, Blanchester housed a surprising number of photography studios in the early years of the 1900s. At right is an image from Wilkin's Studio, and below is a senior class portrait of Robert Ross Simpson, Blanchester High School class of 1932, taken by Spencer's Art Studio. Simpson later became vice president of the Labor Union International Association of Machinists (IAM).

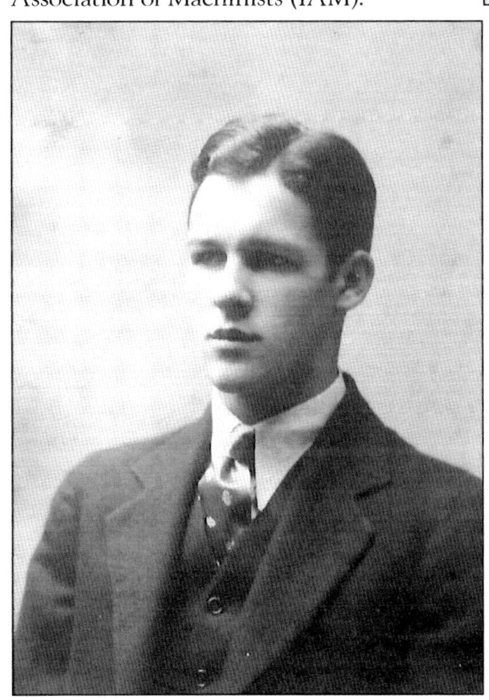

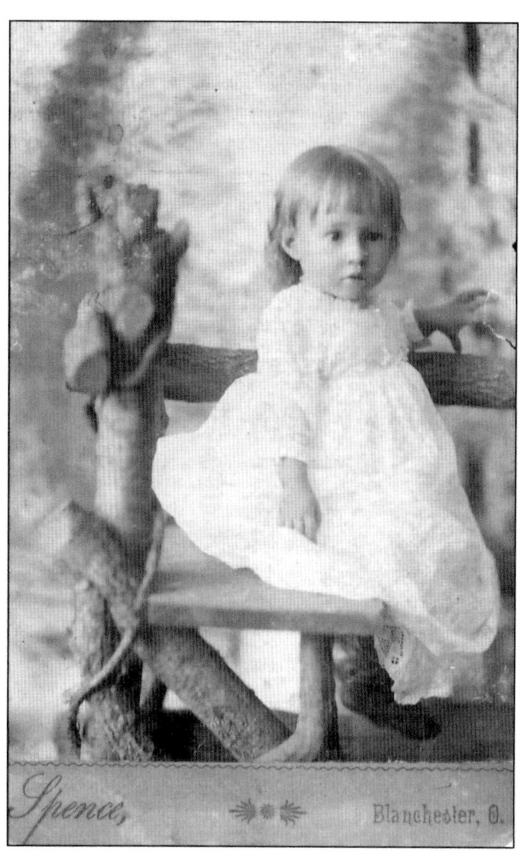

The Spence Studio was located in the upstairs portion of 115 South Broadway Street, one of a string of studios to occupy the space. At left is Christine Wilkins. Posing below are the Ross brothers: Guy, McCluney, and Fred.

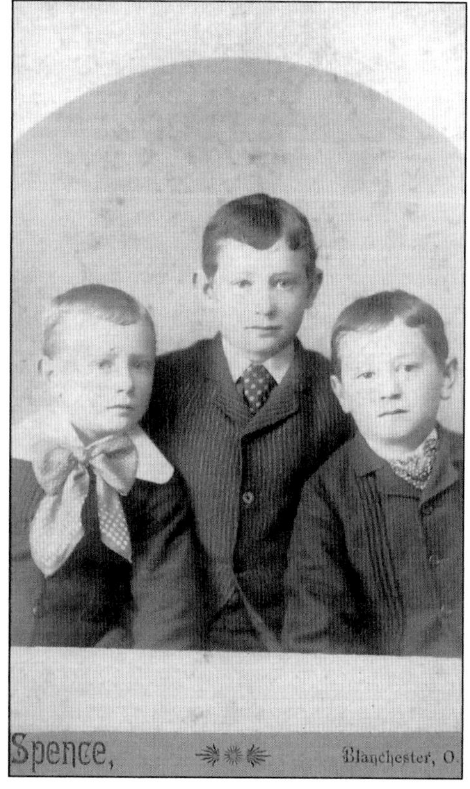

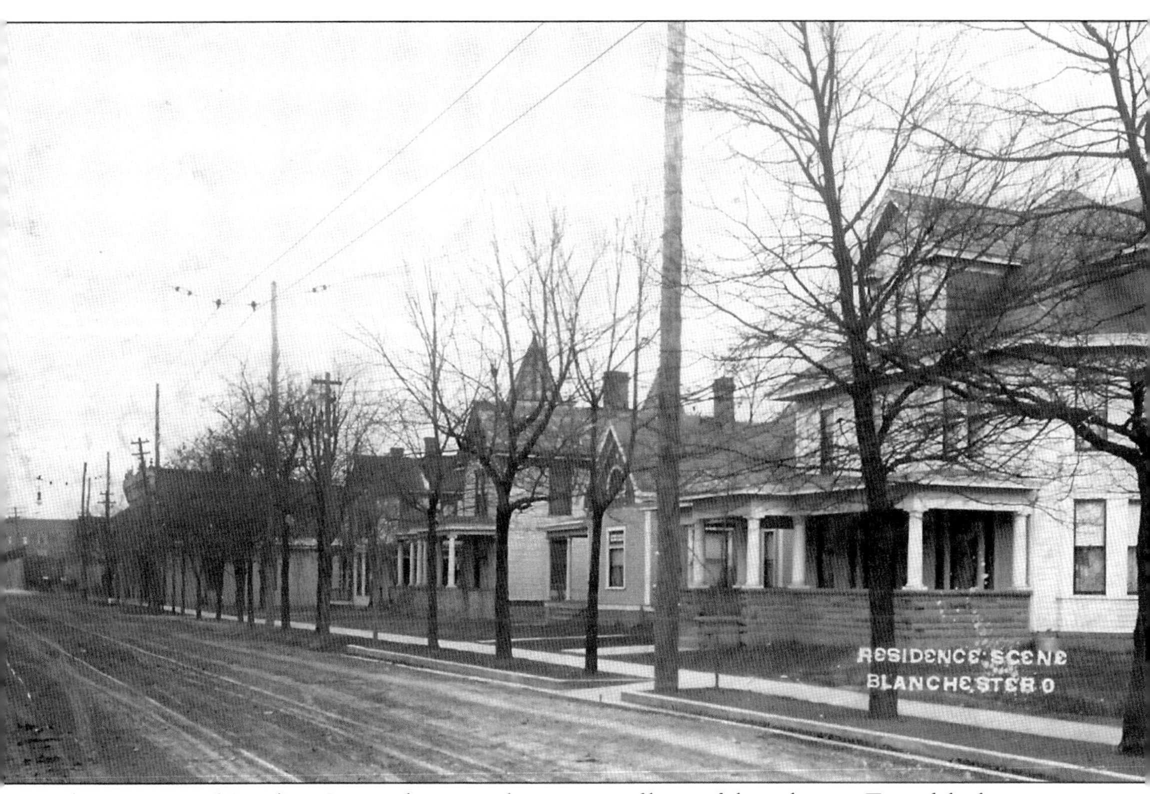

This is a view of Bourbon Street, showing a long string of beautiful residences. Two of the homes in the foreground are still standing today.

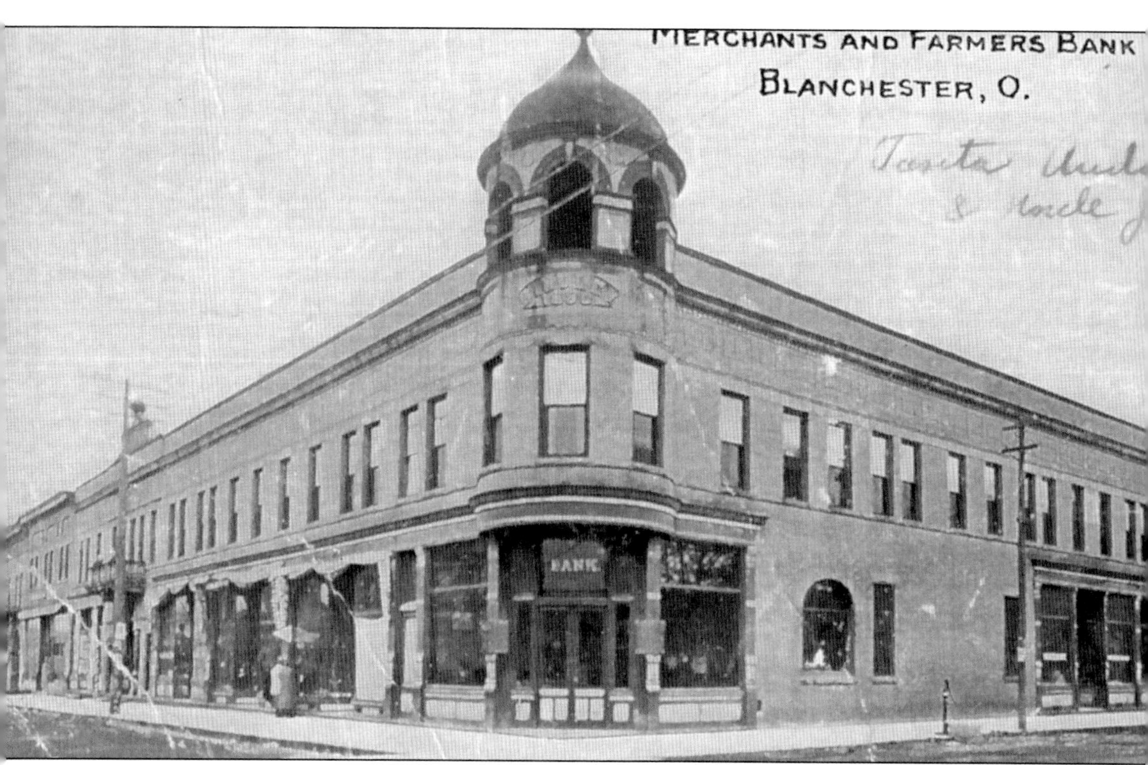

This is a view of the corner entrance to the Merchant and Farmer's Bank, which closed in 1928 but repaid 86.6¢ on the dollar to all customers by October of 1936, a surprising return in hard times. In the cupola is "M&F," and there is a weather vane on top of the building also sporting the bank initials, which is still there today, but the diagonal entrance to the Bindley Block is not.

Nine

Street Fairs and Celebrations

Community celebrations have always been common in Blanchester. Reasons for street fairs have been many and varied over the years. When a town is small, it is easy to spread the word of an event and get most of the inhabitants involved. From the weekly band concerts mentioned earlier to the spring and autumn yard-sale weekends, and many and varied events in between, Blanchester is a more exciting place to live than many would assume of such a small town.

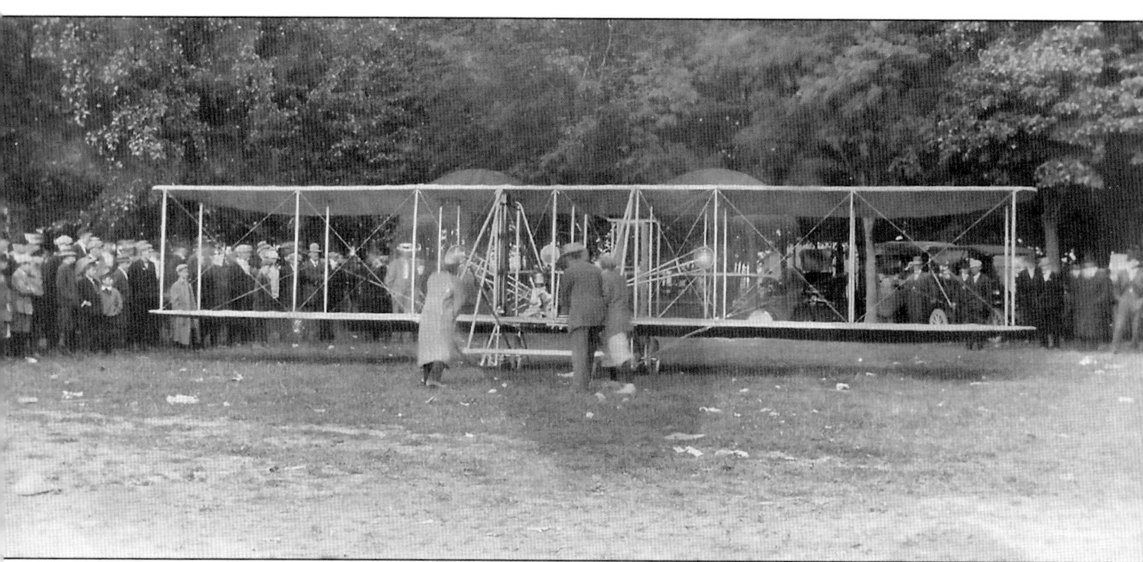

Sometime between 1909 and 1910, the Wright brothers' plane, the *Wright Flyer*, was brought to the Blanchester Fairgrounds to be placed on exhibit. Ohio is proud to remind the world that flight truly originated here, even if the first successful flight was in North Carolina. This pride even extends to small towns.

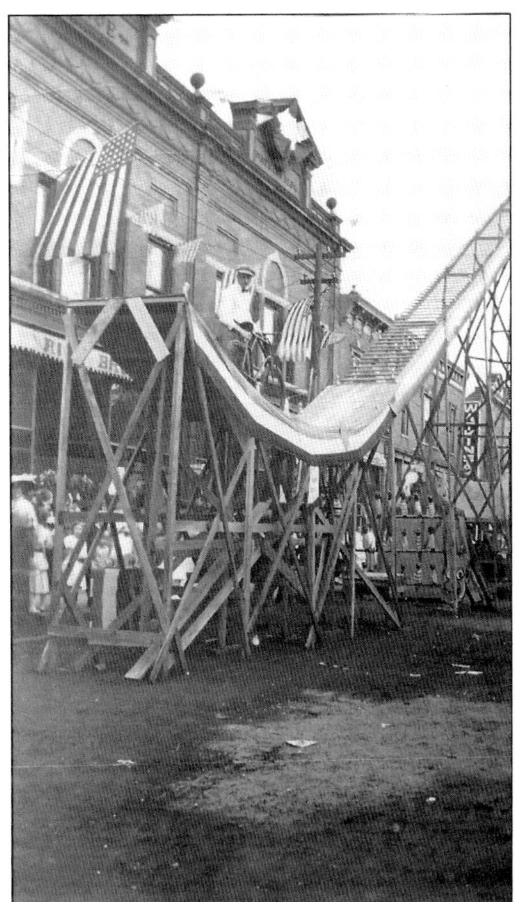

In 1929, the Blanchester Fair closed, but that only opened the opportunity for the fall festival, which ran during the late 1930s. There was demand for a thrill seeker, so Daredevil Doherty was brought in. A huge ramp was erected on the closed South Broadway Street. The local drugstore and cameraman shot the photographs to sell as postcards. One can only assume that the jump itself was successful.

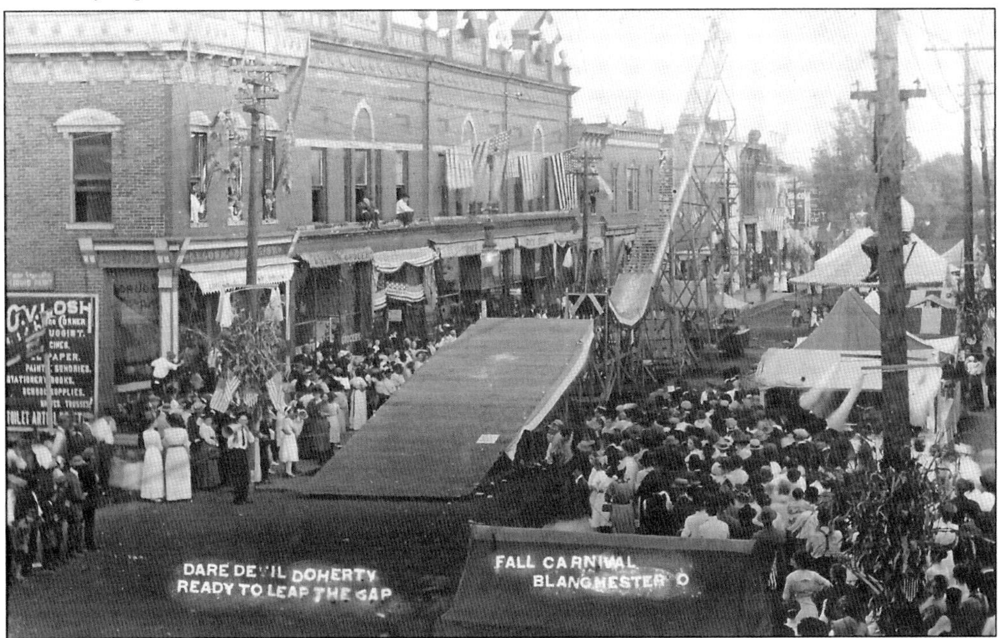

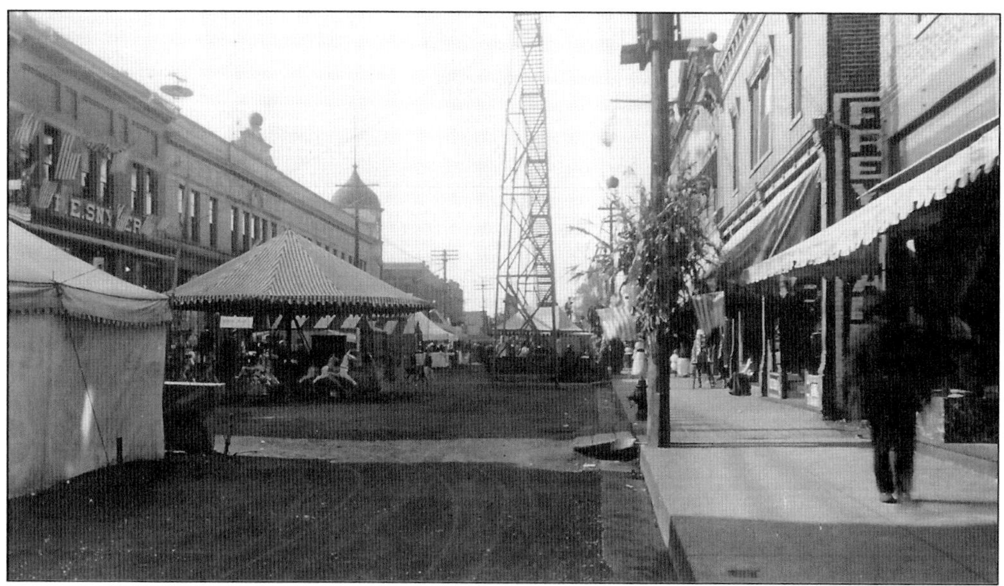

The Blanchester Fair was held from 1857 to 1927. After 1935, the Blanchester fall festival took its place. In the background of this image is a steel structure, which was the ladder ascent for the Daredevil Doherty ramp.

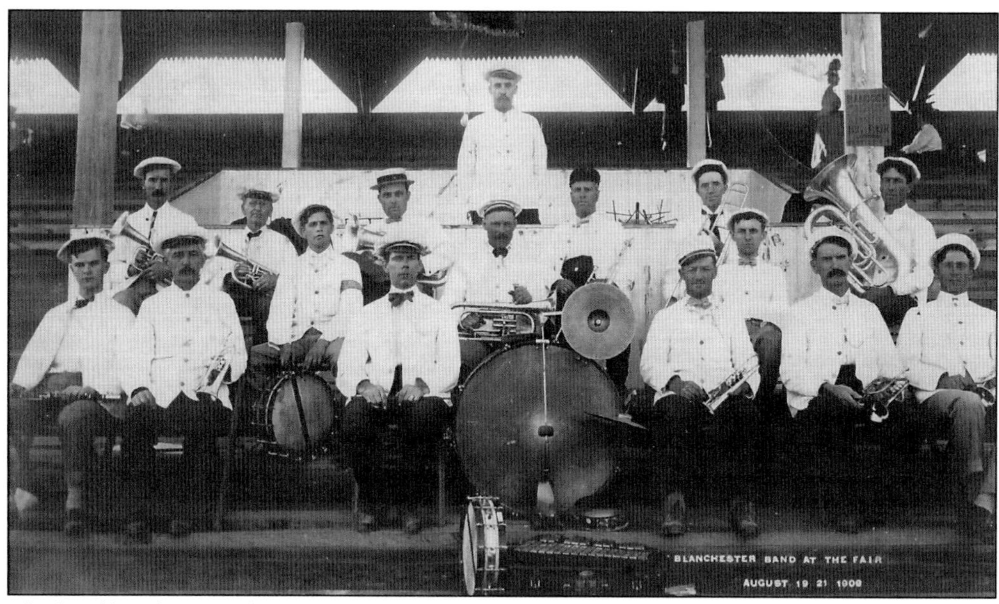

The local band was made up primarily of high school students and musicians. They are seen here at the Blanchester Fairgrounds bandstand. The fairgrounds also housed a racetrack, but today at the site is a housing development called Fairground Acres.

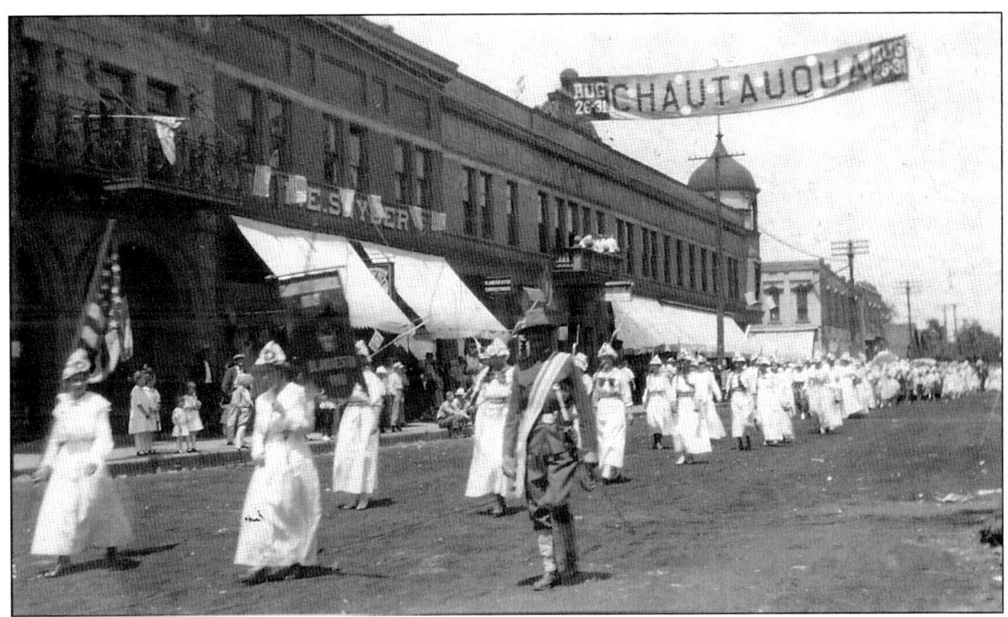

This is an image from a Chautauqua parade during the 1920s. The Chautauqua was a presentation of speakers, musical performances, and dramas held on the school grounds. During Chautauqua days, there were weeklong activities, a preview of which would be at the fairgrounds. The event stopped shortly after World War I but was revived in 2000, with various towns around Ohio taking turns hosting.

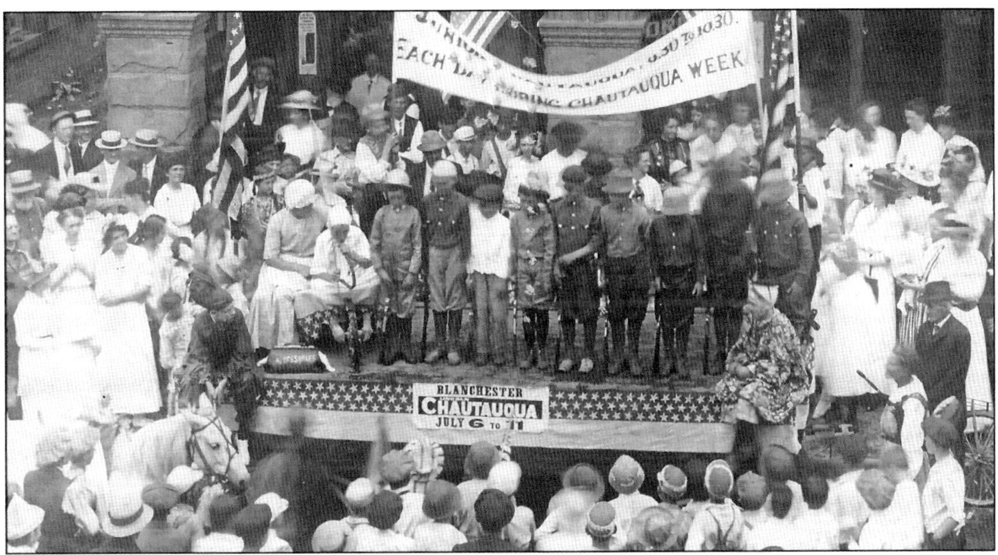

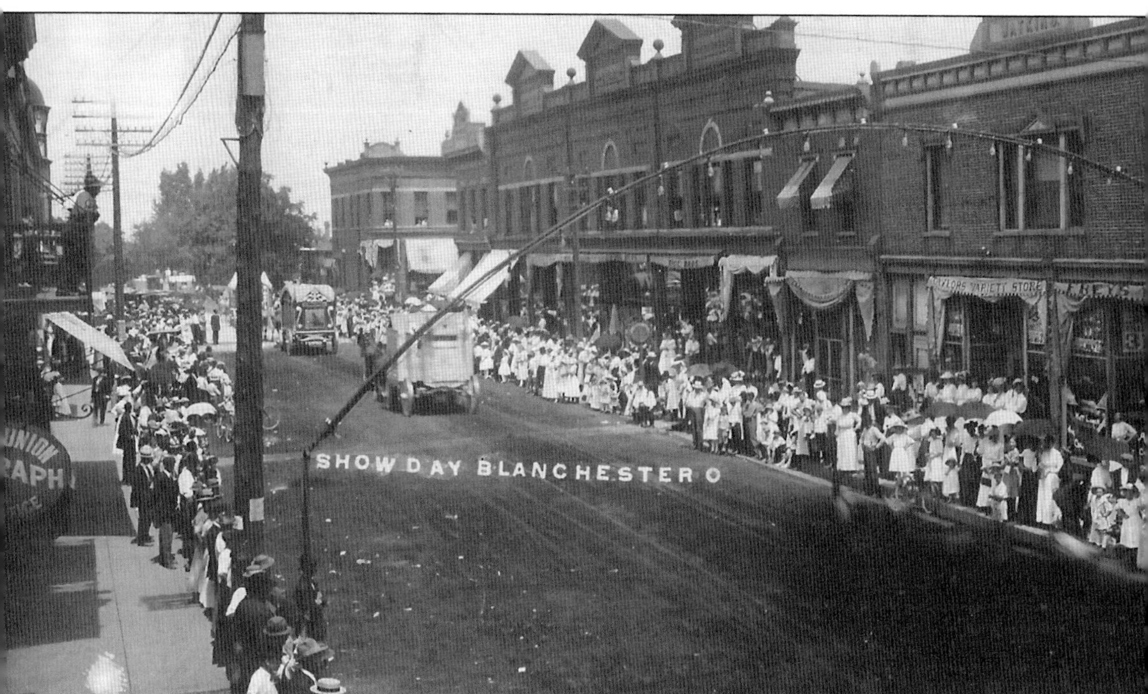

In 1912, a circus wintered on the farms and fairgrounds around Blanchester. The railroad would bring the circus troupe to town, and there was a parade down South Broadway Street as the performers and their equipment made their way to their winter lodgings.

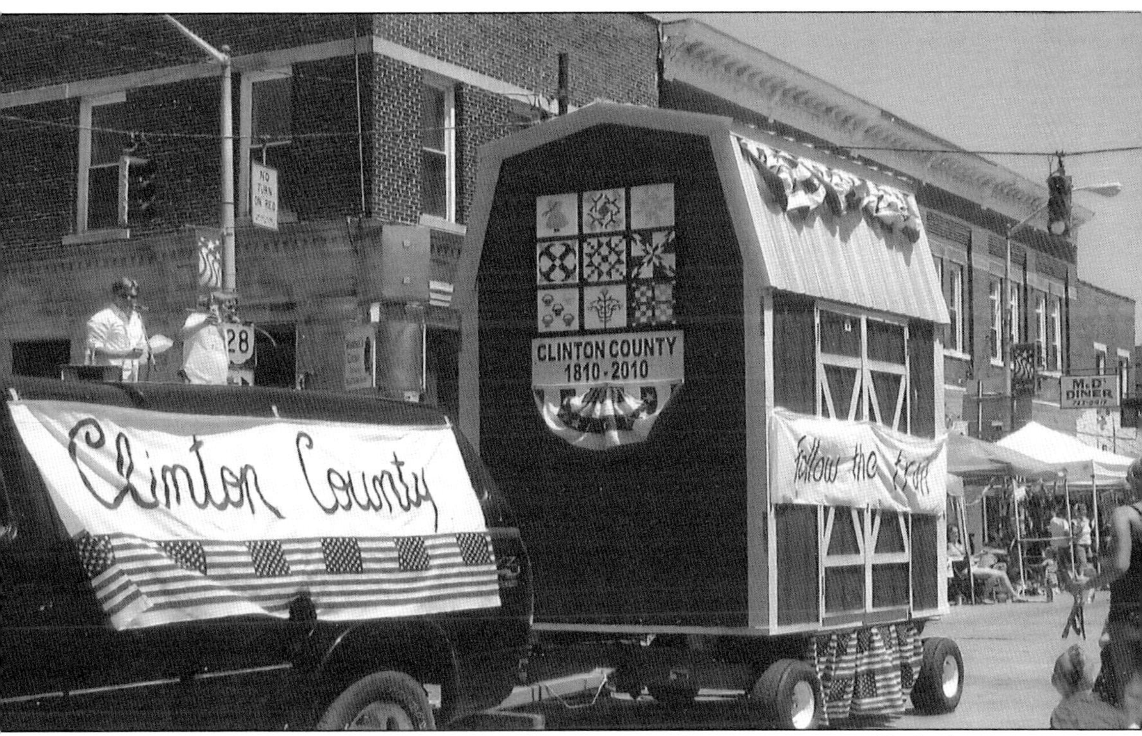

In 2010, Clinton County had its bicentennial celebration. The county was established in 1810, and though Wilmington is the county seat, Blanchester had a parade to the delight of the locals who came in to view it. This float with the quilt block barn represents the quilt block tour route through the county for the bicentennial. A celebration that hearkened back to rural roots, as well as the excitement of previous parades, it was a day for joy.

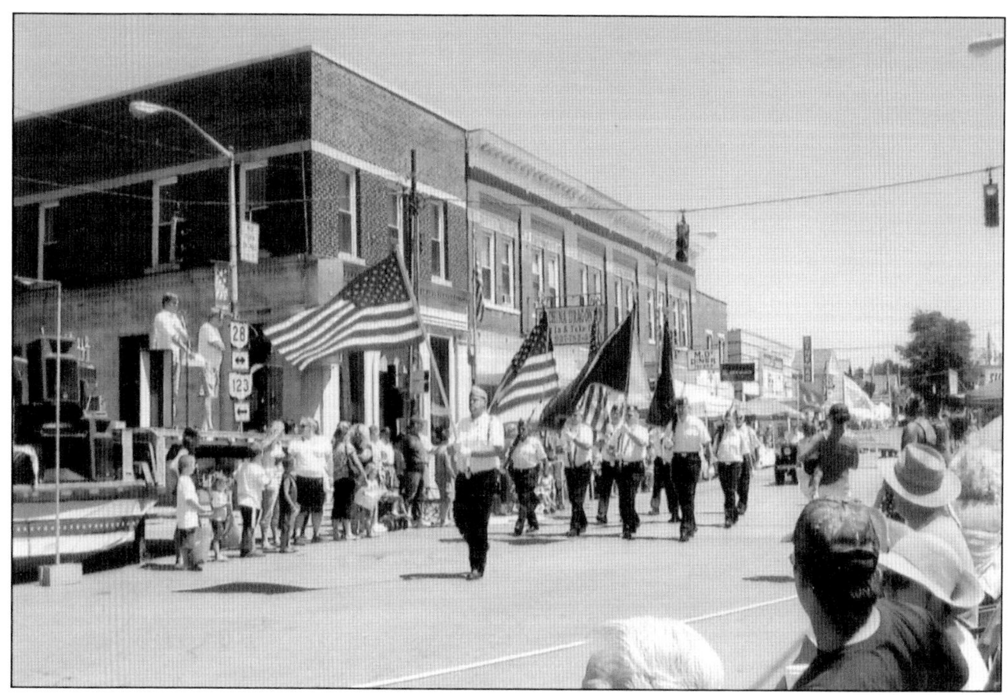

As with so many parades in previous years, local veterans and the Blanchester High School Marching Band made appearances.

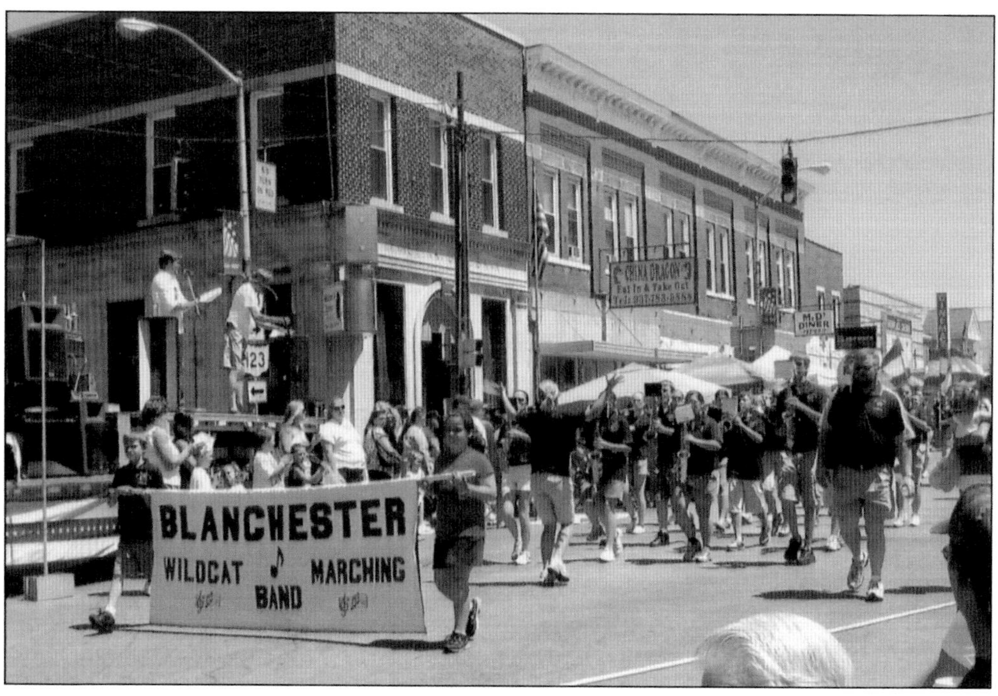

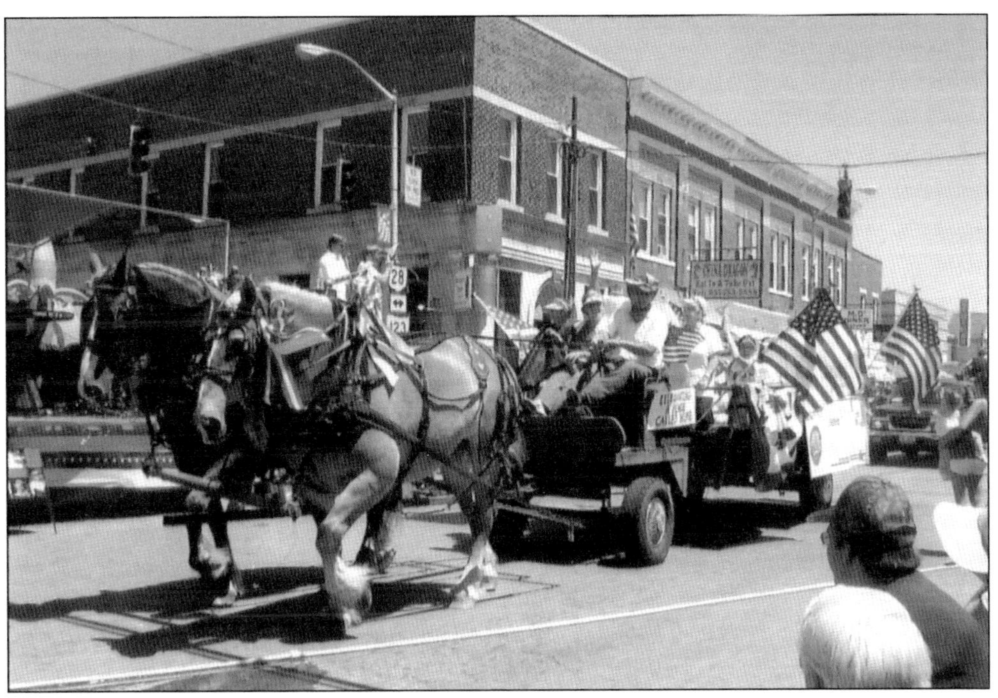

In addition to the quilt barn on the bicentennial float, there were horse-drawn floats and a display of quilts made by local artisans.

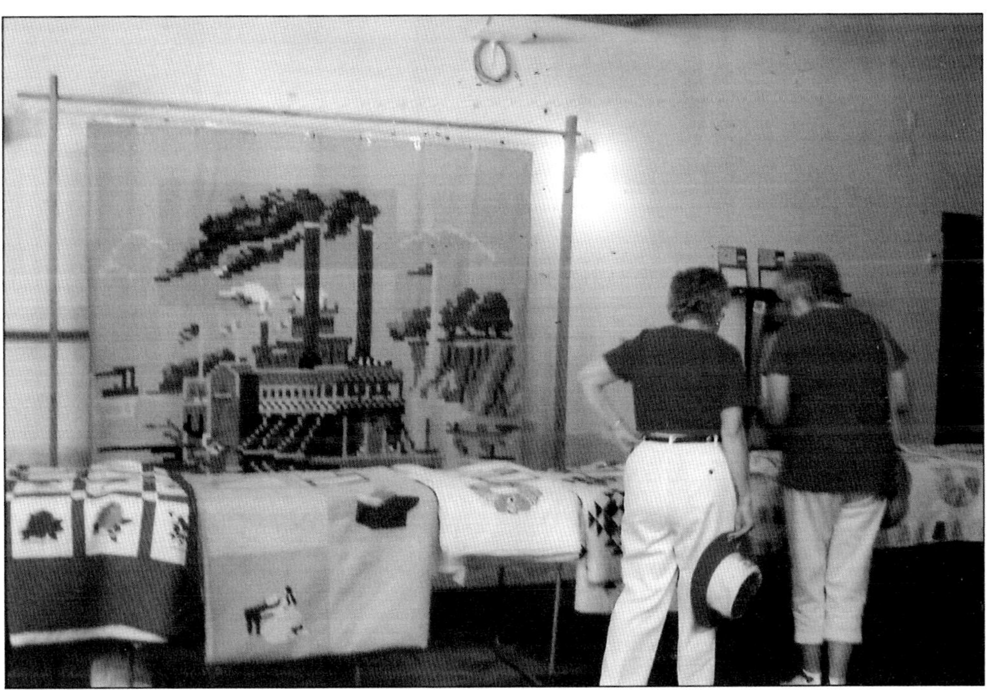

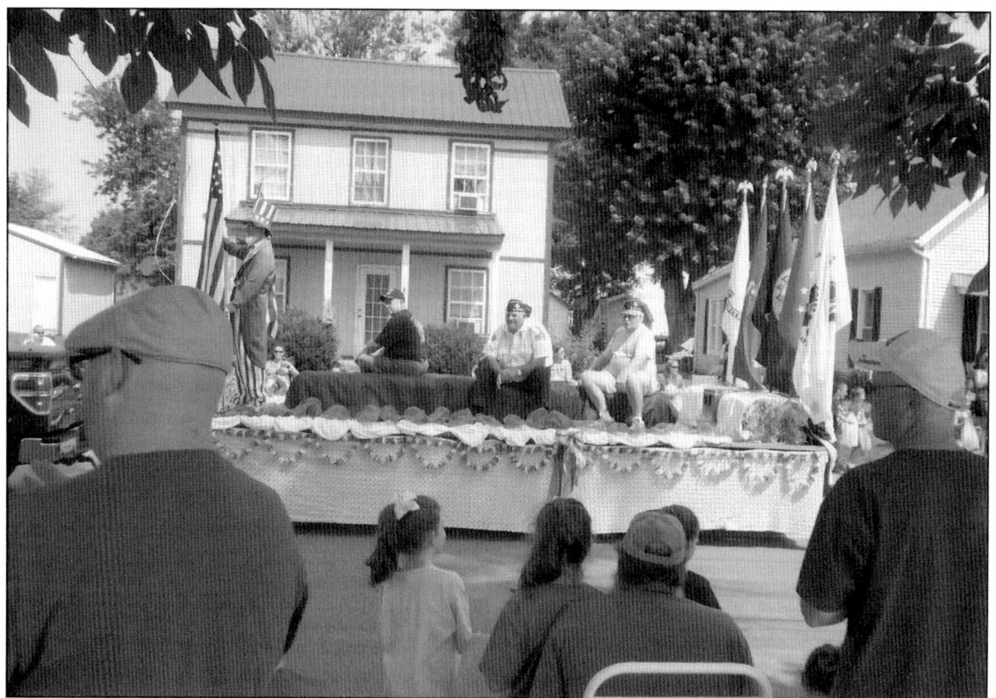

Veterans have always been an important part of Blanchester history and community. At the 2015 Fourth of July parade, they were represented several times on several floats, including a tractor decorated with flags to remind people to support their Vietnam veterans. (Photographs by the author.)

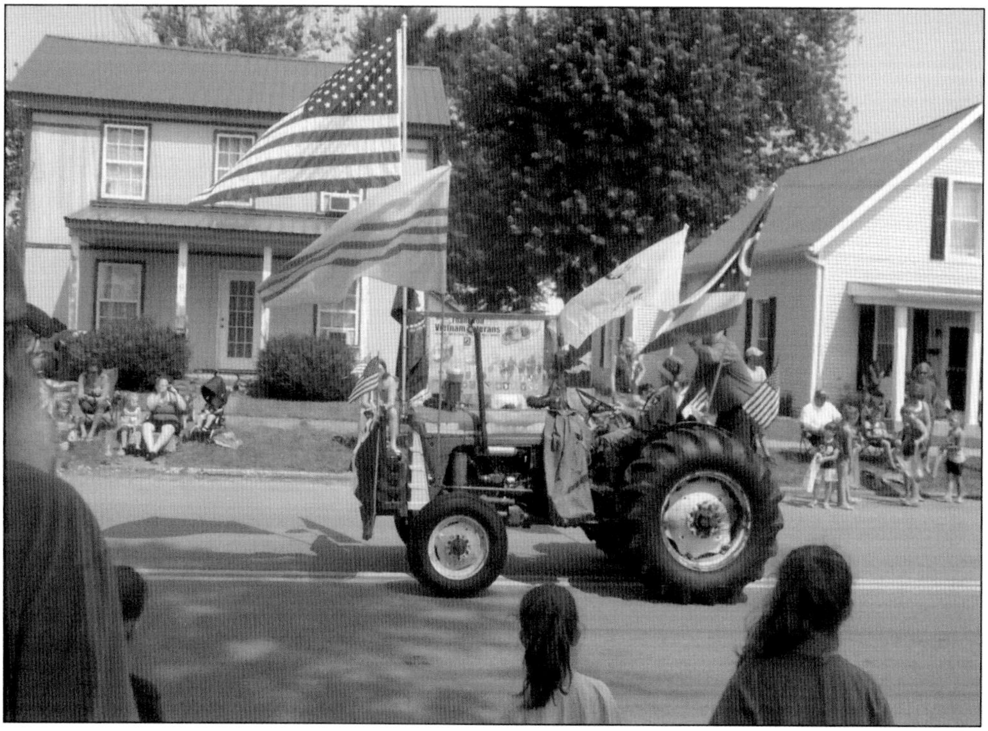

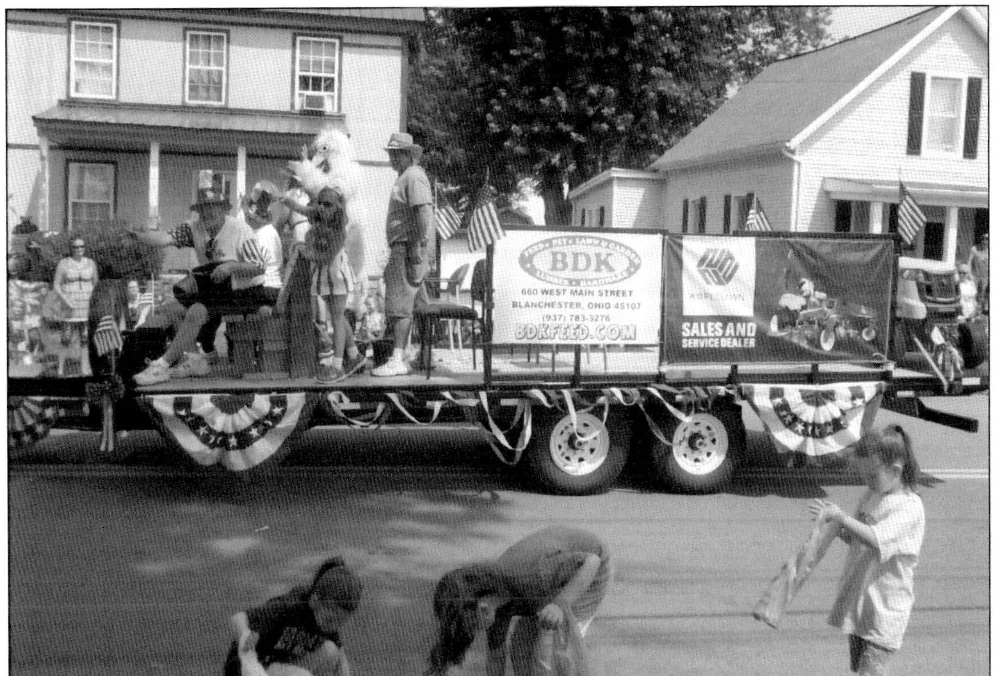

Just as in years past, local businesses have gathered to create floats to advertise. Once these floats were pulled by horses—today they are pulled by tractors—but the rural implications remain the same. This float appeared in the Fourth of July parade in 2015. (Photograph by the author.)

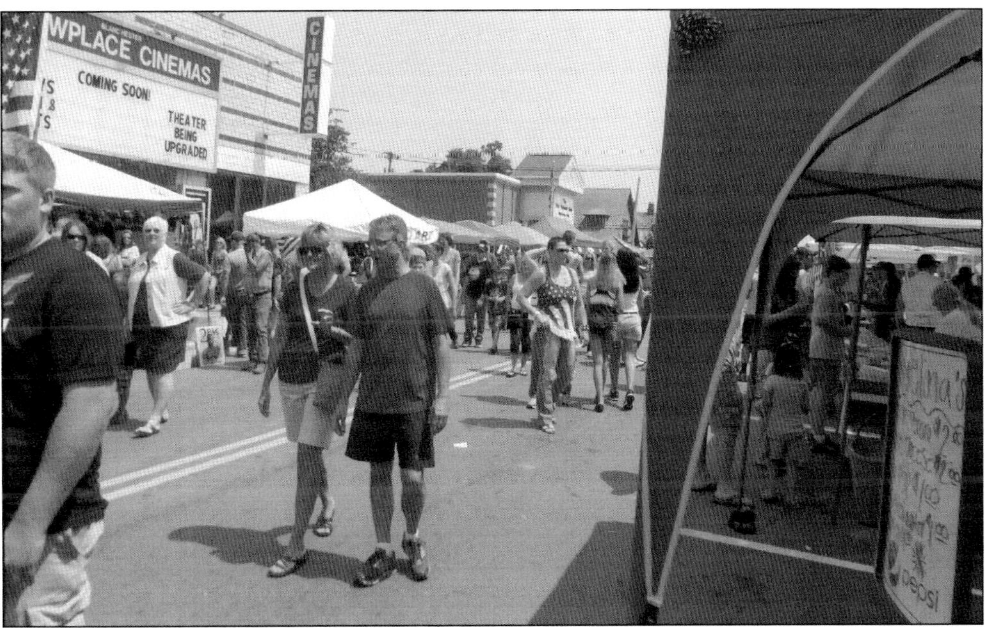

The streets are routinely closed for local restaurants and shops to set up for the revelers at the Fourth of July celebration. In 2015, the streets were so crowded with people and booths it was difficult to walk. The author has attended this festival many times in her life but has never seen it so crowded as it was in this photograph. (Photograph by the author.)

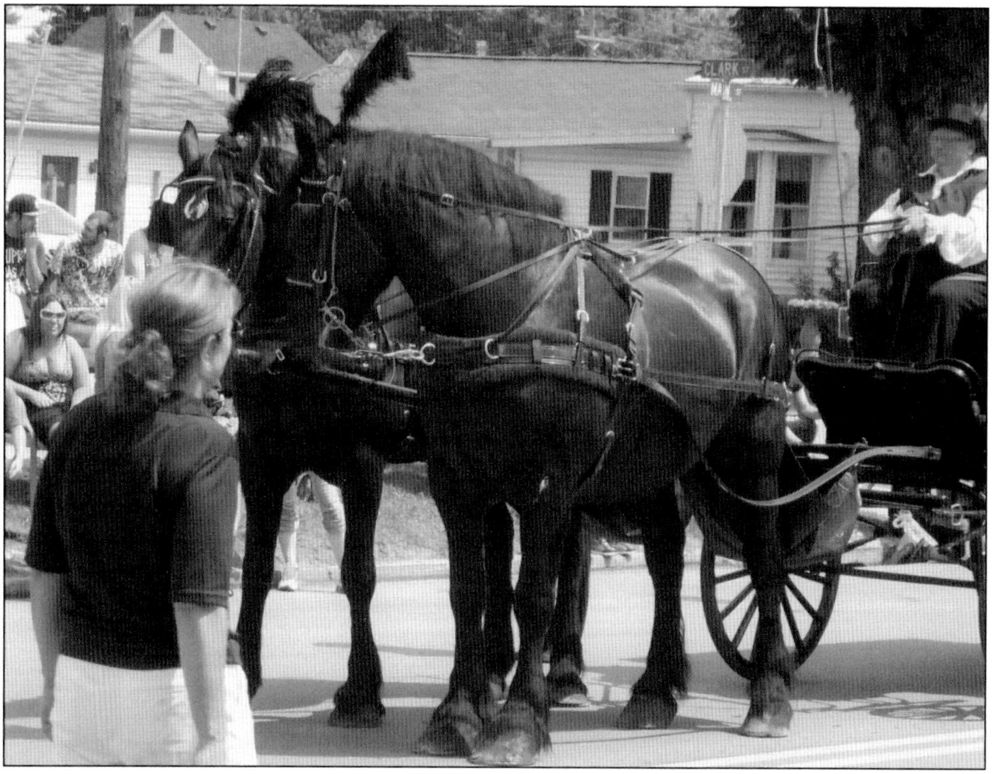

Though the Hannah Funeral Home is no longer in business, its successor, the Tufts Schildmeyer Funeral Home, honored the past with their floats in the Fourth of July parade. In addition to the horse-drawn hearse reminiscent of the floral display of yesteryear, the business followed it with other old-fashioned hearses, ending with a modern model—though nothing was as striking as the horses and carriage. (Photographs by the author.)

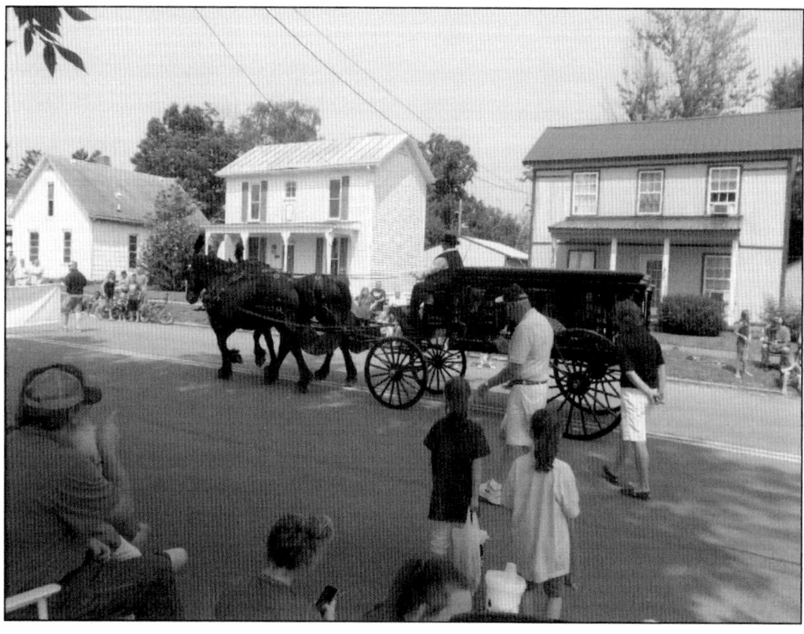

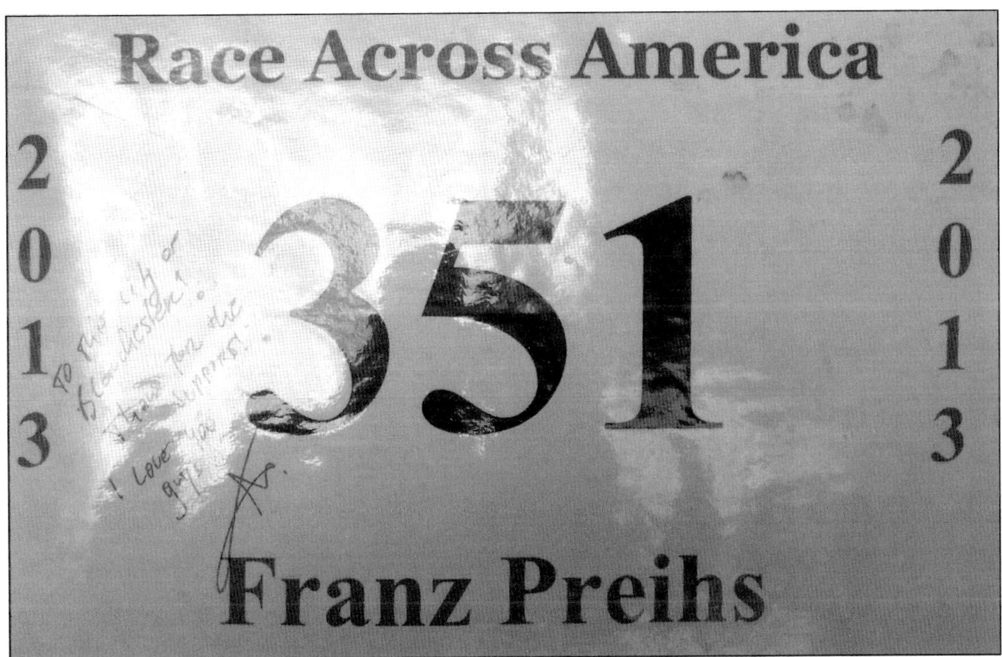

Race Across America, an annual bicycle race from Oceanside, California, to Annapolis, Maryland, has made Blanchester a stop on its route for several years. Viewers line the streets to watch racers bike through town. The Blanchester Area Historical Society has a section in its museum dedicated to the race, and racers have kindly stopped in over the years to visit and gift the museum with mementos. Seen here are race bibs from 2013 contender Franz Preihs and 2011 contender Christoph Strasser, who has made six attempts at the race, finishing four times and setting records in 2013 and 2014.

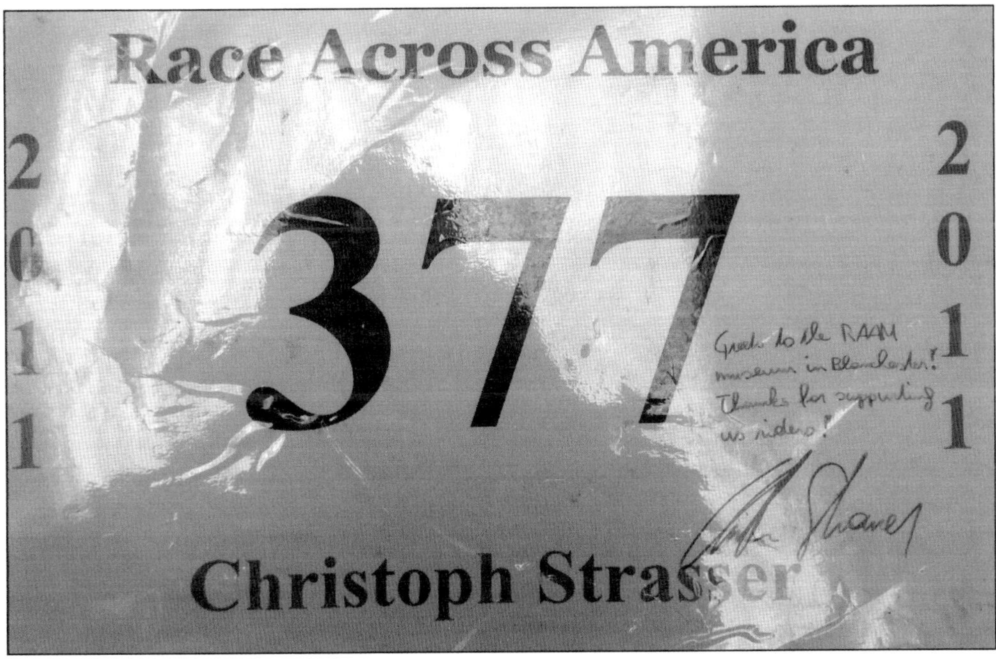

BIBLIOGRAPHY

Blanchester Area Historical Society. *Blanchester Area Heritage*. Blanchester, OH: Curless Printing Company, 1994.

Carnahan, J.E. *History of Blanchester, Ohio: In Two Parts*. Evansville, IN: Unigraphic, 1979.

About the Blanchester Area Historical Society

The Blanchester Area Historical Society formed in 1967 in response to the Main Street High School and Elementary School building being razed. The alumni of Blanchester High School decided to band together to preserve the history and heritage of the area, with special focus on the school system, which links so many area residents together.

Over the years, much literature, art, memorabilia, antiques, and history have been gathered. The society has hosted pageants and lectures and put together booths for area festivities. It has recorded all those buried in the Blanchester IOOF Cemetery, organized a musical concert of local church choirs, and put together displays for the Chautauqua revival and other events.

The society also petitions to preserve the historic buildings in town and remembers what could not be saved. In 1994, it released the first written collection of area history and has long been at work on a second volume. Despite so much being in print, the society is still taking in new information, going through old newspapers, and happening upon new items at estate sales that sometimes revise much of what was known previously.

Ask around town about area history, and the response is the same, "Go to the historical society. If they don't know it, it didn't happen."